UNLOCKED

UNLOCKED

DENISE REID

Library of Congress Control Number: 202191126020

ISBN:	Hardcover	978-1-5434-9742-7
	Softcover	978-1-5434-9741-0
	eBook	978-1-5434-9740-3

Print information available on the last page.

Rev. date: 09/17/2021

To order additional copies of this book, contact:
Xlibris
NZ TFN: 0800 008 756 (Toll Free inside the NZ)
NZ Local: 9-801 1905 (+64 9801 1905 from outside New Zealand)
www.Xlibris.co.nz
Orders@Xlibris.co.nz
822301

Now the word of the LORD came to me, saying, "Before I formed you in the womb I knew you, and before you were born I consecrated you; I appointed you a prophet to the nations."

Then I said, "Ah, LORD GOD! Behold, I do not know how to speak, for I am only a [woman]." But the LORD said to me, "Do not say, 'I am only a [woman]'; for to all to whom I send you, you shall go, and whatever I command you, you shall speak. Do not be afraid of them, for I am with you to deliver you, declares the LORD."

—Jeremiah 1:4–8 ESV

ACKNOWLEDGEMENTS REFERENCES

nzhistory.govt.nz > politics > women's-suffrage
Tertullian
[Gaithers 1964.]
Archdiocese of Hobart, [Wikipedia]
Saffron rebellion [Wikipedia.07]
Nargis 2008 Wikipedia.
Nepal War 2007 [Wikipedia]
26 November 2008 [Wikipedia] Bangkok Rebellion
4 March 2019 India (International Christian Concern) –
Arrest of Aung San SuuGyi [8 August 2013 4:48 PM
ET Heard on All Things Considered]
Khandhamal Persecution 03/04/2019
(International Christian Concern) –
Why Not Women in Ministry by David Hamilton and Loren Cunningham
[The Gallipoli campaign - The Gallipoli campaign | NZ History, New ...]
Visions Beyond the Veil by H. A. Baker
[Talk to me in Paradise] Angela Curtis
[Wikipedia https://en.wikipedia.org/wiki/Cyclone_Komen]
https://www.aljazeera.com/news/2019/8/16/myanmar-rebels-kill-over-a-dozen-in-attack-in-shan-state
August 8, 2013 4:48 PM ET Heard on All Things Considered

Pyin Oo Win [Anadolu Agency 15 August 2019 Kyaw Ye Lynn]
[nzhistory.govt.nz > politics > women's-suffrage]
Prem Pradhan [Amazon]
[Apr 3, 2018 2015 Nepal earthquake: Facts, FAQs, and how to help | World ...
www.worldvision.org > disaster-relief-news-stories]
https://www.npr.org/2013/08/08/209919791/as-myanmar-opens-up-a-look-back-on-a-1988-uprising
World Directory of Minorities and indigenous Peoples www:/ minorityrights.org).
Wikipedia,
"Myanmar's Nationwide Ceasefire Agreement").
"Prince blamed for Nepal massacre". BBC News. 14 June 2001. Archivedfrom the original on 7 January 2009. Retrieved 31 May 2009. Page 270

Land beyond Evil, Benedict Rodgers.

TRIBUTES

To Jesus and to those who, over these years, have received amazing supernatural touches and seen supernatural events.

To my husband Kevin who has walked beside me, encouraged, served, and loved me. He has cherished, followed, facilitated, and empowered me through these years. He has worked, suffering with diligence and endurance to travel, driving thousands of miles, shifting bags, ministered to thousands of people as only he could to support the ministry. It is with his devotion, prayers, and help that the Lord has empowered me to undertake what together we have accomplished. To my husband Kevin, you are a true trojan and an extraordinary man of prayer. I celebrate you for your sacrifices, that you have allowed the unlocking of God's purpose in and through me. And as that purpose has unlocked you have encouraged and supported me

To Rachel, Aaron, Paul, Kim and my grandchildren who have lived sacrificially, to release us to the purposes and plans of God.

To all those who have allowed their stories to be shared.

To my special friends and to the many nameless ones who have shared our lives and journeyed with me, to see me unlocked from unbelief into faith and glory to steward degrees of glory, as God has unlocked His love around the world.

To those who have gone on to their heavenly home now totally unlocked to His amazing prersence.

To the many in the nations with whom we have worked, loved, and served, those we have watched grow, mature, and love, sons and daughters who are family.

To Veruni De Silva met by divine appointment who has done the graphic work for this book and other book covers, my grateful thanks.

Denise Reid

CONTENTS

PICTURES

FOREWORD

The miracles of Jesus Christ and His resurrection were the evidence that God can intervene in His creation and provide the immutable evidence that He is the Creator. Our lives finds their creative meaning when we connect with Him and His creative power.

Denise 'unlocked' her creative destiny by the grace of God and His unmerited favour, and connected with her Creator in a unique way. The miracles that followed her obedience 'unlocked' new dimensions of the Holy Spirit in the lives of thousands of people in Eastern Europe, Cuba, North America, Africa and Asia.

Sadly, so many followers of Jesus Christ settle for lives restricted by the limitations of earthly laws. The world would be transformed when many more believers in Jesus Christ would 'unlock' their created destiny like Denise has experienced.

Connecting with the Holy Spirit of the Supreme Magnificent Creator of all that is in the universe, who raised Jesus Christ from the dead, is likened to coming home to the One who made us. It was never God's intention that we would wait till we go to heaven to experience an intimate connection with God and the manifestation of His supernatural power.

In John 10:10 Jesus said; ' The thief comes only to steal, and kill and destroy; I came that they might have life and have it abundantly.' The Holy Spirit came after Jesus' resurrection to make that 'abundant life' a reality in the lives of the first new Pentecostal believers. Denise's life demonstrates how much that thief has stolen from so many modern day believers who live a self-obsessed life aimlessly waiting to go to heaven.

Many years ago I had the privilege to stay frequently with Kevin and Denise for a night while on business in Hamilton. During this phase of revival in their lives Denise discovered the divine intent and power of the Abrahamic Covenant Genesis 12:1-10. Her life was never again content to settle for the mediocre. She pushed the boundaries of ecclesiastical restrictions and was 'unlocked' to the nations.

In the years following, a revived Denise was led by the Spirit of God to the places in the world that were on His compassionate and merciful heart. To most of her friends these places were unheard of. Despite this seeming obscurity Denise was led to people who were courageous, and willing to obey the Lord and go with her to places where the harvest was awaiting their Abrahamic blessing. This covenantal blessing was poured out on many indigenous people groups where the gospel had only recently arrived. He provided resources for the many journeys of faith that created adventures similar to those in the Book of Acts.

'Unlocked' will provide evidence of the miraculous power of God at work in the many places the Spirit of God led Denise too. My prayer is that you will experience a revival in your life from reading this book. Be assured that God gives His creative power to anyone who seeks it.

Bryan Johnson
CEO / Trustee
Asia Pacific Discipleship Trust
New Zealand

INTRODUCTION

> For everything there is a season, and a time for every matter under heaven: a time to be born, and a time to die; a time to plant, and a time to pluck up what is planted . . .
>
> —Ecclesiastes 3:1-2 ESV

Prophetic words unlocked situations and came from the beginning, but life was too busy to even consider them. "You will write a book, you will write many books!" Different people had repeated the words so many times in different places! But these words fell on deaf ears as this lady was too busy, too involved with people, nations, conferences, ministry, travel, organisation, and life. How could a book or books be written when every year for over thirty years I travelled around the world, held multiple conferences in difficult nations, spoke and ministered constantly? It needed a year to write a book, didn't it? Time dedicated just to writing! Time out! Impossible! Beyond consideration. Have you found that God delights to do the impossible beyond our dreams and expectations? He wants to explode our vision to unlock our preconceptions.

Could we have ever dreamt no planes would fly? Could we have dreamt nations would shut down, borders would close? Dreamt no visas be issued? Who could have dreamt that moving around the world would become impossible? With tickets booked in January 2020, we ministered in Asia, returning to New Zealand at the end of February. I expected to fly to the USA at the beginning of April 2020 and on to Cuba, the love of my life to minister. In Myanmar, they laughed and told us no need for masks, no COVID here! In Thailand, we wore masks. They checked us for temperatures in the airports. We took care!

Asia was on alert as COVID-19, this additional strain of disease, threatened. Everyone took care, but after all, Asia had dealt with bird flu, SARS, and other viruses and handled them all extra well! Never did we dream what would happen! No checking on arrival in Auckland. After all, this was New Zealand! Marian and I wore masks on the plane to

New Zealand, but no one else did! No temperature screening on arrival. Nothing! No one was wearing masks in New Zealand! On 25 March 2020, New Zealand announced and moved into level 4 lockdown, and the nation shut down! No planes flew in or out! In just twenty-four days, New Zealand went from its first case of COVID-19 to a nationwide lockdown. Never had this happened before . . . beyond our dreams . . . new. A new day . . . for new things . . . time to do things a new way . . . New means no previous history, it's original. We cancelled flights to the USA and Cuba! The day of the lockdown announcement, I told my husband Kevin, "I'm writing a book!" Day and night, I wrote *Heavenly Kaleidoscope,* the stories of heavenly encounters and stories of my life. Finished and published, I wrote *Endless Safari* and *Changing Gears.*

With the realisation many stories were yet untold, I continued to write. This time my life story! Join me and discover the journey. Explore with me the DNA of God, our family's recently discovered DNA, and experience God's supernatural love and power. Journey with me to unlock God's purpose and plan, to unlock and release the mighty hidden things, the secrets only revealed to those who love God!

> From my childhood You've been my Teacher, And I'm still telling everyone of Your miracle-wonders! God, now that I'm old and gray, don't walk away. Give me grace to demonstrate to the next generation, All Your mighty miracles And Your excitement to show them Your magnificent power! For Your glorious righteousness Reaches up to the high heavens! No one could ever be compared to You, who is Your equal, O God of marvels and wonders?
>
> —Psalm 71:17-19 TPT

> Everyone will say, "Come and see the incredible things God has done; it will take your breath away! He multiplies miracles for his people!"
>
> —Psalm 66:5 TPT

Walk with me through the nations, fly with me to heights unknown, discover the dimensions of heaven, experience revelation in your journey with God, unlock your life just as I have unlocked mine. Visit with me to the unlocking of heavenly experiences where the Kingdom of heaven touched earth, all because we learnt to declare and decree and move by faith to see transformed lives. Share with me God's purpose unlocked. It's my prayer, God's purpose and plan will be unlocked in your life as you read my story. May this book not just bless you but stir you as an agent of change. May it unlock unforgettable truths applicable to your life and walk with God.

Denise Reid

CHAPTER 1

Seasons . . . The Beginnings

When you tell the Lord you will go with Him wherever He goes, He takes you at your word. When you devote your life to pursuing His purpose and presence at the cost of everything else, even family and friends, He will lead you into an adventure beyond your wildest imaginings or dreams. When you go where He goes, you position yourself in the line of glory. Basically, that's what I did, with no idea of the consequences. I did not understand what God would do; I did not know the glory He would pour out. As I walked in simple obedience, I could never have dreamt what He would unlock. Looking back, I could never have dreamt the amazing adventures and events that would fill my life. Riding on the world's worst train from Mandalay to Myktina in Myanmar with people fearful it would crash . . . rocking and rolling back and forth as it struggled to remain on the track . . . the first train after a terrible crash when the train rolled off the track. Travelling by bus on the world's worst roads, Kathmandu to Pokhara, where vehicles played chicken and trucks regularly hurtled off mountain cliffs to death in the valleys below!

"Dreams are free" is a regular statement, but I could never have dreamt or even imagined the things I would do and even say or the journeys I would embark on. Interviews with police and immigration, summons and invitations to interrogations we did not attend. Ripping an expelled page out of a team member's passport to enable her to get the visa so necessary for our next stage of travel. Catching malaria and cholera after an emergency relief trip in a disaster zone. Illegal activities became the norm in world travels! More than thirty years a perpetual tourist. Arriving before and leaving after the police sat on the street during meetings in the church! Visits to restricted nations where governments forbade sharing the Gospel, forbade preaching in churches, forbade riding in private cars and staying in houses, and they expelled others for doing what I did and still do! My life so orderly, so law-abiding, became colourfully different from those of my peers. So different that a colleague once said, "Another trip? Throwing Bibles out of planes, that's what you do!" Cloak-and-dagger stuff! Am I whetting your appetite to hear more?

Imagine I could never have dreamt of the thousands who would find new life in Christ or those who would be healed and delivered, visit heaven, see Jesus, walk and talk with angels, and experience the heavenly realm. That Jesus would walk in our meetings, and when we washed feet, those present would experience life-changing supernatural events.

After the prophetic word and reading the book *Red Star over Cuba,* I gazed at our world map in awe and trepidation as I realised that God had called me to go there! Cuba became the love of my life; Russia and Bulgaria, the inner circles of communism, part of my life! Such healings and miracles happened there. The walls gone, but oppression remained. Bucharone was an amazing place in the countryside near the zoo park, about forty minutes' drive, overlooking Guantanamo Bay and Caimanera opposite the US base. These were coffee plantations where we walked down paths amongst coffee trees and smelled the unforgettable aroma of roasted coffee. The views were amazing, especially of the brilliant sunsets and red moon. A place of many miracles. On an early visit to the house church on the hill later demolished in an earthquake, we prayed for a young woman teacher suffering with stomach cancer. We cursed the cancer and told it to go. We spoke healing, and God healed.

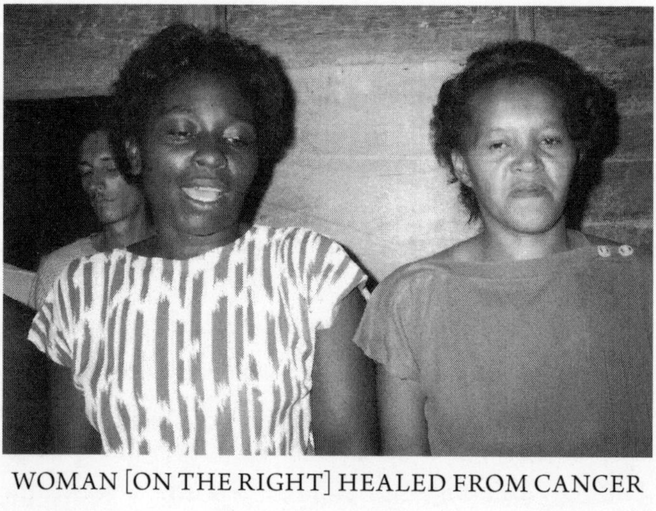

WOMAN [ON THE RIGHT] HEALED FROM CANCER

They brought a small child with cerebral palsy unable to speak or walk, and in the name of Jesus, we prayed by faith for him, speaking the blood and name of Jesus, telling his body to come into divine order; speaking to his brain, commanding it to respond. Ten years later, we saw him totally healed, leading a normal life. During an outside meeting, a man put his hand on his ear and shouted, "I can hear! Jesus healed my ear!" A woman raised her arm, shouting, "No pain! No pain! My arm was frozen, and now . . . look at me, I can raise my arm!" They were so excited to testify to being healed through the name and power of the blood of Jesus.

There was a Chicago prophet who later prophesied I would have to lay down a baby for the fresh developments God was birthing. I understood as it unfolded, that the call of God had shifted to Asia and the mountainous Himalayan region. I would no longer be as free to travel and minister in Cuba. All part of the life that unlocked in answer to the call of God.

Looking back at Asia, especially Myanmar, the first nation visited, I saw an amazing pattern. Interesting, as when we are in it, we don't see it! I first travelled to Myanmar in 1990, after the military murdered children and young people in a rebellion in 1988. I visited a month before the first elections in 1991, which the military failed to honor. I visited right after the Saffron rebellion in 2005. In Yangon, when bombs exploded, closing roads minutes before we could enter, in the Bangkok uprising when no planes flew. Again at Nargis 2007 when the military failed to allow aid to reach millions of people in the Delta and all of whom perished. And again at Chin States cyclone and disaster… and now 2021 when the borders open I must go again… to say nothing of Nepal and the times visited during the war…

But the stories are for later. "Let's start at the very beginning, a very good place to start!" It all began in Graham Street, Dunedin, at the bottom of the world, in the South Island of New Zealand, a tiny nation of two major islands, but one which had favor amongst communist nations because of its continued neutrality and the way it refused nuclear ships! I don't remember if we always lived there in Graham Street, but my earliest memories were, as a child, we lived in an old white wooden one and a half-storied house in a small, short street, at a landing on a steep long stairwell beside lots of prickly bushes. There sat our house with a veranda, where we played, and a path to Dad's large sloping back garden. The bridge between upper and lower classes, it was in a zigzag of paths. Below us lay the worst street in Dunedin, with many problems there. At a restaurant there, they cooked and served cats as chicken! Prosecuted by the police, the city shut them. We read how they brought young women in the early settlement days to the many brothels and boarding houses in this notorious street of prostitution. Men working in the gold rushes looked there for wives. As children, we saw the brothel and several boarding houses. A choice! We did not go there!

EARLY DAYS IN DUNEDIN. ACROSS THE VALLEY

EARLY DAYS. THE ZIG ZAG FROM GRAHAM STREET

Above us, the wealthy stately homes and a private hospital-home at the street corner, where I worked as a nurse's aid in holiday times.

Our grandmother Sarah was only seventeen years and pregnant when she married John David McKellar, twenty-nine years. The baby arrived shortly after. His Protestant family—wealthy landowners, bankers, important people—disowned and disinherited him because he married a pregnant Catholic girl.

John David never spoke of his upbringing. The family until recently thought him an orphan with no family at all. None of us knew this grandfather, who died in 1933 in Dunedin during a typhoid epidemic at sixty-four years. His family had a historical godly heritage from the times of the translation of the Bible in England. They martyred many of them for their faith in the 1500s, when all believers suffered terribly. The authorities chopped and put their heads on spikes and burnt these early believers to death for their determination to follow God. They had pioneer spirits; their DNA was from God.

The blood of the martyrs is the seed of the church. [Tertullian]

Many died for their faith in the release of the Bible for common people to access. What a discovery that it involved our family with early martyrs, like Tyndale and Wycliffe, who gave all to see God's word available.

MARTYRS GRAVES, ENGLAND

Our Irish grandmother's family came from Sydney, Australia, after they received their freedom. From County Clare, Ireland, and arrested for petty crime, the British Crown shipped them to Sydney as convicts. My father's family lived down High Street opposite the corner of Hope Street and the local shop where we sometimes bought things just minutes from where we lived. As children, we visited them and the extended family members who lived down the lane close by. After they moved to Brunell Street, Mornington, we visited until Grandma's death when I was about seven years.

My earliest memories as a child are of running down the steep hill from the cable car stop and climbing big steps to enter an aged brick house. Inside, a very old lady crippled with arthritis sat at the back of a room, my aunt hovering and fly papers with dirty flies hanging from the ceiling. They left a lasting impression, those dirty dead flies! We visited other family who lived nearby in Serpentine Avenue.

My father John Henry (but called Jack) loved to garden and produced prolific vegetables. Everybody in the street loved him. Could it have been because they were always getting vegetables? As a young man he worked as a joiner, but in an accident, lost two fingers, making it impossible to continue his trade. A tall simple man with black curly hair, keen blue eyes, and a bright smile, he had a fiery temper when roused. His two loves, his girls and his garden. He was difficult to live with because of his volatile Irish temperament and job instability. As an agnostic, he showed no interest in God. When his job did not go well, he would arrive home in the middle of the day, saying, "I've finished, chucked it in! Signed up!" Impetuous, impatient, within a few days, he packed and vanished for months on end, working as a deckhand on a coastal vessel. As a tiny child not seeing him for many months, on one occasion when he returned, I did not know him, which caused him to stay home more.

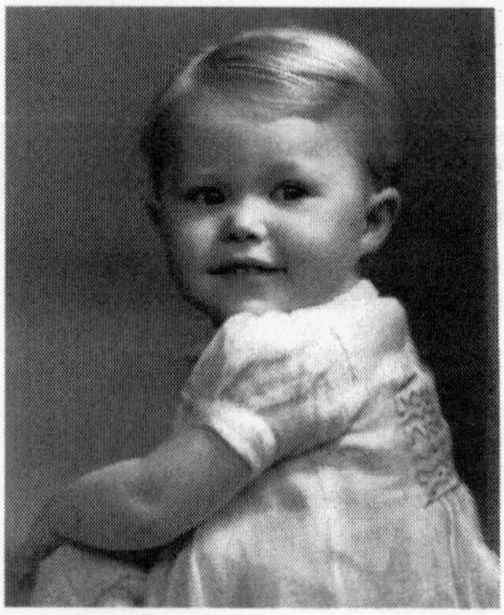

DENISE AT 2 YEARS

He would leave my mother to survive and cope alone to bring up his beloved girls. They handled money with care in our little house on the steps, but we never lacked. He could not swim but worked on a big ship, *Maheno,* in 1935. Decommissioned from being a mercy ship in the war, it shipwrecked off Fraser Island in Australia. He and eight crew members spent several days stranded on the island!

DAD 4TH IN THE BACK LINE WITH THE CREW.

MAHENO SHIP

My sister Lyndsey and I attended the local primary school up High Street, aptly named for its steepness. Grant Street, which we passed when we walked to school up the steep hill, had a large ugly dog, which we feared. It barked loudly and chased us. Sometimes we crossed the road before the hill at Melville Street to avoid the dog.

My mother Iris, with her business skills, ran a small sewing business to support us. When she was just six weeks old, my grandfather returned to the house and announced to Ellen his wife he registered the baby's name! My mother Iris Victoria Helen—named for the pretty flower, the Queen, and a beautiful name—became a skilled dressmaker and sewed for the local shows, the operatic, and ballets. She often sewed all night to complete orders and support us. We always had the most beautiful clothes. My mother made clothes for the wealthy upper-class city people and knew all the latest fashions. She sewed amazing tutus for the ballet shows and exquisite costumes for our ballet events.

Lyndsey and I danced in the overseas shows that had children's parts. In later years, my mother worked in the shoe factory at the bottom of High Street, next to the old site of the Saint James Theatre. When we were older, we would visit her where she worked near the railway station at Thompsons Boot Factory.

FAMILY

HIGH STREET SCHOOL

DENISE [SEATED 2ND RIGHT FRONT LINE].

Included in my earliest memories is saying one day at four years, "I'm off! I'm going to school!" and off I walked, carrying a small school bag. Mum thought I was just playing (as I told her often I'm going to school) and realised when I did not appear for some time. A tram driver who found me halfway to High Street School brought me back home. My father and his entire family attended school at this historic Dunedin building demolished now! Even my sister's children attended there after she married and settled in the area.

If we left home on time, we walked up the hill; if not, we caught the cable car, a tram, which the children all rode and enjoyed the thrills. After the ride, we jumped off! As children, we could not ride on the outside of the tram. After a terrible accident injuring many children, when the cable car came off the track, we rode in the tram cab!

Another memory: I danced in an Eskimo dance, at the back of the line, dancing backwards. Someone had forgotten to move an enormous statue from a previous event. I catapulted backwards into the statue, and what a shock! Behind me, a resounding crash, startling and frightening this small child!

The desire to go to Brownies and on to Girl Guides filled my life. Mother said, "Choose, ballet or Guides?" Without regret, I chose Brownies and Guides, and happily, my ballet career ended.

BALLET. LYNDSEY AND DENISE

DENISE IN SNOW WHITE AND THE SEVEN DWARFS SHOW [DENISE IS FAR RIGHT]

MUM AND DAD

My mother came from Christian roots. Her father, a backslidden believer, came from Ardgow, Central Otago, where his family had a big apple orchard. They sold the farm and moved closer to her mother's sisters in Dunedin. Her mother Ellen died of double pneumonia during the tenth pregnancy, when Iris was almost fifteen years. She carried graphic memories of her mother's death and had a great fear of dead bodies and death until she and our stepfather Basil lived next door to the funeral director's property and daily watched the activities as people came and went.

As our grandfather could not manage four children—Iris, Edna, Joyce (Mona), and William (Bill)—the family broke up. For three years, two children went to a Dunedin orphanage until he remarried, and the family reunited in Christchurch. Iris and Bill stayed with Aunt Emily for a time until she met our father and lived with his family. When she got a job, unhappy with where she stayed, she wrote to Aunt Daisy, a prominent radio talk back host, asking what did she need to do to be independent. After Aunt Daisy's reply and her questions being published, she moved out to live with my father's family.

FAMILY REUNITED AFTER THE REMARRIAGE
[IRIS AT THE BACK BESIDE NAN AND GRANDDAD]

GRANDDAD REMARRIED TO EDITH [NAN]

Granddad lived with us, and I remember he would come with his swag, stay a few weeks, and then go. After his marriage to Edith (Nan), he bought a home in Christchurch but would not live there. He worked on farms anywhere in the country and on the boats. When he tired of it all and wanted to see the family, he always knew there would be a home, a bed, and family in my mother's house. My father and he would drink at the pub and return to fight. Mother would stand between them, breaking it up. Lyndsey remembers standing between our parents, breaking up the fighting! Even though he loved the cat, he and the little black cat would struggle and push for a special hole in the couch. Neither would yield until he almost sat on top of the cat! That cat played a big part in our lives. He perched on the letter box, and when my aunt Ann would come by each day, she patted him. After she did not come for several days, the cat stood on his hind legs, took her face in his paws, and hit her on both sides of her face! Quite a cat. He had an enormous personality!

So we grew up with Granddad and the family, down the steps with all the bushes, between the slum, the lane, the rich above, the poor below. After being away, Granddad would arrive. At the letter box, he would pet the cat, and call out, "Lyndsey, Lyndsey." After hearing the call, Lyndsey would run out to see him and shout, "Granddad's here! Granddad's here!" Since she would lead Granddad in, Mother would allow him to come in to stay indefinitely! Though there were issues, our mother never turned him away. As long as he lived, Granddad always had a bed in our house. He loved to rub his long bristly ginger beard round our faces. Living in Hawea, he always said that he knew when he was welcome. He would throw his hat in the door, and if it came back, he knew whether they would welcome him! My grandfather John Petrie Carew Harvey, born in Albertown, Central Otago, a younger son of Jane and Christopher Harvey, his parents emigrated from a farm in Kent in the Orkney Islands off the coast of Scotland to live in Tarras. Christopher and Jane had a Godly heritage. Christopher, a Wesleyan circuit rider, a reverend, had a deep baritone singing voice and involved himself in establishing the Tarras School.

TARRAS SCHOOL. IRIS IN 4TH ROW 5TH RIGHT.

GRANDDAD AT THE SENIOR CITIZENS' DUNEDIN

GRANDDAD'S WEDDING TO ELLEN SPARROW

THE EXTENDED FAMILY. 2ND ROW ELLEN, BETWEEN HER TWO SISTERS MARY AND EMILY. IRIS IN FRONT OF MARY.

As we could look out our upstairs attic window across the city, we liked it there on the steps. About five minutes from the main street, we could run down to the shops. Whenever the fire sirens rang, our father listened and watched for fires. He would wake us, and we would run hand in hand, coats over pajamas, down the hill in glee and excitement to watch. A highlight in our lives. Even now, we well remember the Whit-Coulls book and stationary fire, His Majesty's Theatre and Saint James Theatre fires. As the flames roared, soaring upwards, we watched wide-eyed, open-mouthed, almost speechless. We joined the crowds and watched as the flames consumed buildings and smoke billowed in front of us. Very exciting to small and growing girls. Yet what excitement we had when we attended the fire sales— everything smelling of fire but so cheap! How we loved cheap.

At about eight years of age, Lyndsey and I went to the local Presbyterian church near to our home. For some time, in hunger for God, Lyndsey and I attended this church children's programme. After this, with my friend, I attended an evangelistic church down the hill, where I found faith in Jesus Christ. As the first Christian in the family, this began the return of my entire family to faith in Jesus. After my sister came to faith, together, we attended youth and church activities in this vibrant Anglican church. At a meeting where Rev John Stott from London ministered I declared faith in Jesus Christ.

SAINT MATTHEW'S CHURCH

At thirteen years, the Lord spoke, calling me to the nations. Whilst reading two books about Jewesses in New York, I heard God's voice to go to nations. To read books became my mission. I drank in anything I could find on missions and the nations, especially about the women pioneers, like Mary Slessor in Africa, Hudson Taylor and Maria, Mildred Cable, Francesca French in China, and the Triumph of John and Betty Stam. Books that impacted my life. I became eager to reach others for Jesus, hunger developed to learn and follow him. An evangelistic group, Open Air Campaigners, that worked on the streets became a huge focus in my life with Friday night and Saturday outreaches. I became part of a team doing a holiday programme reaching families and children holidaying in Central Otago. It was during that time our parents visited us and my father shared that he would have answered an altar call during the movie *Heart Is a Rebel*. But no older people had done so!

There, we experienced a supernatural event. Late one night, with poor visibility as we returned to where we stayed in Alexandra, we came round a steep narrow gorge with a swift, dangerous river far below. Swerving to cross the river at the bridge, a man appeared from nowhere and stood in the road, gesturing us to turn back. The car stalled as the driver assessed the scene, realising the danger. We had turned into a dead end opening onto the river, the entrance to the demolished bridge. Later we realised this man, an angel sent by the Lord, protected and saved each of our lives!

As young women, we attended Otago Girls High School in Dunedin. Whilst my earliest dreams were to be a nurse and a teacher, it seemed impossible. I did not get school certificate, the usual requirement. Only three years of high school attendance seemed an obstruction.

Whilst my father was ill with cancer, I began working as a nurse aide at the public hospital. After a year working in the neurosurgical theatre, my father was dying. Because assistance was needed at home, I resigned from my job as my mother needed support. We felt so happy when he said, "It's great to know where I am going." At only fifty-one years, he died.

I entered the three-year nursing diploma training programme. In preliminary classes, the sister tutor told me, "You must be so careful because anytime something happens, they will blame you because you always smile. They think you are the mischief maker!" I carefully followed her warning.

Student nurses lived in the nursing home until final exams. In my second year of training, an old friend, Paul Davidson, a missionary in Pakistan, returned to stay at our house. He wanted to connect with several hundred young men led to Jesus during his time as Youth Leader at the Y.M.C.A. After knocking one night on my husband-to-be's door, he asked him, "Do you still follow Jesus? Are you doing anything to follow him? Will you help me visit those who came to Jesus through me?"

Kevin replied, "Yes, I can help you in the evenings after work."

Each night Kevin and Paul visited the entire group, reconnecting and discipling them. One evening, as I prepared for bed, showered with hair in curlers, the phone rang on the floor. Someone called me, and when I answered, a voice said, "Come to coffee . . ." But they accepted no excuses; hair in curlers, we had coffee. After three nights, having devotions, sitting above the city, at the lover's leap, he said, "Pray about it . . ." The rest is history. For we had the proverbial matchmaker, and God sent Paul from Pakistan for our divine appointment.

OUR SPECIAL FRIENDS AND MISSIONARIES, PAUL AND HELEN

To study hard was the key as finals loomed close. Kevin was away in Otematata, working on a power project, and visited every second weekend. State finals followed, and we waited anxiously for the results. Excitement filled the air, I passed!

At graduation, on behalf of the graduating class, they honored me by asking me to speak the Nightingale pledge:

I solemnly pledge myself before God and in the presence of this assembly to pass my life in purity and to practise my profession faithfully.

I will abstain from whatever is deleterious and mischievous and will not take or knowingly administer any harmful drug.

I will do all in my power to maintain and elevate the standard of my profession and will hold in confidence all personal matters committed to my keeping and all family affairs coming to my knowledge in the practise of my calling.

With loyalty will I aid the physician in his work, and as a missioner of health, I will dedicate myself to devoted service for human welfare.

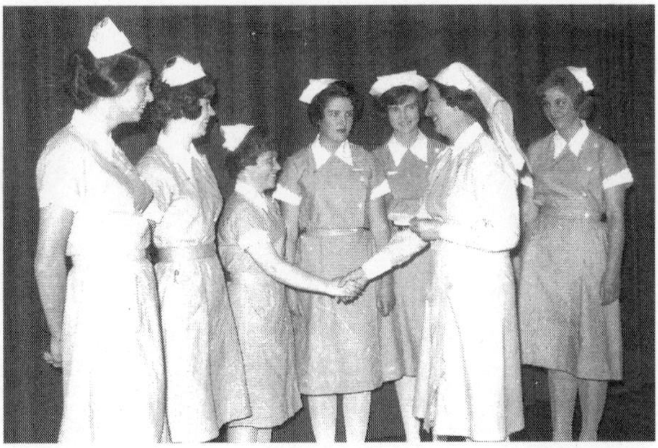

GRADUATION – DENISE SHAKING HANDS WITH THE TUTOR SISTER.

Only two of our original class of twenty-four graduated that year. Those who had not already left for other lifestyles and jobs graduated later. But others who had missed sections previously, joined our class. And all six of us graduated! Our photos were in the paper. So often, when the newspapers wanted photos of nursing events, they chose me! That would never happen now.

After a year as a staff nurse, Kevin and I married. Engaged after courting for a year, we married with all the trimmings. A simple wedding, just an afternoon tea, as my widowed mother had limited money. We loved Jesus, and we would be okay. We had God. What else did we need?

DENISE AND KEVIN'S WEDDING

MOTHER AND DAUGHTER

After a honeymoon around the North Island New Zealand, with its amusing challenging moments, we settled in Otematata, North Otago, living in a compact unit on the power scheme in a project town.

On a visit to Pounawea Christmas Christian camp, in the deep south, God spoke to us to go to the nations, and we had noble plans. The nations were in sight as we planned to obey God.

> If you love God, he empowers you to do what he says.
>
> —John 14:15 TPT

We had the plan—to move north, to go to Bible school in Auckland. As we belonged to the Anglican Church, we desired to serve with their Mission Society. On enquiry, we discovered we needed money and training as doors were open in Africa.

Desiring to be closer to our goal, we moved north, from Otago to Hamilton, for Kevin to work in a Ministry of Works workshop. Hamilton was like a new country, very different from the South Island. They even spoke differently and had different names for things.

We stayed for a short time with new friends. Pregnant and due, my waters broke. The maternity hospital sent Kevin home, saying, "come back in the morning, nothing is happening." At 3:00 a.m., they performed an emergency caesarean section as I had severe pain and complications.

Kevin woke to the announcement we had an eight-pound fifteen-ounce baby boy. Yet at 4:00 p.m., though the baby delivered early that morning, I had not seen the baby. After tears, the baby appeared rapidly to this anxious new mother! We moved into a unit provided by the job and settled there.

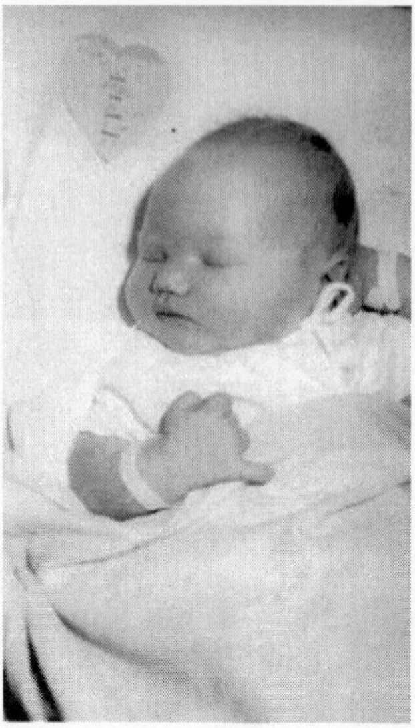

THE BABY, PAUL JOHN REID, 8LB:15OZ ARRIVED.

We named the baby Paul after our special missionary friend Paul who had such an important place in our lives and Paul the apostle. Now focused, we were on our way to Bible college to obey God and go to the nations!

> And I pray that he would unveil within you the unlimited riches of his glory and favor until supernatural strength floods your innermost being with his divine might and explosive power. Then, by constantly using your faith, the life of Christ will be released deep inside you, and the resting place of his love will become the very source and root of your life.
>
> —Ephesians 3:16–17 TPT

CHAPTER 2

Ordinary—Are You Ordinary?

> A time to kill and a time to heal,
> a time to tear down and a time to build.
> a time to weep and a time to laugh,
> a time to mourn and a time to dance,
> a time to scatter stones and a time to gather them,
> a time to embrace and a time to refrain from embracing...
> —Ecclesiastes 3:3-6 ESV

Paul, an active growing child, full of curiosity, jacked up the car and trailer, regularly filled the lawn mower with gravel, the car petrol tank with water, and dare I say endless other things! After several miscarriages and much emotion, another baby came again by caesarean section because of my tiny body size. I groaned when they told me of his daily activities whilst in the hospital with Rachel. Every day, staying with friends, he unscrewed hundreds of screws from an ancient historic telephone. Every night they screwed the telephone case and box back together! By the time I returned home from hospital, this small child had become an expert with a screwdriver! He could use anything—knives, scissors, anything with a flat surface to unscrew doors, cupboards, windows, you name it—anything at all! What a nightmare! And he had an eye now for any screw anywhere!

Life took a normal roll; Kevin working at the Frankton workshop, me at home with the growing baby. Family visited; normal life enveloped us as we lived in suburbia. Lyndsey and Herb at NZ Bible College in Auckland were high on our places-to-visit list. We seemed okay. We all look like good Christians, but often things are not the way they look! We loved God but could not love one another despite our involvement in Christian work, meetings, and church.

Involved in missions even then, we organised other young people, read and prayed and shared about the nations. Anglicans, we met others of like persuasion. Open Air Campaigners featured high in our life's activities, and we enjoyed weekend outreaches.

Three years after Rachel arrived, our marriage disintegrated because of a breakdown, severe postnatal depression, many miscarriages, and much dysfunction. After many problems, much stress and anger, I fled Hamilton with two small children to return to the family in Dunedin. For a short time, we stayed with my sister before renting an apartment nearby. I gained employment at the local hospital, working nights in intensive care. Kevin and I were apart eighteen months; during which, Christians tried to do God's job for him. They cajoled me, talking endlessly about how my place was with my husband. But despite the endless words, they all fell on deaf ears!

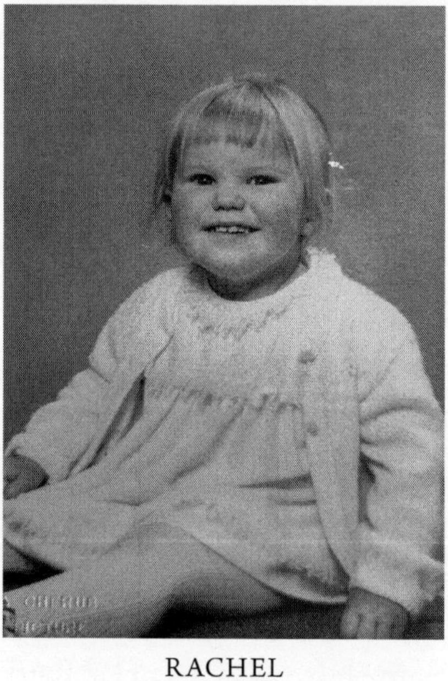

RACHEL

During this time, my mother remarried a fine Catholic widower with five grown children. Basil and Iris lived happily until their deaths within two weeks of each other in the year 1993. They had a beautiful relationship, loving and serving each other.

BASIL AND IRIS.

Returning from school to our apartment one day, Paul said, "Mummy, a car hit me on the leg."

Though only five years old, he walked home each day from the nearby school, where few cars came into the street. Until then, I thought the way very safe!

"What happened?" I enquired, alarmed.

"A car hit me on the leg."

"Did you look both ways before you crossed the street?"

"Yes, Mummy," he replied. "But the car kept on coming!"

After that, I met him each day when school finished.

Such an active child, he tried to light fires under the bed; there were the regular flat tyres when we found small tacks by the car wheels, and one day, just before church, all four tyres on the car were flat as he had placed tacks beside each tyre!

DENISE WITH PAUL AND RACHEL IN DUNEDIN

At the end of the first six months, Kevin wrote, asking if there was any hope of reconciliation. Speedily, I replied to say no chance unless he changed! Towards the end of the following six months, I attended a conference in Christchurch, at which I received much prayer. And the Lord touched me mightily and spoke. “Do you love Me?”

I replied, “Lord, You know I love You.”

“Love your husband?”

“Lord, I don’t love him anymore!”

The Lord spoke again. “Do you love Me?”

“Lord, You know I love You.”

“Love your husband!”

“Lord, I can’t do that. I don’t love him anymore! It’s finished, I can’t do it. It’s too tough. It’s too hard. He hasn’t changed!”

He asked me again, “Are you willing to be made willing to love him by faith?”

I said, "God, I can't do it, but if You can help me, I'm willing to be made willing . . . Even if he is unchanged?"

Came the Lord's admonition, "Allow Me to love him through you."

"Lord, by faith, I can do that. I will allow You to love him through me. Lord, I can't do it, but You can. By faith, I will allow You to love him through me." I cried.

Because of this encounter with the Lord, on my return to Dunedin, I wrote to Kevin, asking, "Can we meet, please?"

Startled and concerned, he pondered over my request and phoned to say, "I haven't changed, I am what I am!"

During the next month, we communicated, whilst I prayed God would solve and bring restoration to our marriage. Finally, we met in Christchurch, a neutral area for a weekend. I travelled by car to Christchurch, believing God would do a miracle. He came by plane, saying, "Unless she has changed, there is no hope!"

On the way to the airport in torrential rain, I misjudged an intersection on a busy highway, ending up the car straddled across the middle island of the road. Two men came quickly to my aid. Like angels, God sent them to lift my compact car off its precarious position. Immediately, they saw the sign on my vehicle, "God cares." They said, "God looked after you, lady!" Indeed, he did.

I collected Kevin from the airport, and we spent the weekend together. He later remarked he met a woman he never knew! God did it; He performed a miracle in response to His promise. After we moved to live in Christchurch to restore our marriage, we joined a Papanui church, where, to my dismay, there were almost no other young couples. No one knew our history. With increasing involvement there, the Lord continued to work in our lives.

> When we love him, he empowers us to do what he says.
> He does not abandon us.
>
> —John 14:15 TPT

Eight thrilling, life-challenging years followed in Christchurch, ministering in an Anglican church at Papanui, where we made many wonderful friends. Shortly after our arrival, I discovered I was pregnant. Alarmed because of the history of our lives and past pregnancies, I visited the doctor, a Catholic specialist known for his conservative beliefs, who examined my terrible history and recommended terminating the pregnancy and having a tubal ligation to ensure no further pregnancies! There appeared to be no choice but to consider his suggestion.

The next day I woke with a heavy black cloud that had descended strongly on me, whereupon I entered a severe depression. Reluctantly, not believing in abortion, I agreed to proceed as planned, even though everything within my innermost being appeared to fight against the plan. The surgery proceeded, the cloud lifted, and I knew I had made the right choice for my mental health and marriage to survive.

ST PAULS CHURCH PAPANUI

PASTORS JOHN & MONICA MEADOWCROFT

After the return to health, our lives continued normally. I worked on afternoons at the gynecological hospital, Kevin, for the Ministry of Works. We ran the huge children's church and became involved in drama. Many Christmas presentations followed in which we adapted children's stories and animal stories from Paul White's Jungle Doctor series and Oscar Wilde's story, "-The Selfish Giant." A fun time with endless opportunities for evangelism and divine appointments in the parish. Our interest in missions exploded. Kevin joined the church eldership, whilst the Lord stirred our hearts to extend our borders to open our home to the needy. Our DNA stirred! Missions were in the blood. As children of the King, we recognised our identity and responsibility to bring the kingdom of heaven to earth everywhere, not just in overseas missions but also in the local community. Missions involved all our lives; everywhere we lived, worked, and moved, we accepted as ministry. We realised the need to do the works that Jesus did and greater works right where we lived to reach and love the lost.

> Enlarge the place of your tent and let the curtains of your habitations be stretched out; do not hold back; lengthen your cords and strengthen your stakes.
>
> —Isaiah 54:2 ESV

In obedience to His voice, "If you love me, I will empower you to do as I say," John 14:15 TPT. He will not abandon us; He empowers us.

God did just that. We had been reading a series of books on family, living as a community, sharing our lives in common. Acts 2:4 speaks of this, of how the believers shared daily and lived their lives in common.

> Every believer was faithfully devoted to following the teachings of the apostles. Their hearts were mutually linked to one another, sharing in communion, and coming together regularly for prayer.
>
> —Acts 3:42 TPT

Because of this, we shared our lives with several single young people in the church. As a home cell, we met weekly with them for fellowship and prayer. Money scarce, we trusted the Lord often for food and current needs. God, Jehovah Jireh, loves us and cares for our needs; thus, we saw Him provide through people in amazing ways.

Sue and Robert were among our new friends and a creative time ensued as together Sue and I made and sold beautiful coloured ice candles for Christmas gifts, and explored doing leather work which I also sold. Both these skills brought us both financial provision in a time of need. I had met them previously at the Conference where God spoke to change my directions.

It was during this time that Sue asked me, "what happened when you had the termination?" I replied and told her of the depression I suffered and how I had no choices in the matter. The following day I felt that black cloud of depression descend on me and that night I had a vision. In the vision I saw some ugly, slimy, dead black ducks down on the ground beside me. As I looked at them they began to squirm and move and the more I looked the more they came to life! I heard the voice of the Lord saying,

"Don't look back it gives the past power over you!" I repented for doing so and never had another problem. This has become a feature in my life when facing difficult situations. The Bible is very clear on this where it says,

> "Do not remember the former things,
> Nor consider the things of old.
> 19 Behold, I will do a new thing,
> Now it shall spring forth;
> NKJV Isaiah 43:18-19

We needed potatoes but had little money to buy them. As we drove to church one day, a truck, carrying just what we needed, passed us. Off the truck rolled a huge sack of potatoes. We stopped the car, jumped out, grabbed the big sack, but when we looked for the truck, it was long gone! Now we had our potatoes. How we thanked God as it had been some time since we had enjoyed kiwi "spuds"!

Kevin enjoyed his cup of coffee, but we had run out again. We prayed for coffee. The answer came when the group arrived one night with a large tin of coffee. Again, we thanked God for His divine provision.

The neighbour, a firefighter, knocked on our door one morning with his arms full of food, groceries, and fruit. "We had all this extra food," he said. "We thought you may need some." Overwhelmed, we thanked him and praised God for His abundant provision. God loves us and knows our every need—Jehovah Jireh, our provider.

DENISE & KEVIN

RACHEL

Joy, with her two small boys, separated from her husband, came to live with us. Now, at more than our full capacity, stretched and squashed, we lived in our small house in an inner suburb of Christchurch. We thought if God is speaking about community, we should just do it here, where we are right now. That's what they did in the Bible, so we did it, squeezed in but happy. We loved her and her two little boys.

Do you believe in the supernatural? Despite having no finance, we approached the church leadership to talk about the house we hoped to buy. A man approached Kevin. "If you need finance, contact this lawyer as he will help you." The following week, the bank refused the money, and when we returned to the church, that same man said he had made an appointment for us with the lawyer. We attended the appointment, the lawyer phoned the bank, arranged the mortgage, and before we left his office, the house became ours! All with no money! Plus, two weeks before closure and moving date, the lawyer called to say, "Get the key, you can move in right now!" God delights to do the impossible! What is impossible with man is always possible to God.

HOLLY ROAD

This house had twenty-three rooms, in a neighbouring suburb to the church, just five to ten minutes' drive. A wonderful time accommodating needy people, loving those who came to our door. In this enormous house, after we prayed to cleanse it of demonic activity, we enjoyed a hospitality ministry. A coal stove kept us cozy, warmed the kitchen, heated the water, whilst soup and food were always ready for those who visited.

Mysterious things often happened in the rooms. Our daughter's bedroom above the front door had a light bulb that repeatedly fell out of the ceiling yet did not break! After we prayed and spoke deliverance, it stopped.

As Kevin lay in bed with an injured back, we called the church. After they came and prayed, he rose, healed.

We had a large lounge and wanted a piano. After prayer, we saw in the local paper a piano to give away. When collected, it did not even need tuned.

Miracles happened all the time, as food continued to arrive at the door to supply our needs. Hamish, one of Joy's little boy, suffered from a hole in his heart. We prayed over him, and God healed. A young woman needing prayer collapsed on the front door mat. We heard a noise and on investigation we found her rolled up on the mat! She said she couldn't enter as she fell down on the doorstep under Holy Spirit's power! A Dutch couple, tourists travelling through the South Island, arrived with multiple drug charges and court problems. We gave them a bed and prayed. The next day, when they presented at court, they found their case disappeared—acquitted, with no case to answer for.

We wanted a church vegetable garden, so the big lawn beside the church drew our eyes. "Yes," we could do it, we could use the land. But no one told us that underneath the grass, a tennis court! Anyway, with a lot of toil and sweat, they dug out the black-sealed court with a rotary hoe! The hard work completed, we planted a community garden. After prayer, no weeds grew! Only an abundant supply of vegetables, which we gave away!

Jesus changed many nominal believers' lives, as each Tuesday I would visit around the church members.

"Eva needs her hip fixed, she needs surgery, with a plaster cast for months. For many months, she was in a splint. I visited the specialist for her hip X-ray, and he said "The hip joint bulb is too shallow, needing repair. She will be so heavy as she is growing fast. I don't know how I will manage—it will be so difficult." Said Jen.

In response to a call from Jen, filled with anxiety and stress, she tearfully confided in me. Eva, her beautiful ten-month baby, sat in the high chair. "We shall pray, if it's okay with you. We'll ask the church prayer group to pray." Everyone prayed.

A month passed, and in response to Jen's call, I returned to visit the family of four girls. Her voice was full of excitement. "It must have been your prayers! When I took Eva to the specialist, they did another Xray. The hip socket and ball were all normal! God must have healed her."

As we hugged, I praised God that nothing is impossible to Him.

Prue, an attractive ex air hostess and solo parent, had four children. I had been visiting her for some time, reaching out in love, seeking to befriend and lead her to a relationship with Jesus. After my visit, she noticed the goldfish floating upside down, dying. Concerned that it would upset the children, she prayed, "God, if you're there, heal this goldfish!" The goldfish became normal, and as a result, she gave her life to Jesus.

We developed in our relationship. One day she shared with me she had entered a new partnership. I suggested that, as a believer, she should reconsider this by not sleeping with Dave until they married. She scoffed rather loudly, "That's impossible! How can you ask that of me! Don't be ridiculous! I've been married before . . . It's okay!"

Without judgment, in love, I showed her what the Bible said on this matter—marriage, then sexual relationships; intimacy after marriage! Sometime later she married Dave, but within a short time, physical abuse took place. That marriage failed, and she fled Christchurch to return to her family in the far north.

The pastor called to ask would I visit a family in the state housing area nearby. A young woman opened the door and said, "My husband had an accident. He came off his bike and has just come home from hospital. We have two small children but no food to give them. Come in!" We visited often. They grew marijuana in a backyard shed! They had quite a history, but both came to faith in Jesus Christ. The secretary of a major motorbike gang, he married when gang members did not marry. They just lived with the women! He had a heavy chain wound around his neck and arm, used for locking the bike, but it broke his arm in the accident. Both came from prominent Auckland families who had rejected their offspring's lifestyles. The parents committed their daughter, his wife, to a mental institution for two years because of rebellion and noncompliance with family values. We served them, loving them into the kingdom. The husband lived with a shotgun under the bed, prompted by deep inner fear. His wife did not leave the house, afraid that someone would abduct her. Jesus healed and took their fear, filling them with His love.

Dee, a young woman with a baby and two other children, all from different fathers, lived in a state house near the church and wanted her baby baptised. Pastor John asked me to visit, seeking to know if she would start coming to church and make a commitment to Christ. Baptism is a commitment to follow Jesus, an outwards declaration of an inner change. This brings a cutting off the old life and a release of the new.

DEE AND OUR FRIEND MARGARET

Dee would inevitably call us day and night at any hour when she ran out of money! Often! Children's birthdays would come, special occasions would arise, whereupon she would spend her whole welfare payment to buy celebratory food, dolls, and toys to bless the children. In the following days, she would phone with the sad story: "I have no money for food! The children are hungry. I need milk mixture for the baby!" We would have to help! We are His hands and feet, the hands and feet of Jesus. We could not leave a baby or children with no milk or food! She loved Jesus! She gardened with the cutlery and planted flowers and vegetables, digging small areas with the knives and forks! I'm not sure how she did it, but she persevered, and remarkably, the plants grew! We loved her and all the others we visited, some of whom we took in to live with us!

One woman visited suffered severe abuse, and after being in the women's refuge, she lived in the parish. So needy, so lacking in love, thin, frightened of life, she struggled for survival! On this day, absent when I called, I left vegetables on her doorstep. She phoned to thank us. "Thank you for coming, thanks for the food! You are my only friend!" Her gratitude overwhelmed me. We are the hands and feet of Jesus to bring His love. My heart broke for those visited!

Challenges came and went. After an emotional break up of our blended family and household, we moved to Hamilton in the north in obedience to the Lord; Kevin to work as a counselor in a drug and alcohol rehabilitation centre.

Within weeks of our arrival, staying in a house provided by the ministry, we experienced a greatly traumatic attack, which changed the life of our family. Bad things happen to God's people. We can be in the plan of God but still undergo difficult traumatic experiences. I have found through my life *it's not what happens to us but how we deal with it to make us better, not bitter.*

Our son needed to go to secondary school, and newfound friends challenged us to believe God for a private school, for the best! We believed God, tested the *water,* and applied for his entry to the third form class. A miracle happened! He received a full scholarship, allowing him to attend an Anglican school in the city, all expenses paid!

After the horrendous attack at the corner of our street, Paul entered a time away from God, then at eighteen years after he experienced baptism, he briefly returned to the Lord. For the next ten years, he lived a very different lifestyle, opposite to all we believed. A bush man on drugs, alcohol, women, prison, all became part of his complicated life! We prayed.

Again we extended and opened our home to two needy young women from a girls' refuge not without difficulty as they had been abused and one had a baby.

After a return to nursing in a city health centre, I attended and graduated with an infant welfare child health diploma in 1983 to become a Plunket nurse specialising in child health. It had taken three months of commuting to and from Auckland to achieve the diploma. Studying became a way of life.

Paul and Rachel, our growing teenagers, were both at Hillcrest High School, and we now attended the Apostolic church, as the Anglican parish had no programme for teenagers.

A year was spent as the priority area nurse working in a combined role for two different organisations. The principal purpose: to deal with child abuse. I visited the worst-abuse situations in the city, checking weekly on their babies and small children whilst offering counseling that would reverse the deep-seated abuse. There were those who fed their baby salt, shook their babies, who punished their infants by burning them with cigarettes, a starved nine-month-old girl the size of a three-month-old baby, twin babies covered in scabies, and more. They all needed love!

Now a new scene in full-time service, trusting God for our needs, I, doing God's work in nursing; Kevin doing God's work in ministry. Kevin's job provided an older house on a tribal burial ground, where we lived for some time, but not without many issues.

As Christians, everything in life is God's work. Whatever we do is serving Jesus, working for Him.

> Yes, we are all in full-time service when we give our lives to Jesus. When we become a new creation, He tabernacles with us. He lives in us and seats us with him in heavenly places because we have the life of Christ, the DNA of God in us.
>
> —Ephesians 2:6 Paraphased.

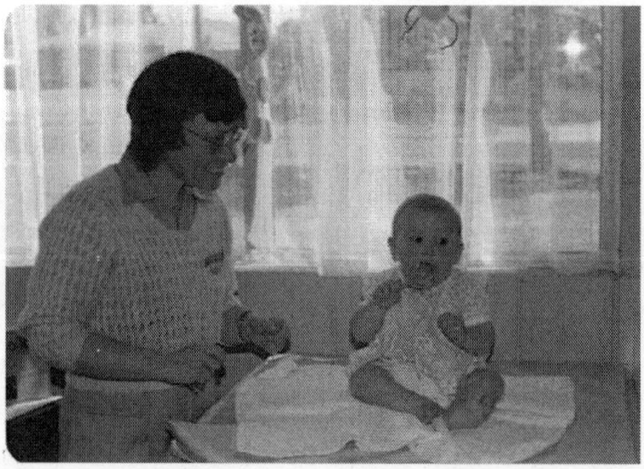

DENISE WORKING AS A PLUNKET NURSE [1983]

A new day and a new season for the unlocking of His purpose and His plan.

> There is a time for everything, a season for every activity under the heavens . . .
>
> —Ecclesiastes 3:1 ESV

Camping with an ancient Kombi Van on the Coromandel Peninsula, we explored on two motorbikes, with the kids pillion passengers on the back.

KEVIN, PAUL AND RACHEL WITH THE CAR AND BIKES.

Oh what fun we had, fishing, a popular pastime on the west and east coasts, and panning for gold in the streams.

During this time, we bought and settled on a sandy property at beautiful Whangamata. Just five minutes away from the ocean, we walked, surfed, swam, fished, boated, and did almost everything anyone could do at such a magnificent beach. Friends and family visited us to enjoy the scenery and hospitality. What a fantastic time! After starting with only two caravans, we built a garage and a framed house and planted an abundance of fruit trees on the property. Such a blessing to have a regular orchard with luscious, tree-ripened, fresh fruit! In Hamilton, we made friends at church, leading to Kevin being invited to go turkey-shooting with a new friend.

KEVIN, PAUL AND RACHEL, SHOOTING TURKEYS WITH OUR SPECIAL FRIEND PETER

Here at the beach, during the time with the caravans, at 1:00 a.m., loud hammering and banging on the door rudely awakened us. That night Kevin had been to the shops and, on his return, mentioned he witnessed a man steal a motorbike then abandon it. Kevin intervened in the situation by taking the bike to the police station. With the police officer unwell, his wife advised Kevin to push the bike onto our property for safekeeping 'til they could deal with the matter in the morning. Kevin opened the door, only to be dragged outside by an angry drunk man who cruelly and viciously beat him around the head. We prayed in the name of Jesus and screamed for help, all the whilst trying to stop the violent beating. Our son ran to the neighbour to phone the police who later apologised. "We're so sorry, but . . . the man came looking for his bike, so we told him you had it in safekeeping at your place!" When he found it on our property, he thought we had stolen it.

Attacked and assaulted here at our beautiful retreat property at Whangamata. Such a terrifying experience for us, the innocent victims. Kevin lost a photographic memory that night. He suffered considerable brain damage from the head injury; that he would carry for the rest of his life! With this injury, life now out of control, his struggle to remember day-to-day things prevented him from obtaining work.

KOMBI VANS CAN DO ANYTHING... ESPECIALLY OLD ONES! WHO NEEDS A TRACTOR WHEN YOU HAVE A KOMBI!

HOUSE AT WHANGAMATA

KEVIN & DENISE

Here, we spent time in relationship, seeking God. Here in this beautiful place of relationship, when I rose early to seek the Lord whilst gazing in awe at the magnificent glowing sunrises, Jesus spoke to guide, lead, and direct. Time on our side to walk the beach in the summer sun, float in the ocean, lie on my surfboard in the clear cool water, all the whilst having a heart-to-heart talk to Jesus. Though we did not realise it, vision unfolded, as pioneers rise to vision.

> At each and every sunrise you will hear my voice as I prepare my sacrifice of prayer to you. Every morning I lay out the pieces of my life on the altar and wait for your fire to fall upon my heart.
>
> —Psalm 5:3 - The Message.

KEVIN AFTER FISHING

We moved again to rental accommodation in Queenwood, Hamilton, as Kevin returned to secular work as a management officer with the local government but remained extremely unwell.

After an interview at the local polytech, I had a career-change to work for ten years in nursing education. Finally, after all these years, now not only a nurse but also a teacher! My earliest dreams realised. My hope for the future coming into full view.

> For I know the plans I have for you, declares the LORD, plans for welfare and not for evil, to give you a future and a hope.
>
> —Jeremiah 29:11 - NIV

> Never doubt God's mighty power to work in you and accomplish all this. He will achieve infinitely more than your greatest request, your most unbelievable dream, and exceed your wildest imagination! He will outdo them all, for his miraculous power constantly energizes you.
>
> —Ephesians 3:20 TPT

At Queenwood Avenue, that vision of God for nations returned. In 1989, an e-mail arrived from an organisation, stating Myanmar is opening to the gospel; they would arrange a team to go. My heart leapt within me! Shortly after this, three of us from the family attended the Armed and Dangerous Rally to hear some powerful New Zealand speakers, Winkie Pratney and Trevor Yaxley, and there, God spoke. When the meeting concluded, I turned to my accompanying family members, declaring, "God spoke to me! He told me to go to Myanmar."

"Whatever He says to you, just do it! Do whatever He tells you! Do the crazy thing! Don't wait! Just do it! Don't consult anyone. Just do it!" came the pleas of this dynamic, hilarious preacher.

> Before I formed you in the womb I knew you, and before you were born I consecrated you; I appointed you a prophet to the nations.
>
> —Jeremiah 1:5 ESV

Positioned by God, I sent a message to the organisation, asking when the group expected to travel. They quickly phoned to say April! I considered the issues. Already in February, I had no passport and had not yet shared my heart with Kevin!

Friday night in the car, we travelled to the beach; Kevin drove as always. I chose the moment. "God spoke to me at Armed and Dangerous—He told me to go to Myanmar! I just heard from the group who are going in April . . . but I can't go!"

"Why not? If God spoke, you must do it! Ask your boss for leave!" He calmly replied.

And so it all began. God revitalised, renewed, restored that call to nations with travel to Thailand and Myanmar (Burma). At work, they denied my request for leave. After three visits to the institute principal, on the final day for sending the money, he phoned and granted the leave against all protocols. It took persistence, prayer, and fasting, but praise God, granted at the eleventh hour—God released the miracle from heaven! When provisions of money came in for my airfare, my faith boosted.

April couldn't come quick enough! A team of fourteen ladies and one man flew out for two weeks' ministry in Asia to a restricted nation . . . but just three days in Myanmar! I looked at the team, surprised to find all but me had travelled frequently before! The question arose: "Will I do this again? Is this what my future holds?" They all seemed so familiar with the plan, having taken part in this ministry repeatedly, whilst here, the "green horn" doing this for the first time!

In our Bangkok hotel room, I woke at 4:00 a.m. with a choking attack! Dramatic, the first of many incidences when the devil tried to kill me. Coughing uncontrollably, unable to breathe, vomit rose into my throat, immobilising me. The gasping for breath so immense and loud it woke my roommate Jen. She ran for a bucket and prayed, speaking the name of Jesus, pleading the blood of Jesus. I could hear her calling on the name and blood of Jesus, commanding demons to flee! As she held the bucket under my head, Jen shouted the name of Jesus whilst slapping me on the back to dislodge any foreign matter. I could clearly hear desperation in her voice, but unable to breathe, I could do nothing but gasp and choke, immobilised. It took over thirty minutes before I recovered from the exhaustion and drama! But praise God, the devil lost that battle. There is power in the name and blood of Jesus; He does all things well.

FIRST TEAM TO MYANMAR

We met with believers secretly in the dark just after the 1988 uprising, when children and students in the nation had protested about the military oppression. The army responded by force, entering universities and schools, shooting young people and protestors. A bloodbath in which thousands lost their lives. The Red Cross did their very best to rescue as many as possible.

STREET DEMONSTRATIONS

They "bugged" the old Strand Hotel downtown where we stayed. When we talked, we resorted to the bathroom, turned on the taps, and whispered. Military personnel were everywhere when we entered the nation. The generals were all lined up at the airport, and it being the annual water festival, the atmosphere electric, full of excitement, spurred me on to fire my water pistol. I had a squirt bottle full of water, which I aimed towards the generals, but they had the last advantage, with inspection of our bags severe!

The pioneers of Hebrews 11 had vision, experienced revelation, and saw into the unseen. That happened for me on the visit to the Shwedagon Pagoda after a revelation of God. I recognised that only in the name and blood of Jesus could one receive salvation. As I gazed at the magnificence of the pagoda with its gold and gems, I looked at what I could only describe as a minor display of Solomon's temple. The beautiful flowers, the smell of incense filled the air, the various offerings all sparkly and bright—and the money given out of total poverty! But as I surveyed the sad scene of hopelessness hidden beyond the glamor, my heart cried within me. "There is only one way—the way of Jesus and the cross." How could they receive an answer when praying to gods of wood and stone? Jesus is the only answer. It is solely in the name and power of Jesus's blood that they could receive the promised salvation and indwelling, life-giving Holy Spirit.

SHWEDAGON–A WONDER OF THE WORLD.

MONK

NUNS

Thirty years later, we revisited the beautiful old Strand Hotel, where we stayed in Yangon on that first trip. After a delightful morning tea, we enjoyed the atmosphere as we listened to an enjoyable musical presentation.

NEW STRAND HOTEL

The hotel was renovated and restored from its former filthy state that I remembered so well—taps didn't work, no showers, rooms damp, towels needed laundering, the rooms bugged with secret microphones, and lightbulbs so dim they cast shadows over everything. In this restricted period, when they forbade churches to meet, with military on patrol at every corner, spies watched our daily movements, and we could only travel on government-arranged tours. Undaunted by what we saw or the strict conditions we adhered to, this was a journey of discovery on this first trip from New Zealand. Though wide-eyed and awed, I loved every minute. Each morning I rose at five o'clock to walk the streets, explore my surroundings, whilst witnessing to the people of the love of Jesus. Old and new greeted me: poor straw houses beside beautiful new buildings. Ancient decadent stately houses, unkept in total disrepair since the British left in 1948, showed no maintenance or upkeep ever undertaken.

On this first trip to Myanmar in 1989, I met Doctor Tu, a Kachin pastor, with an organisation in Thailand, assisting restricted nations. Senior pastor at a Myanmar fellowship there, he shared years later that I prayed for him in the kitchen, and Jesus baptised him in the Holy Spirit. He asked us to check on his wife and young family, still in Yangon, unable to join him. Thus, we assisted her survival in this tough season of restriction and persecution. Doctor Tu became a long-term friend, later confiding that his brother, a conservative Kachin pastor, Lazum Lahtoi, and his family lived in Yangon, working with a doctor there.

DOCTOR TU WHO WORKS IN BANGKOK & ACROSS ASIA.

DANIEL FROM THE KAREN TRIBE

On our return to New Zealand, sitting beside me on the long flight from Bangkok to Auckland was a man in national costume. Daniel, a Karen believer on his way to Bible school in New Zealand, shared many amazing stories as we sped through the night sky towards our journey's end. That began a relationship with this precious believer and his family, who came later from Yangon.

After this visit, I heard from people in the Philippines inviting me to mission work, trekking in the hills, but this "Kiwi foot soldier" was not going there! My family hooted at the thought of their mother trekking over rough terrain!

Through a prophetic word later that year, God spoke again to call me to the four corners of the earth through prophetic leaders in New Zealand. "You must go to the four corners of the earth. Myanmar is only the beginning. You will go again and again. You will see signs, wonders, and miracles." After the word, I gazed at the world map on our kitchen wall, and to my amazement, there were four corners: Russia, the Middle East, New Zealand, and Cuba! After this, I prayed and fasted, rising early in the morning to seek God. In prophetic acts I declared and decreed God would do it, daily speaking by faith, I asked God for nations. I laid hands on the world map on our kitchen wall and declared that I would see signs, wonders, and miracles in these places. God would do these things! No one wants to know you at 4:00 a.m.; the phone does not ring at 4:00 a.m.! At 4:00 a.m., I prayed!

> You will decide on a matter, and it will be established for you, and light will shine on your ways.
>
> Job 22:28 ESV

I always had trouble with faith. My sister Lyndsey seemed to have no problem believing, and others seemed to have great testimonies of how God did things for them, but me, I had trouble seeing God do things for me. After listening to Derek Prince and the Copelands, I read the Bible out loud and wrote any good verses I found, establishing the power of declaration and proclamation in my life.

Each week I confessed these good verses and declared them over my life. In Hebrews 3 and 4, it speaks of the Israelites who could not enter the Promised Land because they did not combine faith with what they believed; they were full of unbelief. When I realised this, the atmosphere changed over my life, and faith came by hearing and hearing from the word of God. As I spoke the word of God, I heard the word of God, and my faith grew. Later I came into the revelation that when born again, I became a new creation; I received the faith of God, that I had the faith of God!

As one of the few believers in the nursing department, there were many challenging moments. During this time, the associate head of the department came into my office for a matter we needed to discuss. As she looked at the desk beside mine, on which hung a witch's pendulum alongside other objects promoting that colleague's beliefs, she gasped, "How can they do that to you? How can they put someone like that in the same office alongside you?"

"It's okay," I said. "It's not a problem. I have greater power inside me than what she does. I have the power of God."

Distracted by life, family, children, work, church, other plans, we had failed to do what God said. The vision we had did not lie. God had spoken. Something distracted us from it. Not intentionally. Just not doing what He asked, God's ultimate plan and purposes obscured for a season. He waited now for the appointed time as His vision and plan were unchanged. Unknown to me, something fixed my DNA as our family had an inheritance, a destiny. There would be a new season where we responded to the cry of the nations.

> And he said to them, "Go into all the world and proclaim the gospel to the whole creation. Whoever believes and is baptized will be saved, but whoever does not believe will be condemned. And these signs will accompany those who believe: in my name they will cast out demons; they will speak in new tongues . . .
>
> —Mark 16:15-19 ESV

Write the vision. Vision is for everyone. Write it, follow the vision. Good things came, even God things came. We followed Jesus, listened to His voice, did what He said. But our lives obscured the original vision for nations from view! We lost that visionary thinking, which had a greater perspective for a long-term view. We did not see the long-term worldview outside our own connections. Sure, we still had a vision for nations. We prayed, read, and connected with missionaries, but with no passport, no vision for travel. I read missions books, received mission's updates, saw a big picture inside the picture frame, yet we failed to see the wider vision.

> And the Lord answered me, Write the vision; make it plain on tablets, so he may run who reads it. For still the vision awaits its appointed time; it hastens to the end—it will not lie.
>
> Habakkuk 2:2–3 ESV

I wrote the vision.

CHAPTER 3

Crazy Beginnings Unlocked: Bangkok, China, Cancer, Cuba

> Ask of me, and I will make the nations your heritage,
> and the ends of the earth your possession.
> —Psalm 2:8 ESV

When God spoke to renew the vision, "just do it" was the message. And in obedience to the word I asked Him for nations asked Him for the four corners of the earth even to the point that when we started a Ministry we called it four corners, another prophetic declaration. Don't wait, just do it, do the crazy thing! Never could we imagine this became the beginning of a crazy life, doing crazy things, going to crazy places in obedience to the voice of God. Just the beginning of an incredible life around the world every year, travelling to see God do amazing things. The vision for the four corners of the earth filled my life with purpose and passion, crammed my every waking moment, consumed me, as when we unlock vision, we grasp the purpose, take possession of the plan, and possess the passion. Do you have a passion, a vision, a plan, a purpose? Grab it, grasp it, just do it!

Hebrews 11 speaks of people filled with passion, crazy with vision and a plan, the pioneers of faith. Imagine in this hall of fame a person like Rahab, a prostitute, prompted and motivated by faith, an unbeliever when she hid God's spies (Hebrews 11:31). She hid them at substantial risk to her own life and became a woman in the lineage of Jesus; a woman of vision, a woman of faith who obeyed what her heart spoke, a woman who pleased God. Because of her faith, vision, purpose, and passion unlocked in her life. Through her trust and obedience, her entire family experienced deliverance amidst hopelessness and impending death. Her life's legacy still speaks through the scriptures, even in death. We received the release of the legacy. Are you leaving a legacy? Rahab stewarded faith; she stood up for what she believed, declared her intentions and moved into what she felt in her heart. I began to steward faith and God's love and presence.

Now, began life as a perpetual tourist, the following year, there were trips to China, Myanmar, and Thailand for six weeks, with increasing opposition in the work scene. This a life-changer-brought challenge, with Bible delivery from Hong Kong to China with an organisation that later opened the doors to Cuba, ministry in Myanmar, and nursing experience in Thailand. On the many visits to Rahab Ministries in Patpong, I ministered with my friend Patricia Green, a modern-day pioneer, a woman of vision and purpose who left all to follow Jesus, working amongst the bar girls and those coming out of prostitution.

Staying near where she evangelised in Patpong Road, in the early days, I visited in the bars with her, and delighted to share with girls seeking to follow Jesus. When she opened the ministry in Patpong Road on each visit to Bangkok, I would call to see her and minister to the girls.

All preparatory steps for what God would do and what would come! In response to the declaration of God's word, we saw miracles of divine provision and protection, with doors opening in nations.

PATRICIA GREEN AND HERB 1993

We believed God for the money to travel, and all the costs were put on a credit card. When I believed God for someone to travel with me to Myanmar, God sent Jeannie from England. Because of the restrictions as tourists, we entered with a tour group as you could not travel independently within the nation. We were the last group in before the elections of 1990, when the government placed the state counselor Aung San Suu Gyi under house arrest. After a call to a Yangon pastor, he came to meet us with explicit instructions, of how to recognise him: "Go to Emmanuel Church, and when you see me, an Indian man, you must follow me on the other side of the road, and when I get into the cab, you must cross the road get in the back seat to ride with me." We followed his precise instructions and climbed into the cab. "Do not greet or speak to me," he said.

Whereupon the driver commented, "Aren't you taking a tremendous risk travelling with foreigners?"

We drove to his home, past the blind institute and into the small compound. The taxi stopped, and as we climbed out in the Anglican compound, the pastor paid and released the taxi. When it had gone, he turned to us with a beaming smile. "You can greet me now."

That was the beginning of a long relationship with Father Felix and his Indian family. A canon in the Anglican church of Myanmar, very religious with a great love for Jesus, he shared amazing stories of past times of evangelism in restricted zones controlled by the army who stood guard everywhere. He shared and showed me his big water jar in which he kept rice that he prayed over daily and it never ran out.

FATHER FELIX AND FAMILY

JEANNIE, WHEN WE DELIVERED TAPE RECORDINGS FROM MYANMAR TO FAR EAST BROADCASTING BANGKOK

This was the trip that a member of the tour group, a foreign reporter, swam across the lake to get an interview with Suu Kyi under house arrest. Arrested for his efforts, he spent a day in the jail before they expelled him with a warning.

In 1990, the military government finally held the elections first promised in 1988. To everyone's surprise, the world considered them free and fair. Aung San Suu Kyi's National League for Democracy won 80 percent of the parliamentary seats. The government ignored the results and rounded up many opposition politicians, including Suu Kyi. [August 8, 2013 4:48 PM ET Heard on All Things Considered]

On return to Bangkok, Kevin phoned to say he had received some extra unexpected work, which would bring in $5,000, the exact amount we needed to pay the credit card. God is so amazing, He had the plan. When we obey and act, He unlocks resources.

That was the trip in which I gained further nursing experience during a month in Bangkok working in a medical clinic and valuable time in China as a Bible courier. It had meant another miracle for the provision of leave from my employment; thus when I again visited the principal, he commented, "Haven't we walked this way before?"

I quickly recognised the key was declaration, proclamation, to pray and fast! My life overflowed with prayer and fasting! He granted my leave, and I travelled to see God do amazing things.

China was exciting, exhilarating, challenging, adrenaline-punching—all the above! It ticked all the boxes. Entering Hong Kong after the long flight, I searched my brain for what to do. I had no address, only a name! On entry, I prayed, wrote the name of a hotel, whilst pleading with heaven that someone would be there to meet me. Sure enough, a man held a sign with my name! What an adventure, in fact, a series of adventures. Every day more adventures! Such exceptional scenery. How I loved the beautiful Hong Kong Harbour, loved the boats, loved the ferries on which we crossed the harbour every day to and from the office. They briefed us for the assignment; we reported back and packed the bags at the office. The entire group all there with one aim: to take literature to bless the suffering church in that restricted, persecuted nation. Our accommodation comprised a 150-square-foot three-bedroom apartment, which all six of us shared on the tenth floor of a high-rise apartment block.

> A time to love, and a time to hate; a time of war, and a time of peace.
>
> —Ecclesiastes 3:8 ESV

I stared at the radio in amazement! As we rested in a taxi, it sped along the country roads leading to Guanzhou in the south of China. Unexpectedly, a Christian song in English came beaming over the radio! Pat, my companion in the taxi, shared she had been in Hong Kong for two weeks, and every day, as she sought to take Bibles and literature into China, they had caught her at the borders and confiscated everything! Discouragement set in because for several years, she had saved for this precious trip to serve God's plan. The organisation we volunteered for suggested that she take a day off to seek the Lord. She spent the day on a hill overlooking the colony, and during the time alone, God spoke. "You will be okay from now on!" Every day after this, everything she couriered reached its destination.

It had been an early start, at 6:00 a.m., after a late-night of packing precious literature and being briefed for our journey the following day. We walked a long way to the train station, followed by a trek to the ferry terminal, before the two-and-a-half-hour voyage by sea.

I've always said, "Walking is good for the soul!" Truly, we walked miles and miles on those trips! I believe fitness is a key to high stamina for travelling in nations. My vision has committed me to maintain adequate levels of fitness even in spite of difficulties.

What a great day we had together as we travelled back by taxi and train from our entry point at Zongshen to Guanzhou. The hard-seated trains had small compartments seating six, with people having close eye contact, marvelous for communication. A phrase book can be such a help but, oh, so inadequate, with no Christian language available. With limited communication, we talked to many other travellers, but one young business executive helped us. He spoke some English, and as he stood up to get off at the station, I took his hand and said, "I'm so glad to have met you. I am a Christian. I love Jesus."

"I know!" he replied, his eyes moist with tears.

It was a moment tinged with emotion as we stood looking at each other, our hands clasped together, saying farewell. He thrust a business card into my hands and vanished into the crowds. Later we sent some literature to the address on that card.

THE YOUNG BUSINESS MAN AND PAT

A young woman, who had been cautious, softened her attitude after he departed, and told us she suffered back pain. We rubbed her back, all the time praying and asking God, the God who heals, to touch and heal her. She took my hand, and as we prayed, something beautiful and glorious happened; as she changed. She had a new radiance beaming out from inside. When we pray, atmospheres change, and God comes.

Faith without action is dead faith. Only active faith pleases God. Mary's faith pleased God in Luke 1:30. An outstanding young woman, she found favor with God with a faith that has blessed the entire world.

This was a new season—a time for excitement, a time for exhilaration, a time for new experiences, a time for little sleep, a time for much activity, a time to meet new brothers and sisters in the Lord, a time to be stretched in the unfolding plans and purposes of God, a time for extra steps of faith, and a time to see God do impossible things.

Dorothy, an older woman with a gentle spirit, slept in the room next door to the tiny apartment we shared with other short-term workers. We spent a memorable day together. Early risers, we travelled the two-and-a-half-hour journey by train to Guanzhou. As green fields, fish farms, and the villages flashed by, she shared how God had brought her to serve Him in this way. "I had become a hopeless case," she said. "My family gave up on me! Depression and anxiety filled my life! For years medicated, I suffered terribly. I had to find my salvation by delivering Bibles to China."

This brave lady, who seemed perfectly normal, appeared to have no signs of the psychiatric problems that had plagued her for years as she travelled now on her third trip to China.

DOROTHY [AT THE FAR LEFT]

> But God chose those whom the world considers foolish to shame those who think they are wise, and God chose the puny and powerless to shame the high and mighty. He chose the lowly, the laughable in the world's eyes—nobodies—so he would shame the somebodies. For he chose what is regarded as insignificant in order to supersede what is regarded as prominent.
>
> —1 Corinthians 1:27-28 TPT

We presented to customs and filled out the usual forms. I tried everything to avoid their eye contact, walked straight past the guards, omitted to put my bag on the X-ray conveyor belt, stacked my bag on top of other bags, but it was all hopeless—they detected the books! "Bibles! Bibles!," the guard said.

I pretended to be unaware of what they were! I talked to him about New Zealand, all the time praying!

"We only allow you Bibles for personal use," he stated. "You can take some for personal use!"

After I scooped up some of the biggest ones, he didn't even bother to check anything else. All the rest of our precious books got through—half of mine and all that Dorothy had! After we delivered what we had to a hotel lockup, we were free to explore before returning to Hong Kong. Near the hotel, we walked to an enormous park where we met some people we thought were beggars who came out of the trees when they saw us, but they were believers. What a joy to give them the few pieces of literature we had kept. It was a special day as we walked, talked, and shared the goodness of God.

Pioneers do anything required to begin a new move of God. With versatility to unlock God's purpose, they move towards the goal, controlled and sustained by faith. They release supernatural power and events. We can look at Moses, who, in obedience, refused to accept impossibilities. Aroused by faith, he refused to accept the conditions, the culture, the difficulties, the impossibilities, but looked to the purpose and plan of God, holding steadfast to the purpose of his calling. Giving up was not on his agenda. He trusted God (Hebrews 11:24 ESV).

Motivated by faith, Moses left Egypt undismayed by the wrath of the king. As he gazed upon God, he unlocked purpose, which he staunchly held, as he endured steadfastly. I was to learn these lessons as I moved to the next stage!

Motivated by faith, my life continued to be one marked by fasting and prayer as every morning, I rose at four o'clock to pray and seek the Lord, and most days I fasted. Some weeks, I only ate one or two meals as I led a fasted life. Earnestly seeking God, I cried out for more of His presence and a greater release of glory. One meal a day was a pattern.

Focused on missions and the call, we embraced a sacrificial lifestyle and opened a special missions account to save $100 each week towards travel and ministry.

I woke at 4:00 a.m. at the beach, knowing in every part of me, I had a lump in my breast! Sure enough, when I touched my breast, I felt a minute hard lump! "Someone was looking after you!" doctors said.

"God!" I replied.

Because it was a fast-growing tumour, I had a rapid hospital admission, and three unexpected surgeries followed!

After cancer invaded our home, people phoned; everyone spoke of cancer! I declared, "By Your stripes, Lord, I am healed. Cancer goes in Jesus's name. The battle had only begun.

> Blessed is the man who remains steadfast under trial, for when he has stood the test he will receive the crown of life, which God has promised to those who love him.
>
> —James 1:12 ESV

> For God gave us a spirit not of fear but of power and love and self-control.
>
> —2 Timothy 1:7 ESV

Thankful for medical insurance, I faced the future with confidence. I woke after the first surgery feeling a little uncomfortable, but soon the pain came, and it was back to theatre as the area bled.

Our daughter drove me for the biopsy results, and that was stunning, life-changing, etched in memory forever! Too much for my mind to process. The surgeon who was so sure of an innocent lump pulled out a report sheet and sternly announced, "You need more surgery and radiation! We should remove the breast and all the glands! It's a fast-growing infiltrative cancer . . . but take your time . . . think about what you want to do!"

Stunned, filled with dismay and disbelief that this was happening, I tried to ask all the relevant questions. Finally, I left the surgery overwhelmed by the news. "How would I go to Cuba? How could I carry on! And what of my call to the four corners of the earth?"

God gave me many verses as I read His word:

> *But we had the sentence of death in ourselves, that we should not trust in ourselves, but in God which raiseth the dead: Who delivered us from so great a death, and doth deliver: in whom we trust that he will yet deliver us . . .*
>
> *—2 Corinthians 1:9-10 KJV*

> It felt like we had a death sentence written upon our hearts. It has taught us to lose all faith in ourselves and to place all our trust in the God who raises the dead. He has rescued us from terrifying encounters with death. And now we fasten our hopes on him to continue to deliver us from death yet again.
>
> —2 Corinthians 1:9-10 TPT

These verses came to mean so much to me as I declared them over my life because they speak in past tense, present tense, and future tense. I took it as a promise that, though, in my heart, I felt the sentence of death,

I did not have to fear as God would deliver me. And that is exactly what He did.

"Are you sure you won't consider removal of the breast? Are you ready to change your mind?" the surgeon pressed as he did not agree with my decision.

"No!" I said resolute. "I don't want that! I want to keep my breast!"

Having done my research, I had decided this decision was right for me. The thought of a lopsided swimsuit was too much for this lady to bear!

It was only minutes before the surgery when the surgeon announced, "You may lose feeling and use in your arm for a while."

"Why is that?" I asked, shocked at this latest blow!

"We may damage the brachial nerve!" he stated.

After the doctors left, I fell apart and sobbed uncontrollably. The staff, very concerned, postponed the event 'til the surgeon returned, to discuss again my decision and reassure me I was in the best hands. After prayer, calmness returned, and the surgery proceeded without complication. Afterwards, the surgeon arrived to tell me of the successful results. "It was the most radical surgery without taking the breast," he announced. "We took every node, everything under your arm! And took special care not to touch the brachial nerve!"

In Whangamata, in this beautiful place, I recovered from the recent surgery. Here, the journey's fight and release of the vision continued. Kevin asked God to give to him the pain. God did just that; He gave him my pain as I walked, rested, read, prayed, and fought for recovery, not only for restoration of health, but also for the renewal of vision and the unlocking of the purpose of God. By faith, I held to the purpose and plan of God, trusting God for the future and indeed for life itself.

Radiation was a life-changer, with the simulation an appointment of almost abuse! Stripped naked to the waist and painted with indelible ink leaving permanent marks! What a reminder forever of a painful experience! Indignity and loss of identity at every turn! The forecasts by doctors and specialists at every appointment haunted my life: It can come back! Cancer written constantly on all their reports and medical forms! I told them, "Do not write cancer on any of my blood work. You can write has had cancer!"

Because of the radiation, it locked us in to Hamilton for six weeks, as in exhaustion, I slept, rested, watched videos, and lay on the couch between treatments. Each day Barbara, a precious lady, an angel sent by God who supported us through this experience, met us at the oncology department. There when we arrived, not leaving 'til we left, she never missed a day. This angel prayed and showered us with love, whilst holding up our hands so we did not get weary and fall down!

BARBARA [IN THE CENTRE] AT ELIM

AFTER CANCER DENISE AND KEVIN

As I rose from the table at radiation, tears filled my eyes and rolled over my cheeks. The worried staff asked, "Are you okay?"

Was this depression? As I lay there, I looked above me at a great beam in the ceiling from which the radiation came. In those few moments alone, I said, "Lord, use this beam for Your good. Do whatever You want in my life. Cut off everything not of You. Do more work in me. I am Yours. I surrender, Lord."

In that room, I met with God. God took me at my word. I rose that day from the table to a changed, unique person. Not hungry, but desperate for God, I wanted only Jesus. Life changed forever! How many changes do we need, to change? (Read more about it in *Endless Safari*.)

Radiation was tough with oppression and exhaustion. At the final oncologist appointment, I received instructions: "You will have regular monthly then three- to six-monthly appointments. And you must return to see us every year for fifteen years!"

A spirit of oppression and death that had come over me from the beginning lifted that day, never to return!

I requested that my health details not continue to record me as having cancer! Don't write cancer on my blood work. I have had cancer. I don't have cancer now! It's gone!

Despite these requests of don't write cancer anymore, the declarations by doctors continued for fifteen years, and even two years ago, our family doctor said to me, "You are one of the few survivors." It was war—war against the devil, war to regain and unlock the plan, the purpose of God. Over the period, my right shoulder became painful until I could no longer clean my teeth, comb my hair, lift my right arm, or put it behind my back! The doctor announced, "You have a frozen shoulder!"

"God," I pleaded, "how can I go to Cuba with a frozen shoulder?"

Unable to move the shoulder or lift my right arm, I faced two enormous battles: first, restoration of normal action and function to my arm; second, a war against the devil. Despite the excruciating pain, with strenuous exercise, I forced my arm to move, forced it to rotate. Every day, as I lay on the floor, forcing my arm, my shoulder to move, I declared by faith, "I declare and decree I will go to Cuba in the name of Jesus. Jesus finishes cancer. I am healed in the name of Jesus." Focused on the call, motivated, and single-minded, I fought and endured to see my shoulder able to move normally again.

The second mountain involved fighting the devil daily. He came every day. "You'll never have another birthday, never have another Christmas. You will die. You will never see your grandchildren!" Every day, many times a day, I stood against the demonic forces that assailed me, that sort to lock me in to negativity and death.

But every day, standing on the word of God, I declared scriptures over my life.

> I shall not die, but live, and declare the works of the Lord.
>
> —Psalm 11:17 KJV

It was a constant battle! Eight months later, healed, I travelled for the first time to Cuba. For two years, daily, I fought the devil many times a day as he attacked the purpose and plan of God. Every visit doctors spoke of death. Constantly, I heard it: "It can come back, you must take tamoxifen for five years." On and on, it went, at every stage a body blow! After each appointment, I returned home crying and declaring, "I'm healed, it's never coming back, I'm free in Jesus's name. I am covered by the blood!"

In prayer, I resisted the devil. I fought off his negative words. I fasted and prayed.

Cancer never returned because God healed. In this, I learnt to fight, to stand and keep standing, to declare and decree God's word over my life.

After two years of suffering clots in my legs from long air flights, against medical advice, I quit the tamoxifen. It was not innocuous, with many other side effects. The fight against the devil continued: Satan tried to kill me, to thwart the purpose of God, but as we declared the word of the Lord, we saw him heal, and it never returned!

Joyously, I could proclaim, "God healed. Cuba, here I come!"

In Canada we met. Fiona, a Canadian nurse and a Baptist; and Denise, a nurse from New Zealand and a Pentecostal—what a combination. God does all things well. We travelled for two weeks, every minute together.

Our itinerary came from the Open Doors organisation. They later shared that two ladies they had sent previously had argued and fought the entire trip. They were more than happy when we returned with positive stories of a wonderful trip and a tremendous time. They waved us goodbye, wishing us, "Happy swimming!"

Arriving at the beaches north of Havana, we stayed in a hotel far from the city. With clots in my legs, I slept at night with swollen oedematose legs elevated on pillows and prayed. It thrilled us, swimming at a beautiful beach! But it didn't take long to figure that we were not there to swim! We needed to get to the city speedily. Reluctant to get an expensive taxi, we caught a bus much to the surprise of the hotel staff who said, "Tourists use taxis!" But we were tourists in name only! This was challenging and fun, and our US dollars were too precious to waste on taxis. The bus travelled in the wrong direction, so after that discovery, we hopped off, crossed the road, and boarded another bus. With a little Spanish between us and the help of commuters (I had learnt Spanish for a year), we reached the city just a block away from where we needed to go. We caught a taxi to the church, and there began our journey of divine appointments. These two weeks became the beginning of many trips to Cuba, most of which became ten- to twelve-week itineraries.

It was in the east of the island we saw new events unfold that opened a doorway. What happened stunned us. It changed me. We were so blessed. I could never be the same!

We stayed in the Santiago First Baptist Church, where the pastor was wonderfully hospitable. With no blankets anywhere, we settled for the night to sleep under clothes and towels. It was there I had the dream, which was to unlock new purpose and change my focus once again; my DNA for missions now supernatural. In my dream, my finger moved around the coast of Turkey to a country bordering Turkey, and I heard an audible voice. "Bulgaria." I had no knowledge if Bulgaria was next to Turkey. But that night I met the Bulgarian woman Yulia who was to open the door to Bulgaria. Yulia spoke to me in English, and not many people spoke English! When I asked her, "How come you speak English?"

She replied, "I come from Bulgaria!"

How startling was that! After God spoke in the dream of Bulgaria, I recognised I must go! There is a time to act, and this became one of those times. I thought I would go quickly because now I had met Yulia. But my friend Bryan discerned correctly. "It will be some time before you go!"

Where was Bulgaria anyway? Somewhere in Europe? I had limited knowledge of this country. Russia oppressed Bulgaria, but not since communism fell in Europe. The people destroyed the walls! In Havana, we discovered Bulgaria was right next door to Turkey, and a prophetic word saw fires across Bulgaria and Turkey and predicted moves of God in both nations. Two years later, I met Yulia in a different city and church, where she gave me the address of her pastor in Bulgaria. Prompted and actuated by faith, I knew I would travel there. Sure I would go there next, I was expectant, eager, full of vision and purpose. But my friend and mentor Bryan cautioned, "I think it will be about two years before you go." How right he was. Two years declaring I will go to Bulgaria in Jesus name I will see miracles, signs and wonders.

FIONA, WITH ALEHANDRO NIETO AND HIS WIFE ALIDA AND HECTOR IN HAVANA

THE BULGARIAN WOMAN YULIA

Cuba became the school of God in my life; my love for the nation exploded with every trip. It was here I learnt most of what I know about ministry. How astounded I was one year when leaving the nation. The church was saying goodbye when I looked down to see a small child clinging to me, sobbing and sobbing, not wanting me to leave. It broke my heart.

CHILD WHO SOBBED

Cuba was in my heart; there was no other nation like Cuba in my life. It's there I saw signs, wonders, and many miracles. When Kevin visited later, he testified after the visit to Cuba, it changed his life. After Cuba, you can never be the same.

Cuba beckoned and called. After the first trip of just two weeks in 1991, it focused me on asking our friend Bryan, "Please teach me about deliverance."

In our circle of friends, no one moved in deliverance, only he, so his reply surprised me. "No!" he said. "You don't want to get involved with deliverance."

However, I learnt this ministry in Cuba because everywhere we went, people needed deliverance. After I resisted the devil in meetings and declared the power in the name and blood of Jesus, people slithered like snakes, manifested with demons, but deliverance immediately set them free. I learnt the significant power there is in the name and blood of Jesus.

"The climate for women's ministry is difficult," Bryan advised. "The anointing makes way for itself, but as a woman, you cannot minister all around the world without some credential to make you credible!"

Everywhere we went, they asked Kevin, "Why don't you travel? Why don't you go with Denise?"

His reply was always the same: "God spoke to Denise, not me! When or if He speaks, then I will go!"

After more study and accreditation of previous study in 1992, I achieved a Bachelor of Arts in biblical studies.

AT THE GRADUATION. BRYAN WHO GAVE SUCH WISE ADVICE

GRADUATION GROUP

A colleague at work jokingly remarked, "Throwing Bibles out of planes!" In the early days, Bible delivery was a critical part of what we did.

During this time I was ministering around New Zealand, and on the invitation of a friend in the north we traveled to Whangarei, where we held meetings and spoke in home cells which my friend Kay arranged. We tried to visit with the senior pastor of the area, but he declined to meet us. Shortly after our visit we received a complaint that we had ministered in his home groups without his permission! Concerned as to what to do we prayed, and I sent money to assist him in his mission trip to India.

Our daughter received a call one day from his wife to say," We received a check from your mother, maybe there was a mistake...

Rachel replied, "No this was not a mistake. My mother sent the money to bless you"

CHAPTER 4

Early Years, 1992-1993 - Extraordinary Unlocked - The Summons - Cuba - Diez Mero Repentance - Myanmar - Family

Extraordinary! My statement "Ordinary!" received challenge! A man visiting from Canada challenged me! "We are all extraordinary!" he said. "When Jesus comes into our lives, He makes us extraordinary as we have the life of Christ in us! We can never be ordinary again." We were just 'normal Christians' or were we?

Suitably rebuked, I never confessed to being ordinary again! We become a new creation, extraordinary like Jesus!

Unbelievers came in from outside and crowded to the front. They reported never had they felt such a great power. Many saw visions and brilliant lights. People said a great power came. Because of the glory of God, goose bumps appeared all over their arms, and the hairs on their arms stood up on end! The Holy Spirit came in power. He moved amongst the people, with many falling under the power of God and set free from curses over their lives. Two girls testified that they felt chains fall off them.

UNBELIEVERS

In a small room in the back streets of Diez Mero Hector shared with us, "I shook when I opened an official letter. I read it carefully—a summons requesting my presence at the police office in the district. I gave that letter much prayer. On the day and time appointed, I presented at the office and sat in the waiting room. An official asked, "Why are you here?" I gave him the letter, which he opened and read. He excused himself, vanished, and I could hear many voices. On his return, he invited me to follow him into the next room. There they were, seated around the table, the officials of the region. The man obviously in charge held the letter. He said, "This appointment is for tomorrow!"

"I'm so sorry," I replied.

"What do you want?" they said.

Puzzled, I asked, "Why did you want to see me?"

"We just want to know you," he replied. This senior pastor I met on the first trip wiped away beads of perspiration. The small fan failed to cool the stifling hot room. He continued, "Well, I just want to know you."

I said to them, "Tell me about yourselves." What an amazing opportunity with every official. Each one in the entire room told me about himself and herself.

Finally, they said to me, "We just wanted to talk to you. The electors are complaining about the church! There is too much noise! The music is too loud, the services to noisy."

"Who is complaining?" I asked.

"The electors," they said, nodding in agreement.

I shook my head and declared, "One elector is complaining! It thrills all the others, all five hundred of them. The people love the church, they enjoy the worship, and they love the music!"

"We must listen to the electors," said the officials in agreement.

Silence reigned as they thought about this. Then they asked, "Would you turn the noise down?"

I asked, "Why, when everybody is happy?"

"We can hear the noise from here!" they said. "We can hear the music, the songs, the preaching."

The pastor laughed as he said, "I became excited as four enormous blocks from the church, they could hear us. With the entire area silent, the sound reached them. Praise God," he said.

He continued the story. They pleaded with him to turn the sound down. He told them, "We only can do it just a little."

"We shook hands," he said, and I thanked them for their time. They thanked me for coming.

Pioneers do anything it takes to achieve their goals, to begin a new move of God. With versatility, they move towards the goal, controlled and sustained by faith. This releases supernatural power and events. Moses knew the power of the blood for deliverance. After a revelation from the Smith Wigglesworth book of the power of the blood, I read an amazing book on the blood of Jesus by Maxwell White. I travelled to Cuba believing that God would do amazing miracles when we stood and confessed the power of the blood and the name of Jesus. Pioneers know how to bring deliverance through the power of the blood (Hebrews 11:28 ESV). Now I learnt and experienced the power of the blood for deliverance and healing.

The second trip to Cuba cemented the plan and purpose of God. Miracles signs and wonders happened everywhere from the moment of arrival. From the beginning, God provided the money. After a call from the church, I raced across the city to collect a cheque worth $3,200, which a woman miraculously changed into US dollars just hours before departure. We believed God for the team, and that year $23,000 came in for four of us. We flew from Auckland to Mexico, to Havana, and on to the east of the island.

THE FOUR LADIES

After arrival in Havana and a long wait with a mountain of baggage, huge bags stuffed full of precious Bibles, medicines, and gifts for pastors, and only one address, which we found out later had changed, we attracted a lot of attention.

When the van finally arrived, we hurriedly loaded our stuff, pleased to get it out of the public view. I froze as someone tapped my shoulder. A voice said, "Sister, I think I know you."

When I turned, to my relief, not the police, but a young man I had met the previous year.

ARRIVAL HAVANA 1991/92

"Sister," he said, "come with me quickly. The car is here. I will take you to my father."

"How will we ever fit in?" I asked.

"No problem," Joshua assured us. "Everyone in the back and we place the bags in the front and the boot."

Squashed travelling along the bumpy roads, he told us the miracle of our arrival! The church sent him to the airport at 9:00 a.m. to collect people from Miami. He waited the entire morning and phoned his father three times asking, "Can I come home? They are not coming, and I'm hungry!"

His father kept telling him, "Just wait, they will come soon, wait a little longer."

Ready to leave the airport, we came but not from Miami as expected! God yet again proved His miraculous intervention and provision as He alone knew our arrival.

As we proceeded on deserted roads with few cars, a car passed us going in the other direction. The driver hooted and waved out to us. "That's my brother!" Joshua exclaimed.

After thirty minutes' travel, we approached the church in an area of narrow streets full of gaping potholes. Finally, the car stopped outside a compound with a narrow gate and steep stairs leading to an upstairs blue house. As we turned the street corner, the pastor appeared and ran down the stairs. We climbed wearily out of the car. "It's you! It's you! It's you!" he cried excitedly, amazed that God sent four ladies from New Zealand.

Excited, Joshua's brother had phoned him, saying, "The people from Miami are on the way, the car is bulging with bags and people everywhere!"

This amazed the pastor. He had received a call from Miami to inform him the people missed the plane and wouldn't be coming! It perplexed him. Who could be in the car?

"It's a miracle," he said. "God sent Joshua to the airport just for you!" A miracle, as the pastor for whom I had an address was no longer there! He had moved.

We stayed with our new friends in Diez Mero. As we brought school materials, books, pencils, and erasers for the children, Hunter said, "Come, we will take them to the school to bless the school. My children have suffered so much there. They penalized and did not give school materials to Christian children when other children received them."

> Speak blessing, not cursing, over those who reject and persecute you.
>
> —Romans 12:14 TPT

By car, minutes later, we arrived at the local school. The head teacher called all the children. We presented the materials, prayed, and left. Within minutes of our arrival back at the house, the phone rang, and

Pastor Hector came running to tell us, "The school phoned. Someone reported foreigners were at the school, and the police arrived." We praised God for His protection, leading, and timing. He does all things well.

HECTOR HUNTER GIVING SUPPLIES TO THE SCHOOL

THE SCHOOL

HUNTER ADDRESSING THE SCHOOL

The children's meeting started late because of power cuts. Except for a powerful kerosene lantern, darkness prevailed in the church. We used a gospel glove, a special plastic glove with fingers of different colours: red for the blood of Jesus, gold for the glory of God for heaven, black for our sin and wrongdoings, white for the cleansing Jesus brings when He forgives our sin, and the glove is green to symbolize growing to follow Jesus. Such an effective evangelism tool that explains how to follow Jesus. I told stories and shared how to find new life in Jesus. What a wonderful response, with many children born again. The people loved the glove.

In an old theatre, where there had been revival and thousands became believers, we experienced marvelous moves of God. Orderly, the people stood in lines six feet apart, about five distinct lines across the platform, and we walked along each line to pray for them. They fell down, and we walked to the next line until we prayed for hundreds of people the Holy Spirit touched sovereignly. Our God is the God of the impossible.

"You only need five minutes for the power of God to fall," Bryan, my friend and mentor, said. "That's all you need."

"Come on," I had said, "that's okay for you, you are used to that sort of thing, but for me, it's a different story! I'm not a preacher!"

We stood in the dark with a lantern. I looked out on this almost-completed church filled with people. People were everywhere, even looking in the windows. A sense of excitement and expectancy arose within me. At 11:25 p.m. on New Year's Eve, I knew we must finish by midnight. I spoke for just five minutes and called for people to respond to come forward.

Catherine sang a beautiful song about the Holy Spirit, and His presence came.

> Come, Holy Spirit, I need you. Come, sweet Spirit, I pray. Come in Your strength and Your power. Come in your own special way.
>
> —Gaithers 1964

They all came, and so too did the power and presence of God. God moved, and many fell to the floor touched with His wonderful presence. God transformed and changed lives.

CATHERINE SINGS

The message spoke of surrender, and the entire congregation responded by coming to the front. I imagined it must have been like the early days of the Pentecostal revival, and it filled me with awe that God would take women from New Zealand, moving by faith in obedience to His word, to this island nation on the other side of the world.

When I visited this church the year before, it was a decrepit old ruin. For forty years, the government forbade maintenance to the churches in Cuba. Now a large two-storeyed concrete building, built by faith to seat one thousand people, in response to a prophetic word three years before, the pastor shared how the prophecy said he would build a large church to which people from all walks of life would come. "Today God fulfils this prophecy," he stated.

Unbelievers came in off the street and reported that the hairs on their arms stood on end with the power of God. A young man, a nonbeliever, saw a brilliant ball of light over the church, and someone saw tongues of fire on our heads.

This the fourth corner of the earth, the place of birthed vision and birthing of God's purpose and plan with the realization of God's DNA. Suddenly, accelerated into miracles, signs, and wonders, all of life becoming ministry to the Lord and the surrounding people.

At Guantanamo, the pastor didn't want us, but that changed after his wife attended a circus service, or should I say a zoo service, where I felt like an animal at the zoo, where everyone stopped to gaze at the animal to observe all it does. All the unbelievers came in off the street and gawked at everything happening. People fell in all directions as God moved to touch, heal, and transform. How bad I felt, like I was on display, like I was an animal and this was the zoo! I just wanted to get out of there and as quickly as possible! Afterwards, God spoke to me and said, "If I want it like the zoo, that's my problem, not yours . . . just do as I lead!" I repented of my rotten attitude.

For God had His plan and purpose, and He unfolded it there in Cuba. Miracles, signs, and wonders happened everywhere. When we walked on the streets, people fell under the power of God. Poverty was everywhere in a nation once rich in everything; they allowed no red meat to be eaten as the government owned every cow. They rationed food, churches were restricted, all looked impossible, but God moved.

We experienced such miracles with multiplication and provision of supernatural gasoline and car repairs. Our doctor driver said, "Let's pray! We need gasoline! US dollars are too special to waste on government gasoline. You must pray."

Pray we did declaring multiplication of the fuel. As Western women, we had never seen a car run for six hours on supernatural fuel! We travelled all the way with heavenly fuel, and our driver returned almost all the way back. Our newfound pastor friend in Guantanamo gave him a tiny amount of fuel, which he used to finish his journey. God provides all our needs far above what we can ask or think. Cars were old and always breaking down! They could only buy fuel dirty and expensive with US dollars or on the black market.

PASTOR OSIAS AND MAGIN OUR SPECIAL FRIENDS -FAMILY IN CUBA

THE FAMILY

On a roll, Hector told us story after story like never before. A car stopped outside the church. Several people climbed out to stand looking at the church. They walked around, talking and looking at the property beside the church.

Here, on an empty property owned by the lady next door, we held outdoor services. He said. "1500 people came twice a week to these services."

The previous year, Fiona and I had been to these services, in which we presented the gospel to the entire neighbourhood.

Hector said, "I met with them to see what they wanted. My son came with me. They said that they were checking out the noise. Why did we have meetings outside? We moved into the church, where we could talk in private. I sent my son to walk on the flat roof. I explained to them, 'Look at this building. It's old, ancient. This concrete building is ancient and needs repair.' The roof shook, and many large lumps of plaster crashed down! The women, faces white with fear ran from the room! I said, 'The building is dangerous!' That's why we meet outside. With over five hundred people, the church is too small, and the roof unsafe, we need a new building! Hundreds of people come, and we must meet outside. They retreated with no answers. God had the final word."

Honored and blessed, we listened carefully as he shared his story of the early days in his ministry.

Diez Mero's Repentance

Only twenty-five years when his family came to the church. The Assembly of God national youth director, as he stood on the church steps, God spoke to him. God had already prepared him in Camaguey, where he had a grand church and said to him, "Prepare to go to Havana."

"We had no house when we arrived," he said. "There were three children, boxes, a table, chairs, the beds, and no house to put them in! Just some rooms at the back of the church, and the doors did not shut! Several families controlled this difficult church! Our stuff had to be stored in the church! After two months, a young man told us to build. In a miraculous way, the government gave all the permissions in one week. With no money, the materials came in, and within a year, we finished! Two days after they finished the church, the Ministry of Justice came to close the church and could not do so as we finished it! The government permitted no repairs and no new churches built! I thought I will only stay one or two years as a great family spirit ruled the place. Five young men and their families dominated the church. I knew I had to take control, but this worried me. I had to discipline their children, and it was very difficult. They did not dare attack me but attacked my wife and my children!"

A prophetess in a prayer meeting said she wanted to pray for him. They prayed, and he broke down! The bitterness that built in him broke. She prophesied and told him from God what to do. Close to these families, she advised him to stay in the trenches to wait and watch for God to sort out the problem! He told her she might not like what happened, but she said she knew.

Shortly after this, an old retired evangelist came on his invitation for a weekend of ministry. The meetings were very ordinary. Sunday morning, the old man said he would finish by midday. The service started. He climbed on the seat and stood shouting, praying, pleading the blood of Jesus. The place broke. They stayed from 8:00 a.m. to 4:00 p.m., weeping, praying, crying out to God, falling under God's power. The offenders came at the end. Two who came about midday were immediately slain! Others wept as they walked in the neighborhood. God moved on them all powerfully. Great repentance came with weeping and joy. The prophetess told all the young men that they must leave!

Each of the six young men came in repentance, and within weeks, God moved each family away from the church. The people said the Holy Spirit came upon them in their homes and as they walked on the streets, urging them to go immediately to the church, coaxed them to repent and compelled them to change. They came weeping, running to the church.

Another church in Havana had a problem. As they worshipped one night, an angry neighbour came with a gun. Angry with the church and the music, he shot off the gun, and a brother was injured shot in the leg. With blood everywhere, the pastor and people took him to hospital. A court case followed. The church prayed and presented to the court. The neighbour said, "The bullet ricocheted across the room from one wall to another, hit this and that, finally hitting the injured man! Such an accident. And it hit the man!"

He told lies as he had come into the church in an act of aggression! He won the case and only got nine months jail sentence! It upset everybody! The police celebrated the victory when a bull escaped from somewhere nearby. His threatening display began as he arched his back and with his eyes protruding, he was ready to attack, and all his hair on his back stood on end. Pawing with his forefeet, he sent dirt flying behind and over his back and rubbed and horned the ground to advance and attack the police officer. After he knocked him to the ground, gored him badly, he stood on him with his front legs several times. After stomping on the man, the bull ceased all activity, stopped, and then trotted peacefully away!

Everyone knew God did it! They took the police officer to hospital, blood poured profusely from many wounds! The whole family came to Jesus as did the police officer.

With reluctance, we had to leave our friend to return, to pack, to leave the island at the close of the ministry there. After this trip, considerable suffering arose as the group taken discounted the move of God.

I sat in church in Hamilton late one night with the two pastors. Tears poured down my cheeks. "I never asked for this anointing!" I cried. "I never asked to be called!"

"Neither did we," they agreed.

"It's so painful," I cried. People gossiped and criticised, no matter what I did. I said to the pastors, "Please allow me to go to the ladies in the church leadership to ask them to speak into my life, to forgive me if anything has been done to upset or wound them."

I met with the key ladies and did just what I asked. I believed this action of humbling myself brought a measure of healing to the situation, but my friend Joan came to me a few months later to say, "It's no better, there are still problems." After obedience to the Lord, I left the results with him.

In response to urging from our friend and mentor Bryan, I graduated that year with a Bachelor's in Biblical Studies.

With my sister Lyndsey and brother-in-law Herb and a woman from Raglan, in 1993, we visited Myanmar. Daniel, who had returned from study in New Zealand, collected us at the airport, and after a succession of little old blue taxis belching black smoke that broke down constantly, we finally arrived at the Sakantha Railway Station hotel. An experience not for the fainthearted! Later we discovered the water they told us we could drink was not safe as it was not purified. The rooms had ants, cockroaches, and phenomenal noise. Lyndsey, after showering, used a towel to discover it covered her body in ants! Herb needed rehydration at a Christian hospital because of bugs—from the water. In the early days in these nations, diarrhea was part of the deal, and we usually succumbed. It's different now as purified water is widely available.

When we visited Brother Ronnie, a true pioneer, a descendant from the second Burmese convert to Christianity of Adoniram Judson, the first American missionary in the nation, he showed us the miracle well. Exceptional that in a zone classified by the government as a no water polluted area, after a gift from an American, he drilled a well. Convinced the well would be a failure, the drillers demanded he identify the exact spot for drilling. He walked to the corner of the property, drew a circle on the ground, and said, "Drill here, drill here!" When the drillers wanted to quit at 120 feet, he told them, "My God says there is water! Keep drilling!"

As he prayed and prayed, they drilled and drilled, and up gushed the miracle water. That well, deeper than any well in Yangon, gushed pure clear water. No sooner we turned the tap than the water poured forth, spurting across the ground.

HOREB'S WELL

BROTHER RONNIE

He showed us a room in the recording studio where the young men slept to hide from the military as they would come late at night and round them up for slave labor, porterage, and working the roads!

At another house meeting we prayed for two women with cancer. One we visited in New York many years later, alive and well. With a breast tumour, she refused surgery, refused any treatment, believing God would heal. Heal he did, when we came in obedience to the Lord and prayed by faith for her! The other, a young woman who had just had a baby, God miraculously healed her of a rampant, aggressive, fast-growing breast cancer!

MYANMAR MAY 1993. COLLEEN AND LYNDSEY AND HERB.

TRANSPORTATION

We trusted God, but bad things can happen to God's people! Every day Kevin spoke the name and blood of Jesus over our son Paul. We did not know where he lived! After three years away, living as a hermit at the bottom of New Zealand, unexpectedly, looking like a hillbilly with long ginger hair, he turned up at our door. Now he ran to hide from people there. After building a big case like a coffin made of used doors on his van top, he toured the country stealing marijuana crops, filling the vehicle with weed. Like a modern-day Robin Hood, he gave away the ill-gotten goods. Unloved and chased by the drug dealers, he retreated to our house for safety, with plans to start up again when everything became quiet! He needed to return to the far south to collect his seven dogs! We agreed he could bring two dogs only! Kevin decided he would go with him to support him, until I challenged him, that Paul unrepentant only wanted to start up again!

Kevin and Paul had a conversation. "Your mother says you are unrepentant! And only want to start up again."

Paul said, "You just want a scalp for Jesus!"

He left alone for Dunedin with the mobile phone and instructions, "Contact us if there are problems!"

Three days later, he returned with a puppy in his jacket and two big dogs, one of which was a pit bull and killed our kitten! But best of all, he read the last pages of a Christian book at my sister's house and gave his life back to Jesus! Within weeks, he entered Bible school and demonstrated a changed lifestyle.

After the second trip to Cuba, it became harder as fierce criticism continued. The greater the move of God, the greater the opposition! When my friend Joan warned me it was happening around me I had failed to notice as focused 'cause pioneers are focused visionaries. Single-minded, misunderstood, I had not noticed. Forging ahead with the vision, the nations captured my heart, the vision consumed me. I visited our pastor and asked him what I could do to stop the relentless raging criticism. He said he would meet with the leader and me to ensure my protection. We met with this leader who denied any problem! Some months passed, and the issue recurred and kept on recurring.

Just because we are believers does not give us immunity to pain, even shame and suffering. The Bible is very clear: The apostles suffered and died for their faith. They were imprisoned, terrible things happened to them, and the same happened to those who loved Jesus.

In the Old Testament, a prophet's widow had no money and needed to sell her son into slavery to pay a debt! In our family history back in the fifteenth century members of our family were martyred because of their faith, choosing to suffer as they followed Jesus. None of us is immune.

Historically, two young Christian women suffered. They killed saints Perpetua and Felicity for their faith. At the beginning of the third century, they threw them to wild animals during Roman games in Northern Africa (Archdiocese of Hobart, Wikipedia).

In more recent days, a young woman in the USA was shot and killed in a school massacre for her uncompromising faith, and at an Amish settlement, schoolchildren were killed. Others today across the world are suffering in prison and are shamed for their faith.

A story I heard featured the Lord speaking to a persecuted believer in a freezing area with a blizzard. He told him to load the sled with food and take it to a very distant area many hours away, where the believers were starving. The believer replied, "Lord, I might not come back!"

The Lord said, "I asked you to go, I didn't ask you to come back!" He obeyed and obviously came back!

That is obedience! Faced with absolute suffering, he did what God said.

> If we love the Lord, he empowers us to do what he says!
>
> —John 14:15 TPT

> If we don't love him, we don't do what he says!
>
> —John 14:22 TPT

He empowers us and does not abandon us! Remember, the mark of loving Him is doing what He says—if we don't do what He says, it shows we don't love Him.

CHAPTER 5

Early Years, 1993-1996 - Miracles - Books And The Family - The Eyes - Bulgaria - Russia - Cuba - Supernatural Strength

"Look!" the very excited lady exclaimed. "Look! I visited the doctor, and he wrote me this paper." She had knocked on the church doors at 2:00 p.m., demanding to see Mary and myself. She waved the paper in the air. "Look at this!"

"What is it?" we asked, gathering round to see what the paper said.

Tali translated it for us. "This woman had a fibroma, and today it is gone! On examination today, there is now no evidence of the fibroma."

The lady received prayer the previous night during the altar call. We prayed for hundreds of people during the tremendous move of God. Crowds of people presented for prayer. Line after line, they came, people falling in all directions, weeping, crying, shaking, dancing.

She shared she came to the front believing God for a miracle. She had been hit in the stomach and had heard many words as she received ministry. As she lay on the floor, she felt the fire of God burn into her body! When she recovered, she knew in her heart Jesus healed her. She said to her husband, "I'm healed!"

He replied, "Oh yes!"

That night, when she woke, black blood filled the bed! She rose saying, "The tumour is gone!"

The doctor who examined her said, "You must have an ultrasound."

After she drank all the water and had the examination, they would not believe the results, and she had to drink the water all over again and be reexamined. They found nothing! She praised God, grateful for his faithfulness and might. Another woman previously healed of infertility brought her baby to show us her miracle. Revival prayer brings transforming power. Faith without works is dead, action is the key. When we declare and act on the word of God, this brings results.

MIRACLE IN CUBA. WOMAN HEALED OF A FIBROMA WITH DENISE AND MARY

MARY, DENISE AND THE WOMAN HEALED OF INFERTILITY

Books, books, books—I couldn't get enough of them. An avid reader, I devoured, drank the books. Pilgrim missionary women had inspired my earlier life: Mildred Cable, Francesca French and China stories, Mary Slessor and Africa. These women moved by faith and obedience in substantial power and authority. Katherine Kuhlman, Maria Woodworth-Etter, and Aimee Semple McPherson, YouTube videos and books inspired me. The women in the Bible stirred my spirit. An unnamed wise woman saved her city by faith and vision as she acted to go to the leader of the besieged town and acted by faith to throw the head of Sheba over the wall! Jael in Judges 4 acted in the wisdom of God when she sheltered and killed Sisera with a hammer whilst he slept, after he ran from the army of Deborah and Barak. Women pioneers of the time showed us faith and action.

After I ministered, people would say to me, "You remind me of someone," and they would pause and say, "I can't remember who."

I would smile and say, "Is it Katherine Kuhlman?" And they would nod and reply, "That's it!"

I knew in my spirit the importance to read all the books. Wigglesworth books were high on the list, and every day I read in my search for a deeper relationship with God, to learn how they moved in power, the secrets of the power and presence of God. So many wonderful life-changing books set the seal for what God would orchestrate in nations we visited; miracles, signs, wonders. What of modern women, Malcolm Muggeridge wrote a most beautiful book about the Albanian Catholic nun Mother Teresa who pioneered a transformational work with the poor, the desperate, and the dying in Calcutta, which much later we visited to gaze in awe at her tomb and the writings of things she had said. What of Heidi Baker and the amazing work she pioneered in Africa with over ten thousand churches, a woman who exemplifies the love of God, showing us what it means in practise to be his hands and feet! Women of faith and vision, examples of moving in obedience and love out of devotion for Jesus. How inspirational are their lives!

Life became full, accelerated in purpose, with travel, work, ministering at weekends and during the week, study, marriage, and family; a time of working full time, studying in the evenings to achieve two more degrees, visiting refugees, running an ethnic ministry, plus travelling overseas. This once tired woman unlocked to be empowered, and energised, became unstoppable!

But for all pioneers, the work is hard, the way tough, the hardships insurmountable, the opposition fierce, and for us no different. I am a pioneer. Pioneers are foot soldiers continuing against the odds. Breaking ground is hard!

> He lifts up a banner for the distant nations. He whistles for those from the ends of the earth.
>
> —Isaiah 5:26 ESV

Is He whistling for you?
A pioneer leaves all to birth their vision.

> Now the LORD said to Abram, "Go from your country and your kindred and your father's house to the land that I will show you."
>
> —Genesis 12:3 ESV

Some translations say, get out. I like that as it takes away the options! It's so much stronger than go! When we say go, it seems to imply we have a choice, yet he had no choice! Abram abandoned everything familiar to birth his vision. He obeyed God, leaving all his security, his family, everything familiar, his home, his activities, his occupation to travel into the unknown, to a land he did not know, to a people he did not know, to unfamiliar conditions. He did not hesitate or delay or ask himself why. He obeyed. No arguing, questioning, doubting, or asking could that really be God. No, he was eager to follow the Lord, obeyed His voice, always calm and secure because God had spoken.

After several trips to Cuba, trips to Myanmar, Bulgaria, Russia, and Nepal beckoned. Kevin prayed, and I travelled. God always provided companions for the task. And as time developed, so did the teams. You can't choose your family, nor did we choose the people on teams! God chose them and chooses them! If you could choose, you would leave some of them at home! Over the years, until we left New Zealand in 1998, teams arose, and I took people to nations. I chose none of them, God did! Sometimes I think if I had chosen them, I would not have done so!

Between 1992 and 1998, there were four trips to Russia and more to Bulgaria plus Myanmar and to Cuba every year.

Joan, Jane, Elisabeth, Rachel, Paul, Lyndsey, Herb, Belle, Catherine, June, Deborah, Shirley, Mary, Val, Chris, Ros, Peter, Susie, Kay, Dayle, Carol and so many others travelled to empower these nations. What a list, and did we get on? Did they argue, squabble, get sick, go to hospital, have problems? Were they a problem? Did they complain? Could the food be a problem? Endless issues and problems. I told them this is a test. If you don't pass the test, you have to sit it again. I told all don't drink the water, but did they listen? I said don't clean your teeth in the water, but did they listen? Difficult? Sometimes! But God.

A woman I took to a nation cried all the time! She constantly cried, day and night. Finally, as it became extremely noticeable, the senior pastor in the region told me to give her the choice to return home. After prayer and giving her the choice, she stayed, and the crying stopped!

There were the ones who wanted to anoint temples and began cursing everything everywhere they travelled! As this attracted much attention wherever we toured, we reminded them we are to bring blessing and speak blessing, not curses, we are blessed to be a blessing and bring blessing.

Some told stories altogether irrelevant to the culture they were visiting, and we needed to remind them that things meaning lots in our culture often mean little in other cultures.

Some did not want to drink the very strong, sweet drinks offered and walked to the passage where they had seen a water fountain. They wanted to weaken the solution. This embarrassed the family who supplied the drinks as they thought they did not like the drinks! Sensitivity is so important. Whatever they offer, we need to eat. Whatever they serve is given sacrificially.

There were those who offered money and help and did not deliver and gave money secretly against ministry protocols; those who wanted two meals at meal times and some who thought we should get special transport for them as they were tall and had long legs; those who suffered travel sickness and expected to always sit in the front seats; those who, when tired, lost the plot and screamed and yelled inappropriately! This world would be a great place without people! Yes, if I could have chosen some of them, many would never have travelled, but God chose, and God enabled, often despite the difficulties! He empowered us all to pass the tests!

Another young woman would not eat the yolks of the eggs and wasted them each morning at breakfast until the national leaders spoke to her and told her eggs were expensive and what she did was unacceptable!

And there was one, who, on admission to hospital the people lined up to see her. They had seen no one as large! She walked in the market in Myanmar and people shouted, "Elephant woman! Elephant woman!" and came into the aisles to see her.

The foods and the bathrooms were always ever challenging, and the total lack of bathrooms and only bushes available troubled many! What a test! Most did well. In fact, they were such a blessing we just wanted them to travel again and again! Some even caught the vision that they had a green light and nothing would stop them, but most settled back into suburbia and life as normal on their return. We could only pray that they would catch and carry the vision to love people. Most people are followers; few catch the vision to be pioneers.

During this time, Rachel married Aaron in April 1992.

RACHEL AND AARON

KEVIN AND RACHEL

THE WEDDING

The car pulled into the drive. Rachel and Aaron arrived to visit, and they said to each other, "They're watching Benny Hinn again." They told us later, "You could hardly stand in the room, the presence of God so great."

We spent hours watching videos of Benny Hinn and Rodney Howard Brown as we were hungry to learn all we could about the presence of God and the ministry of the Holy Spirit.

God spoke, I had to go. Kevin had no hesitation in releasing me. He was very clear: "God said you have to do it!" Unquestioned obedience. That's how we lived. Easy? Absolutely not!

> You will never worry about an attack of demonic forces at night, nor have to fear a spirit of darkness coming against you. Don't fear a thing! Whether by night or by day, demonic danger will not trouble you, nor will the powers of evil launched against you. When you sit enthroned under the shadow of Shaddai, you are hidden in the strength of God Most High.
>
> —Psalm 91:5 TPT

When we dwell in the secret place, He will protect us. He will be our refuge. He will be our fortress and our hiding place. Declare with me, "Thankyou Lord you are my fortress, you are my hiding place."

Choking in the night happened often in so many nations. After the first attack on the first trip to Thailand and Myanmar, it happened often. Regularly in the night, I would struggle to breathe as the devil repeatedly tried to kill me! In Cuba one night, wheezing and gasping for breath, I woke the entire house. We agreed that someone should share a room with me. It immobilised me. I was unable to do anything to save myself!

> By faith, Abraham obeyed when he was called to go out to a place that he was to receive as an inheritance. And he went out, not knowing where he was going.
>
> —Hebrew 11:8 ESV

Another translation speaks of how faith urged and influenced Abraham, and he travelled with no anxiety or stress to begin a new life, a new move of God!

All these qualities of a pioneer were there in Abraham and Sarah's lives. They had the urge to set ablaze a new trail towards their dreams; they were versatile and flexible to move to their goals. Their determination charted the course for them. They would not settle on excuses. They had an ability to advance ahead and instill confidence. They provided groundbreaking influence to affect the society into which they were moving. Their determination and obedience caused them to go forth and receive the inheritance of many descendants. If our vision is to be birthed, we must ask the Lord for these qualities in our lives. To see my vision birthed, I asked the Lord for those qualities in my life.

A pioneer is one who leads the way, who paves the way for others to follow. They start, they open up, they forge ahead, they found, they break new ground. That's what we did. Everywhere we travelled we broke new ground, forged ahead, opened up unfamiliar territory. My great-grandfather, a circuit rider, preacher, and farmer, paved the way in Central Otago as an early pioneer. My other grandfather's family settled and did brilliant pioneer work in Southland with lakes and areas named after them, leaving a historical DNA for the family. All of them pioneers coming as early settlers from Britain who left all behind to seek a new life in New Zealand.

In the early days of each trip to Cuba and Myanmar, there were the bugs, and the water was always contaminated! No matter how careful we were, I would return with Caribbean salmonella, diarrhea, giardia, chest infections, and on the list went. Some got amoeba, but thank God, I never did! But they were nothing, just part of the deal! Later the more serious issues occurred. In spite of all the difficulties we pushed in and carried on. I learnt never give up!

During this time, my mother celebrated her eightieth birthday, in 1993, the year she died. There were many flights south that year: for the birthday celebration, before she died for a week to see her, for her funeral, then two weeks later for Basil's funeral. Only on the advice of family friends and our pastor did I fly the last time for Basil's funeral. The whole situation was too traumatic! Such a time of great trauma with my entire extended family totally alienated. What a year! Two weeks later, I flew for three months to Cuba.

GRAN'S 80TH BIRTHDAY 1993

Pioneers are unstoppable! Despite sickness, disease, hardship, difficulties, troublesome people, family alienation, deaths, and demons, nothing stops them. Nothing stops a pioneer! Focused, they carry on!

During this time, we received a few pieces my mother always said I would have. Some lovely crystal bowls and a lamp, and some pieces for decorating a duchess top, which we brought home and put in the bedroom. After that, strange events happened.

Spooky! Strange! As though there were eyes watching me, following me everywhere, a strange sensation. I shared this with my friend Bryan, and he said to me, "I could've told you, but I didn't want to. It's demonic! It's witchcraft. You have to get rid of that stuff. It's a great familiar spirit your mother had over her."

Startled, I said, "How could that be? My mother loved God. She followed the Lord in her later life."

He replied, "It's over the family. It's always been there. It's a great family spirit, and it's come on the stuff that came from her house, and you need to get rid of it all, even the rings. Take it out and smash it!"

I was reluctant to do this because it was from my mother, and I had always wanted the stuff, so pretty, and now I had to get rid of it because the eyes keep following me. What a strange sensation. Finally, I gave it all to Rachel because she wanted it and didn't want me to send it back.

A few days passed, and she phoned to say, "There is a problem, eyes follow me everywhere I go!"

In the house, eyes were following her, and she felt strange. Like being watched, spied on, she felt as though somebody stood in the room. Very unusual, so demonic, hard to explain. After two weeks and prayer, she picked everything up, put it in a box, and sent it to my sister.

Friends asked, "Why couldn't you put it in the garage, pray over it, and bring it back six months later, break the powers over it?"

Again, our friend, skilled in deliverance, said, "Absolutely not, you can't do that. Get rid of it."

You could ask, "Well, did your sister have any problems? Did those eyes affect them in their house?" No, I have to say no. There were no further problems.

You could ask, "Why was there no problem?" Well, it's a long story and goes back many years to early childhood when I had an elder sister and a powerful mother. Our mother took control with our father absent most of the time! Because of the controls exerted by mother to daughter,

daughter over sister as the youngest child, it oppressed me. Nobody intended or meant to do so. A spirit. It happens in families, oppression, control, intimidation, familiar spirits, soul ties.

Unaware of this, when I married Kevin and we moved north, he said after every visit to Dunedin, it seemed like he lived with my mother and sister! He said he seemed to live with three people all at once! I know that after I returned from my great visits to see them, there were uncanny feelings! For weeks after, when I spoke I would think, "Wow, I sound like Lyndsey, I sound like Mum." Gradually, it wore off! After my mother died and the family alienation, I had a strange dream. God often speaks to me in dreams, and my dreams continue to be significant. In this dream, my mother stood on the landing of a house at the corner of the property. I stood with Kevin's brother at the far end of the property. My mother, a tiny woman, became very tall in the dream, towering there on the balcony. She pointed at me and said, "It is finished!"

Startled, I woke, saying, "What is finished?" I understood this to mean that it finished my extended family relationships, this filled me with sadness as I have only one sister and her family.

I shared it with my friend Bryan, and he said, "No! No! It's not finished. It doesn't speak of your family! The great familiar spirit is finished. It's broken! It's broken! There's no longer any power over you, any power over your family."

Six months later, God did a work in my sister that reconciled the families.

Prior to leaving for Cuba on the request of a phone call, Kevin visited our landlord who lived in the house behind us. We prayed as it seemed unusual, and maybe he wanted to raise our rent! He returned excited. The landlord had reduced the rent by $60 a week! God is so faithful, that rental continued for many years until we moved again, this time to a house we purchased.

Unforgettable, Hosea Luis, Idalia, and I still laugh at the time when Belle and Shirley travelled with me to Cuba. We were at dinner, and we sat outside in the yard by the light of a lantern under a long cord where they hung clothes and washing. Around the table loaded with food, we all ate and talked. Chickens and hens roamed the yard. As we ate, a hen flew to perch on the cord above the table. Positioned directly above us, the inevitable happened! As I watched, the hen descended, ran right along the table. Its wings fluttered as food flew in all directions! We laughed and laughed so much, tears rolled and even more so, when one of the team laughed so hard, her false teeth fell out onto the plate! The family entertaining us were horribly embarrassed.

Because of the specific directional dream and prophetic word in Cuba about Bulgaria, Rachel, Joan, and I travelled by faith to Bulgaria in 1994 to see signs, wonders, and miracles there just as in Cuba. We discovered we could go on to Russia, the fourth corner of the world, without additional flight costs (spoken about in *Heavenly Kaleidoscope* and *Endless Safari*).

> Without faith, it is impossible to please God.
>
> —Hebrews 11:6

We travelled like Abraham, not knowing where we were going. The walls had not long come down, and everywhere people destroyed the statues of communism.

YULIA AND HER FAMILY. MET BY DIVINE APPOINTMENT IN CUBA.

No plan! No bookings made! Nowhere to stay! Enormous bags! Only one connection! Just the plan of God! Crazy people! Were we crazy? Or what? Who would do it? Only one address as we trusted God for provision! By divine appointments, I met Yulia and then Pastor Elenkov who opened the door to the Roma churches throughout the nation. Poor, big and small, hungry churches where we experienced signs, wonders, and miracles.

"It's a miracle! It's a miracle!" Said Pastor Elenkov, who led a national organisation and kindly provided accommodation for us over many subsequent visits. He cried excitedly, "I received your letter, but it did not say where you were coming from or the flight details! I phoned the airport this morning. I asked them, what time does the plane come? They told me no planes come from New Zealand!"

BULGARIA 2ND CENTURY CHURCH

BULGARIAN PARLIAMENT BUILDING

PASTOR ELENKOV AND FAMILY

My friend Joan said you needed three months training at the gym before such a trip. Travelling through the nation by train, we stopped at many little stations. We pulled our bags down cobbled streets and dirt roads to Roma pastor's houses where we slept on couches and air beds. The process repeated daily. After the meeting, we slept and moved on the next day. Adept at bag handling, in calculated efforts, we threw our bags on and off trains, especially when they only stopped for a minute or two.

We experienced a boiling hot summer of 40-plus degrees! On every corner were watermelon mountains, and the man selling slept on top. Peaches, we spotted a block away, almost smelled them, we loved peaches. Grapes were painful, so we avoided them! After walking miles, we would stop and sit in the gutters! People smiled as they walked past and said, "Foreigners!" They never sat in the gutters! Sometimes in desperation for somewhere to relax in our walking, we sat in the lounge foyer of the posh downtown hotels!

BLACK SEA, RACHEL, ANNIE AND DENISE

Stuck, we stayed in a little cottage in a Christian camp at the Black Sea, far from town, with plastic bottles we cut and used as pots! With a travel stick element, we cooked instant things like Uncle Ben's rice in a bag and vegetables, ate lots of Bulgarian goat and sheep cheeses and ham. For three weeks whilst blocked there and unable to go on, we explored the city, swam, prayed, and walked!

WHERE WE STAYED AT THE BLACK SEA
CHRISTIAN CAMPING GROUND

We returned to Sofia by train and to the apartment in the immense building on the city outskirts near the airport. After a great evening meeting in a Roma community, When we waited for the elevator, all lights in the building stairwell died! Stranded on the ground floor in the pitch-black, we tried a torch and wondered what to do! Reluctantly, we started the long climb to our apartment, many floors up. After we climbed a few steps, the lights appeared. We breathed sighs of relief as we stopped the elevator. Just as we were to get in, the lights were gone again! In the deep darkness, we heard peels of loud laughter. We looked over the stairwell, and a man played with the switchboard. Now concerned, we speedily climbed the stairs! Off again, and this time he climbed the stairs, chasing us! Somehow now he appeared above us, so we ran down quickly to the bottom. What a problem.

Worried, frightened, anxious, we ran up the stairs again, stumbling in our haste in the dark with our one flashlight! He shouted in Bulgarian, chasing us from floor to floor! Thank God we reached Pastor Elenkov's floor and banged on his door. He came to help us. And the man vanished. We breathed sighs of relief, broke the spirit of fear and intimidation operating, and retired to our haven, happy to pull shut the apartment door's great bolts.

After another arduous train journey, we visited Dimitrovgrad, where an older pastor met and happily took us to his home. In most homes where we stayed, were pictures of the sacred heart of Mary, everything very religious, as the communist time had not long ended, and few pictures were available.

We prayed for a young pregnant woman who repented for seeking to take the life of her unborn baby. She said she had tried several times to kill the baby. I spoke that night on curses that oppress when we disobey. God touched her and gloriously set her free after we broke the curses of death and hell.

Russia amazed us. So beautiful, so vast, so grand. A tourist's heaven. Endless sightseeing, much to see but too little time. A land of immense steppes, vast forests, major highways, magnificent palaces, and ornate orthodox churches and cathedrals. The ends of the earth, from New Zealand to the top of the world. To Moscow, we journeyed with love. We travelled by faith with one connection unavailable on our arrival!

> My old identity has been co-crucified with Messiah and no longer lives; for the nails of his cross crucified me with him. And now the essence of this new life is no longer mine, for the Anointed One lives his life through me.
>
> —Galatians 2:20 TPT

We live in union as one! My new life is empowered by the faith of the son of God, who loves me so much that he gave himself for me and dispenses his life into mine! We live by the faith of the son of God, not by faith in the son of God as some translations say.

For faith is not an attitude, it is a lifestyle based on a world view of the power of the word of God. Prompted, activated by faith, in obedience we travelled to Russia as pioneers, exhibiting active faith.

On this first trip in 1994, for just a week, the walls were not long down. What intimidation we suffered, but we change atmosphere when we look at Jesus, not the circumstances, declaring His word. What a shock after the flight from Bulgaria. We walked down steep stairs to look up at the dark brown bottle-shape-ornamented roof we three entered the intimidating long immigration hall! Impressed by the feeling of guilty-'til-innocent-why-are-you here with stern officials on our first entry, wow, we breathed a sigh of relief to exit that airport entry situation.

After we located a taxi with an English-speaking driver, he drove through the city on the way to the hotel and pointed to an immense building known as the White House. He asked us, "How many floors do you think it goes underground? It's the home of the KGB."

It astounded us to know that there were almost as many floors under the ground as above. He warned us to be careful, never to go on the streets at night!

THE WHITE HOUSE KGB BUILDING

HOTEL WHERE WE STAYED

MCDONALDS

We wanted to go to McDonald's, but a queue for two blocks changed our minds. A sign in our room said, "If you are going out, you can have a guide, a bodyguard, or an armed guard for 150 USD." The hotel wanted us to have a guard to go to McDonald's, but we declined as we live by faith, not fear, and knew God as our protector. Across the road, we enjoyed exploring the Kremlin and a big mall.

JOAN RACHEL AND DENISE KREMLIN

ST BASIL'S CHURCH

After only one night at the hotel, our divine connection with Helen arrived. She and Yuri took us to their apartment outside of the city. They had just returned from the farm in the countryside and excitedly served us lunch, a watery soup in which a few vegetables floated forlornly. Until the believers came to transport us to Vladimir, we stayed in their home. When we ate watermelon, abundant in summer, every sore covering the entire body of six-year-old Luni vanished!

Sunday came, and Helen instructed, "Get ready, quick, we have a long way to go to church. Yuri will take you."

Mystified, we quickly obeyed. Together with the family, we left the house, walked to the metro, and rode for an entire-day affair. We passed forests and quaint villages until we stopped and walked through the village. In single file, into the forest, we walked along the narrow track into the forest depths. On the far outskirts of Moscow, what a beautiful time. Amongst tall birch trees, which surrounded and towered over us, believers sat for a five-hour service on silver birch logs. This church declined registration, preferring to meet in the forest during the summer, just as it did during the communist time. On the forest floor, everything green, families spread rugs and sat together in groups. As children played, they listened, ate, and drank.

The simple speaker system hung from a tree, and we sang that beautiful old hymn "Blessed assurance, Jesus is mine, O what a foretaste of glory divine . . ."

Women did not speak here, but they asked me to share for a few minutes and said I could pray for the people when the service finished! I spoke for all of two or three minutes, brought greetings from New Zealand and the nations. I said, "God is healing today in Cuba. I have seen many healed, delivered, and set free. If you would like prayer, I will pray at the end of the service."

The service ended, the leadership called me forward to pray as they gathered many people at the front. People knelt everywhere: on moss, fallen leaves, and the rough dirt forest floor. In reverence, we prayed and laid hands on them. After about an hour, the watching pastor stood up and exclaimed, "Last prayer!"

The entire group fell on their knees, the ladies put scarves over their heads, and I prayed a final prayer. Wonderful. A most holy occasion, one that I will never forget. No, I didn't see signs and wonders or miracles but the Holy Spirit's beautiful manifest presence. He touched those people. Many were weeping.

KREMLIN, CZARS PALACES AND CHURCHES

The police officers staggered in the street, drunk, laughing, shouting, falling down in the road, and we didn't want to proceed to the police station. There were three of us women, and even though somebody travelled with us, we were all concerned. At immigration, they had told us we must report at the police station if we changed our accommodation or moved to another area. When we arrived to report, we were absolutely shocked because we had to go down this long alley and deal with all these drunken police officers. After some discussion, we decided safer not to report, and we left, never to return. Later in Vladimir, the pastor took our passports and reported our presence.

As we drove along the huge highways, we noticed container shops and cars stationed with crystal all over them and huge soft toys and rugs! On enquiry, we discovered the factories paid the people for their work in crystal or rugs or toys! To survive, the workers sold the items! After three hours' travel through extensive fields and forests, we arrived in Vladimir.

"She's short, small, powerful, and from New Zealand, just like you!" God must have a sense of humor as the believers told me after we arrived to stay in the apartment of an absent New Zealand missionary. I had contacted Lesley before our travel, and she helped us by opening up Vladimir. We stayed in her apartment but never met her.

We spent many hours counseling and praying for people who came with hopeless issues. There were no answers! Only God. After we listened and prayed, we left the results with God!

Powerful altar calls followed each meeting, with joy and weeping always apparent. Iron sharpens iron, and that is true when you work with prophetic people. As Joan moved incredibly in the prophetic, the flow became tremendous as we ministered together.

> Iron sharpens iron, and one man sharpens another.
>
> —Proverbs 27:17 ESV

Danger on the Russian rail! Different to every other country! We noticed people expressionless from disappointment and loss of hope, and experienced no eye contact or response when we smiled. Sturdy, stout, strong-bodied people pushed against us as we were overwhelmed and pressured by the magnitude of the crowds at only 7:00 a.m. Crowds rushed for the day ahead of them, everywhere around us in the metro. We boarded the train, sat on each side of the compartment, facing but unable to see one another because people stood all around. Suddenly, a man in the aisle pulled out a rolled newspaper, out of which he drew a long-bladed knife! Two of our group witnessed this and became very alarmed. Immediately, as the man showed the knife, a man standing beside him showed his strong disapproval and made these "tut tut tut" noises. Before the man could make his next move, our guide called out, "This is our stop!"

Rachel and Joan recognised the dangerous situation as he moved to slice the strap and snatch my video camera. They shifted quickly to surround and protect me as they rapidly ushered me off the train to escape his clutches.

The following year, 1996, Joan and I returned to Russia. The ends of the earth called again, the four corners beckoned.

With ice on the veranda, I slipped and slid across the landing and down the stairs. Almost crippled, I hobbled to the car and drove to work. During a meeting, suffering much from pain, I excused myself and returned home to rest! The next day, Tuesday, I visited the doctor, who told me I must rest as I had ruptured the ligaments in my leg and I needed to go to bed!

I told him, "I'm flying to Russia on Friday!"

He replied, "You will fly nowhere if you don't rest!"

I rested. Friday morning, rising at three o'clock to travel two hours to the plane, with a backpack, I stepped out on the landing outside our bedroom, tripped, and rolled down two flights of stairs. As I rolled to the bottom, our daughter in the next bedroom woke and said, "Sounds like someone fell down the stairs!" Me!

Kevin said nothing, just drove me to the airport, and I flew to Russia as planned! My leg had no further pain or problems. I asked him later, "Why did you say nothing?"

He replied, "What could I say? Commiserate and then it would have been worse, or ignore it and pray?"

Prompted, actuated, motivated, urged on by faith, I travelled regardless of the difficulties. We pick ourselves up, shake ourselves off, don't look at the circumstances, don't look at the difficulties, and we move forwards because we move by faith.

> Without faith, it's impossible to please God.
> —Hebrews 11:6 ESV

We must have active believing faith. Abel brought God a better and more acceptable sacrifice than Cain, because of which, they called him righteous Abel (upright and in right standing with God), and God bore witness by accepting and acknowledging his gifts. And though he died, yet (through the incident) he is still speaking (Gen. 4:3-10 ESV). Faith prompted and activated me. Like Abel, it gave me identity and purpose. Pioneers have identity and purpose.

Joan and I had a tremendous trip in Russia and saw God move.

JOAN, RACHEL AND DENISE KREMLIN

Etched in my memory is a visit to an orthodox church where the priest stood in the entrance. Solemn worshippers bowed in reverence, lit a candle, before proceeding to the front where they knelt to pray. So many candles burning as they prayed. Yet such reverence! What a sense of the holiness of God. Unforgettable. Despite this, the darkness, heaviness, and coldness of religion blanketed us, and the snares of fallen communism reached out to clutch us. Poverty everywhere in free Russia! We reflected, what could it have been like in the communist times? It must have been tough! Yet they had food and work, now nothing.

Cuba continued to have first place in my life, with trips every year taking many people. Belle and Shirley, Mary and Val, Carol and Dee, and of course Kevin all of whom were part of tremendous moves of God. Cuba won their hearts. An intrepid traveller who had recovered from surgeries for a malignant brain tumour, Mary loved Cuba. She had travelled with her husband to North Korea and many other nations with an organisation where they served faithfully taking Bibles into restricted nations.

We noticed such a sense of excitement and anticipation as God's presence filled the old block church. People overflowed out of the church onto the street! Three rows sat on old wooden forms outside, and many looked in the windows. "A wall of prayer! A wall of prayer!" Pastor Hector shouted.

All the leaders, including myself, gathered at the front to form the wall of prayer! After a service of prayer, praise, and worship, we moved amongst the people, ministering to them. Believers wept, cried out, shook with the tremendous sense of God's love and presence. An altar call followed the cry for salvation. Not a word had been preached. That night twenty people came to know Jesus as Savior and Lord. They were born again of the Spirit of God, transformed in a prayer meeting!

Pastor Hector, coordinator of the Assemblies of God and in whose home we stayed on arrival, said, "Don't spend the money to fly! We need to deliver Bibles and literature in the East. Would you pay the fuel for the truck to travel east? It will deliver you to Palma Soriano!"

When we asked, "How long will it take?" his reply was "Maybe twenty-four hours, maybe more!"

Game for anything, we agreed and paid the fuel! Finally, leaving at 3:00 p.m., we climbed aboard and hit the road. What an adventure: no seats, just hard wooden forms with other believers. Shaking and rattling on the back of the enormous truck under the red canopy, watching the stars, we took out our blankets and slept when we could! At 5:00 a.m., we stopped for a brief break, a comfort and food stop. When we looked in a small wall mirror, we laughed at ourselves as black faces, necks, arms looked back at us as we were entirely black covered by road dust and exhaust. After a rest and food, we journeyed on. Mary, unstoppable, a pilgrim, a true pioneer who completed her journey some years ago, is now with Jesus. Together in the month she stayed, we prayed for hundreds of people and saw tremendous miracles.

THE TRUCK

In 1996, with Mary again, what a privilege! When I preached on Isaiah 6 about the fire of God and Isaiah being broken, about twenty persons came to Jesus with a significant move of the Holy Spirit. The fire came so wonderfully. Much gold dust appeared all over my arms and on others; tremendous fire came as many shook, wept, and fell down! Jesus healed many, and a man testified he had a leg problem for months, which caused constant pain, and he could not walk properly. After prayer, no more pain, the leg problem gone! Amazingly healed. In answer to daily declarations by faith, God had told me, "Signs, wonders, and miracles!"

It was during this time God spoke to me to take off my jewellery which I did not realise had been offensive to the leadership. For the following two years I wore no jewellery at all. Graciously they had never mentioned that for them it was a problem. The church in this nation hungry for God had many rules!

Cripples walked so often in the districts we visited. In Holguin, I could not see why the crowded church was clapping and cheering, but there was a man with his crutch raised high in the air walking, healed! Here too a person with a frozen shoulder lifted their arm totally healed. In Minna Harlem, there was Roberto, robbed of his healing the year before because of demonic activity. Now healed, he pushed the wheelchair back to the hospital where he lived. In the Maffo District, another man was healed, picked up his crutch as he left the meeting, and sadly, we watched him start to use it again!

Does God answer your prayers? I declared and decreed miracles, signs, and wonders.

> The fervent prayer of a righteous man [woman] avails much.
>
> —James 5:16 ESV

The old camion or church truck stopped outside a large church in this city we were visiting for the first time. "It's safe there," the leader of the district had told us as we set off for three days of ministry. After greetings and drinks, we discovered the praying service underway.

We followed a worker into the church and immediately sensed the presence of God. What a great time with the Lord, and after speaking over and praying for all present, we returned to the house to drink and relax. The ladies followed us in and exuberantly shared about the meeting. There appeared to be no signs or wonders or anything visible happening and no obvious anointing! Yet during this time of prayer and seeking God, God touched one woman's hernia, healing her, and all around the room, ladies shared how God brought health to their bodies.

Yes, we can lay hands on the sick, and heal them. When we change atmosphere and bring God's presence, there is healing power released.

Wedding dresses are a special luxury to women in Cuba as they are too expensive to hire, and you cannot buy the dress nor the materials to make it. For years, I carried wedding dresses and ball gowns to Cuba. The senior pastor's son was getting married, and Josh, the bridegroom's brother, told us of the bride's need. We said, "We have dresses in the cases, you can have one!"

Outside the airport, we thrust a beautiful dress into his arms, and a few minutes later, we were gone!

Six weeks later, we attended the wonderful wedding to see the girl in her beautiful dress provided by a caring New Zealand woman. The transformed dress now magnificent with beads sewn all over.

The enormous box contained a tremendous amount of baggage: dresses and many New Testaments with a small car motto on the front. Unaware that inside the books were ten pages of testimonies from the persecuted churches of the region and Asia, we entered as usual, but the bags remained in Mexico! The following day, when we arrived to collect the bags, officials asked, "What's in the box?"

We prayed and said, "Dresses!"

On arrival, where we stayed before going east, we opened the box. There were the books and when we opened them, the forbidden car motto and the testimonies even from Cuba! Our friends said, "These would have meant your instant expulsion if they had opened the box!"

With a blade, we sliced out all the testimony pages. How we praised God for his protection.

In Cuba, the most incredible significant thing happened. Cuba changed, empowered, and affected the remainder of my life. Because of this, I have lived at another level, a supernatural level, for over twenty-five years of life in ministry.

> So I kneel humbly in awe before the Father of our Lord Jesus, the Messiah, the perfect Father of every father and child in heaven and on the earth.
>
> —Ephesians 3:14 TPT

> And I pray that He would unveil within you the unlimited riches of His glory and favor until supernatural strength floods your innermost being with His divine might and explosive power. Then by constantly using your faith, the life of Christ will be released deep inside you, and the resting place of His love will become the very source and root of your life. Then you will be empowered to discover what every holy one experiences: the great magnitude of the astonishing love of Christ in all its dimensions. How deeply intimate and far-reaching is His love! How enduring and inclusive it is! Endless love beyond measurement that transcends our understanding—this extravagant love pours

> into you until you are filled to overflowing with the fullness of God! Never doubt God's mighty power to work in you and accomplish all this. He will achieve infinitely more than your greatest request, your most unbelievable dream, and exceed your wildest imagination! He will outdo them all, for His miraculous power constantly energises you.
>
> —Ephesians 3:16-18 TPT

A life change, empowered with supernatural strength, just like in the Bible. Remember Caleb, he, at eighty-five years of age, stayed as young at eighty as at forty years. Empowered, strengthened by God, we can be the same.

Caleb's faith is on full display in these verses:

> *Just as the Lord promised, he has kept me alive for forty-five years . . . so here I am today, eighty-five years old! I am still as strong today as the day Moses sent me out; I'm just as vigorous to go out to battle now as then. Now give me this hill country [mountain,] that the Lord promised me that day. You yourself heard then that the Anakites were there and their cities were large and fortified, but the Lord helping me, I will drive them out just as he said.*
>
> *—Joshua 14:10-12 KJV*

Notice that in three out of the four statements in this section, Caleb mentioned the name of the Lord: "The LORD promised . . . the LORD promised . . . the LORD helping me." Here is a man who learnt to trust in the promises of God and stake his entire future on them. He knew the Lord's help and trusted that the Lord would do so. This is exultant, powerful faith prior to the event. It sounds like bragging, but it is faith bragging on the power of God to keep His promises. I like that kind of faith!

> *Then Joshua blessed Caleb, son of Jephunneh and gave him Hebron as his inheritance. So Hebron has belonged to Caleb, son of Jephunneh the Kenizzite ever since, because he*

followed the Lord, the God of Israel, wholeheartedly. Then the land had rest from war.

—Joshua 14:13-15 KJV

What a dilemma, stuck in the mud, after we left at 8:30 a.m. for the meeting. Nothing we did altered it! Absolutely stuck tight, mud oozed all around the undercarriage, and the wheels were deep in the mud! In fact, we were not just travelling to the morning meeting, but to three meetings, and we would not get to bed until 3:00 a.m.! The New Year services did not finish till very late. But now the jeep stuck made the situation extremely difficult! I looked up at the mountain ahead of us. Obviously, we had a problem: Maybe we would not do this meeting? But no, no! They loaded everything out of the jeep, myself included, and we started the climb. The guys just ran up like mountain goats, they were used to this, but Me not used to climbing, I plodded. It would take us a long time to get up there, about an hour and a half, and we walked, walked, and walked. I became tired. I had no water! It was difficult in the heat, on this mountain, in the equator! Suffering, I just cried out to God because I knew we had three services that day! It was so difficult as I didn't have strength for all that and not used to walking mountains, climbing up steep tracks with no water. I cried out, "Lord, I have no strength. Help me, please. Lord, I need Your strength. This is a long day, and we've been ministering every day now for weeks. Lord, I don't have the strength, but You do. Please give me strength."

Amazed as I cried out to God, it seemed like I had an injection in my arm. Suddenly, I became strong, energised with new vitality and strength. No longer tired, the rest of the day became incredible. With no drink until 2:00 p.m., when we arrived for a brief stop where we stayed, I preached and ministered, lunched, walked down the mountain, travelled to two more churches. I preached, and ministered to hundreds of people, and didn't finish 'til 3:00 a.m. the following day.

After we finished, the senior pastor half my age asked, "How come you're not tired? I was so tired I slept whilst you preached, I was so tired! And you have not even had a rest!"

Phenomenal, supernatural. With God, nothing is impossible as He delights to do the impossible. It's not about us. It's not about how strong we are or how weak we are. It's about trust. As I reached out for God to do the impossible, that became the story of my life. Seeing God do impossible things, moving in divine strength by faith in the assurance of His provision, I have never lacked strength for the tasks, even when they have seemed impossible!

Because of that experience, I have moved and lived in this supernatural strength all the years of ministry as I travelled around the world!

CHAPTER 6

The Early Ministry Years, 1994-1998 - Unlocked Freedom - Ethnic Work - Nonconforming - A New Day - Cuba - Russia - Bulgaria - Nepal - Myanmar

"Did your mother try to kill you? Did she not want you? I see a dagger over your life! A curse of death and hell is over your life. Is someone seeking to kill you?" he said cautiously.

Stunning questions, but I knew the answer. As the service concluded, knowing I needed deliverance prayer, I responded to the altar call for those wanting prayer. After months of repeated excisions and much pain, the bladder tumours kept returning, I needed a miracle. Aware of the risks of recurrence and eventually cancer, I needed healing prayer! Several people had come asking if they could pray for me, but I waited for the one person I knew could help. Only one man in the entire church moved in deliverance.

As I lay on the floor, I knew what he wanted to ask, but as a church leader, he hesitated to ask me the question! I said, "I had a pregnancy terminated several years ago!"

That day, after he broke curses over my life, the bladder tumours never returned, instantly healed. The devil had sought to kill me.

Every day in Cuba, I spoke on release from curses telling stories from my life.

"You think the cancer and the tumours happened because of the abortion and a curse came over your life. But that's not the reason! Have you considered another reason?" my brothers in Cuba who listened daily to my stories said to me.

Every day I preached and told stories of my life, they analyzed the realities. I considered what they said, and agreed that the revelation and conclusions reached were correct!

They said, "When God spoke to you as a teenager to go to the nations, when God spoke to your husband and you to go and you did not, that's when the curse came over your lives! It was disobedience!"

I received a miracle, set free from that day, and from the day, we travelled to the nations, free to release God's DNA of love in nations where He stirred me to go. I operated on the green light of every door is open until He shuts it with a red light! Most believers operate in the opposite way, waiting for God to move their feet out of the concrete!

Garage sales yield more than a sale, more than selling and cleaning out stuff. At our garage sale, we found Dawei and Jian, or rather, they found us. They came to buy and stayed in our lives forever. From China, they settled in Hamilton with their only son Justin and later had a daughter, Holly. Dawei, a believer with a widowed Christian mother; Jian, an unbeliever who discovered faith in Jesus through me. The beginning of an ethnic outreach, we started conversational English classes for new immigrants and refugees. Each Tuesday night, we held a free class, and once a month, we held potluck dinners for friendship and socialising. Culturally, these were expansive as we learnt much, especially about timekeeping! Most of these folks operated on a different cultural value as events people, not based on time like so many of us in the Western world are.

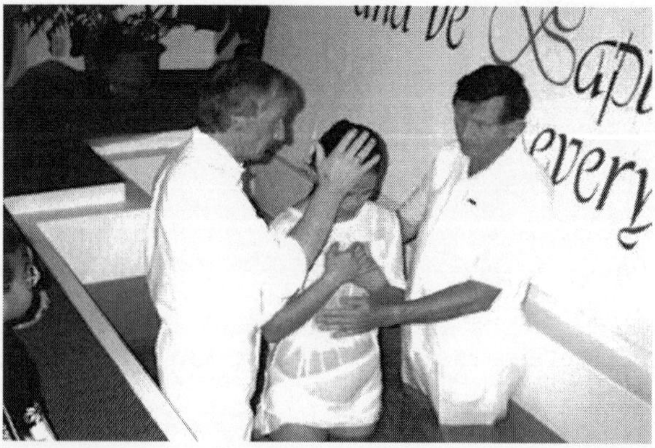

BAPTISM OF JIAN, BY KEVIN AND RODNEY FRANCIS

The dinner started at six o'clock, and they all came, except the Nepalis. What a great night! We had fun, fellowship and food of all cultures. We played games, encouraged them to share, and everyone talked and ate lots! But where were the Nepalis? There were two families who usually joined us. After a fantastic fun evening, it was time to leave as 10:00 p.m. and Sunday fast-approached.

"Ding! Dong! Ding!" the doorbell rang!

The door opened, and the Nepalis arrived with their steaming hot curry, *daal*, and rice!

When you say 6:00 p.m., they come about three hours later! That is so true of Nepal's culture. In Nepal, we say 10:00 a.m. for meetings, and they start walking from home at 10:00 a.m., maybe getting to the meeting at 1:00 p.m.! Some arrive the next day as they often walk long distances!

Each week we did puzzles leading people gently to understand how to find the new life in Christ, what it meant to follow Jesus, and the final week of the class, we did a special crossword puzzle, which explained giving your life to Jesus being born again. How exciting it was when the entire group of these precious people found a relationship with Jesus.

We ran a children's class, and they too were unbelievers. One ten-year-old Chinese boy said, "I want to feel Jesus. If He is real, I want to feel Him."

We prayed for him, and he not only fell down but also had to crawl from the room, astounded that he experienced God's presence!

Dawei and Jiang moved on to Bible school, and they now pastor an Auckland Chinese church, and when we found them again after losing them for many years, we asked, "What are you doing?"

They beamed and said, "The same as you!"

"Ask of me and I will give you the nations," Psalm 2:8 ESV says. We asked God, and He gave nations right in our own town and in our own home and in our own family! Our immediate family now multi-ethnic, with Cambodian Chinese Kiwi grandchildren, and our extended family now interrelated with several other nations. How good is that!

The nations invaded our home. To explain what being a Christian really meant, Kevin held a Christianity-explained course. The church filled with ethnic people: Iraqis, Chinese, Nepalis, amongst others. We reached them all. An amazing season of tremendous fun and enjoyment as horizons extended and our borders expanded right there in New Zealand.

Pioneers possess a spirit of adventure, exhibited in the lives of Paul and the other disciples. Nothing stopped them as they travelled all over the known world. Look at Priscilla, Junia, David, Samson, and Timothy, with lives full of adventure. They knew the revealed will of God. Have you ever thought your life to be dull and lacking adventure? Do you want to change? My life has been full of adventure, sometimes escalating non stoppable adventure! But I never wanted to stop the bus because it travelled too fast or raced out of control! When we put our hand in the hand of God, we lose control we are in His control.

The masters of philosophy in missions completed, next step, the nursing and health sciences degrees. Our friend Bryan had advised me carefully, "If you are going to travel the world, you need to be qualified and credible! As a woman in ministry, they must see you as credible!"

Few women were in ministry, and no women, at least not from New Zealand, travelled the world doing what I did! After I quit studying several times, with much hard work and desperation, I finally graduated with many sighs of relief, with the M.PH. in missions and the nursing and health science degrees, in 1998, a pioneer who broke new ground. People continued to give Kevin a hard time wanting to know why he did not do what I did and why he did not accompany me! He told them again and again the same thing: "God has not told me to do it! God told Denise, and I have released her to do what God says!" This silenced the critics, at least sometimes!

That year, there arose more difficulties at work: I loved teaching in this wonderful job, but the atmosphere became increasingly difficult, almost intolerable. One lunchtime some students came to see me, they were believers, and one student manifested on the floor with demons. As a group, we prayed over the girl and delivered her. The next day my colleague from the office next door came to visit me. She shut the door carefully, and there alone, she asked, "Were you doing a role-play yesterday? I heard the noise, I became worried as all the staff were at lunch, and I came to see if everything was okay. I thought someone was being attacked. When I looked in the window, a student lay on the floor, and you were standing over her shouting. Was it a role-play?"

I looked at her carefully, pondered how to reply, and I asked, "Do you understand about deliverance? Do you know about demons?"

Puzzled, she said, "Yes, I know a little." A nominal Anglican, she loved God.

I said, "That student fell on the floor, oppressed by demons, manifested, shouted, and rolled around. We prayed and delivered her!"

"Oh!" she said, startled.

I breathed a quick prayer of thanks to God that my friend noticed the noise and not some other person who worked in the department. They would never have understood! God is good. He looks after us.

Bad things happen to God's people, even those serving Jesus!

Stressed, I arrived at the lecture concerned at having lost my keys. My colleagues knew I lost my keys. We walked in and sat down amongst the students in the huge lecture theatre and picked up the materials for discussion. Shocked, I glanced at the frank homosexual material! In that moment, I decided on my next costly course of action and rose, excused myself, picked up my stuff, and left! Relieved, I located my missing keys on return to my office!

A few days passed, and a colleague came to visit me. He said, "I think I need to apologise!"

I asked, "Why would that be?"

He said, "I denounced you at the staff meeting for leaving the lecture before it began the other day, for having no cultural sensitivity! But other staff members told me later you lost your keys!" He gazed at me and asked with care. "Did you leave the lecture because you lost your keys or for another reason?"

I considered my reply. He gave a way out of a tough situation, but as a believer, I could not take it. I replied with care, "No! I had lost my keys, but I left the lecture because of the proposed discussion of the frank homosexual material."

In shock at my honesty, he said, "How can you be culturally sensitive if you're not willing to discuss such material?"

I replied, "I'm a believer in Jesus, and I cannot accept that material!"

Because of this conversation and my actions of leaving the lecture rejecting the materials presented, all hell broke loose, and a season of extreme persecution of intimidation and manipulation developed that later cost me my job. God's timing is always perfect, He has the perfect plan, and for ten years, I had wished to quit and become full time in ministry.

A few weeks later, I flew to Cuba. That too a battle! To go to Cuba for three months, I worked through all the holidays that year and saved the time for the leave in December through to February. As I had no reply to my leave application, I visited the head of department to ask about the status of my leave, all set to fly on 6 December. The head of the department said, "I did not grant the leave! You're scheduled to work 'til Christmas!"

I replied firmly, "I cannot work! I'm leaving on 6 December, I'm booked out of the country, and that's tomorrow. This is my last day. I applied for the leave. I am entitled to the leave, and you cannot deny it! You failed to reply to my application! Tomorrow I'm flying!" The next day I flew to Cuba knowing the situation had become untenable!

After an amazing time of ministry and supernatural power in Cuba, I returned to the coal face to discover my job now under threat had become too difficult. Under tremendous stress and with health issues, I visited the doctor and explained the terrible situation! She said, "You must take time off to recover! You cannot work there! I will give you three months sick leave!"

I said to her, "No, that's impossible! Let me get back to you."

On my return to work, I called the pay office. Because of all the sick leave taken when I had cancer, I was sure I would have none available and we needed my income! I was amazed when the pay office replied to my call to say from the previous day, a new allocation of six months paid leave had become available. What a miracle just when I needed it! On my return to the doctor, we agreed I would take sick leave on a month-by-month basis, reassessing the situation at the close of each month.

At Easter, I returned for half the morning and as the situation deteriorated I phoned Kevin to collect me. I left that day and never returned. My job paid me full sick leave until I resigned in July, giving two months' notice, and ended my employment of ten years in August. A miracle, paid in full for eight months and never worked a day, even paid for vacation times. God looked after our every financial need and restored my health and well-being. It took me every ounce of strength to walk across the platform to face the staff when I graduated that year with my nursing and health sciences degrees. This a year of resting and recovery from the enormous stress caused from loving God and doing what He said! I could not remain silent in this matter, I could not accept the department's culture, I had to stand as a believer in the face of opposition. Born to be transformers, we cannot conform. Pioneers often face incredible obstacles but continue, regardless; they never give up.

As pioneers we travelled again to Russia, returning through Bulgaria. In 1997, the year Princess Diana died, three of us, Rachel, Elisabeth, and myself, travelled.

After clearing Russian immigration and collecting our bags, we pushed our bags out of the building, only to be bombarded by many taxis wanting our custom. We looked through the crush for our friends. Yuri and Helen beamed as they waved to us, and to our consternation, they dismissed the taxi.

"Mafia," they said and shook their heads. "No, we will go by metro!"

After fifteen hours on planes, hours in airports, now the metro! We sighed in resignation as we rolled our heavy enormous bags and carry bags into the immense building with people going in all directions. What an experience! Unforgettable! Yuri hauled and lifted all the bags through the gates across the stiles, and we jumped over entry stops. At one stage, I looked back, and there, Rachel attempted to lift a fifty-pound bag over her head to get through the stile. After hanging on the rails as the steep moving stairwells descended what seemed like hundreds of feet into the depths, we arrived at last on ornate platforms with historic carvings and wall artwork designs. After what seemed like forever, we scrambled on the metro.

"Watch your bags!" they warned. "Thieves are everywhere!"

We clung to our bags.

HELEN AND YURI WITH RACHEL AND ELISABETH, MOSCOW.

After about 3/4 of an hour, they told us we get off at the next stop. With bags ready at the door as it opened; we threw them onto the platform. We moved to the escalator. Some bold people in a hurry ran up and down these death traps of steepness. Skull and cross bone signs warned people to hold on to the rails!

After processing the bags in a Samson like manner, we escaped to the fresh air in the street above where older people sat along the path selling cigarettes, papers, food, anything they could to survive. When communism fell, with little social support, they struggled with no incomes. In the distance were multistoried buildings!

"Are we going there?" we gasped.

We pulled the bags down rough streets until, exhausted, we reached massive apartment blocks bigger than anything we had ever seen, and in the midst, they said, "We are here."

Blue cornflowers and spindly silver birch trees filled the grounds between the buildings.

We followed them up the ramp into the grimy building and into a decrepit, smelly elevator to the sixth floor and the apartment. There, we stayed a few days before moving on.

We asked Helen, our great guide, "Please, we want to go to the Kremlin."

"Okay," she said.

Later she told us she endured and suffered going to the Kremlin as everyone she met and helped wanted to go to the Kremlin!

After an hour on the metro to the centre city, we arrived at the square. No dull old Russia. Brilliant colours, amazing scenery. We gazed at the square's corner at Lenin's tomb, with crowds of people lined up to enter. We didn't go there. The brilliant multicoloured Saint Basil's church caught our eyes and called to us. Many photos later, we were so enchanted by everything we caught sight of.

We joined the lines, the four of us, and after a long wait, paid a US$1 entrance fee at the ticket office. The walkway led past the Russian parliament and other enormous official buildings, past the buildings the Tsars families lived in. We passed huge orthodox churches attended by the royal family and burial sites for entombed royalty, palaces of bygone eras. They chased us to go into the gem museum with the royal family jewelry and could not believe it when we declined because of the cost. Wide-eyed and enthused, we rounded a corner. There, to our surprised amazement, were ballerinas in ordinary clothing, dancing, and an orchestra playing. We stopped to watch. Helen explained to us, "This is the preparation for 750 years anniversary of Moscow. It's next week, and they are practising for the tremendous show they will have here."

Pavarotti, the world-famous singer, and the amazing Bolshoi ballet! How blessed could we be! We watched it all for just $1! God does all things well. How He blessed us.

In the crowded trains there were risks, and we experienced this one, the worst of many difficult occasions. We pushed through the crowds to get on trains. With not much time for the exchange, people poured off, and others poured on. To leave the train, the people crowded at the compartment exit, making it difficult for those getting on. Few sat in the seats. We had to get on! The three of us struggled and pushed to the front of the crowd. Easy for me, as I am small and can wriggle through! For bigger people, rather difficult! Like a football scrum, everyone struggled, shoved and pushed. The train stopped, the door opened, people poured off. Now our turn! We pushed and pushed and struggled to get in! I wormed and pushed in around people; I checked Elisabeth had somehow got in, but I couldn't find Rachel. But I looked around everywhere until, to my shock, I screamed as I found her, for she could not enter the slamming door! Outside, the door kept shutting on her! Through the narrow opening, I reached and clung to her backpack with both hands. The door slammed but couldn't shut. On the narrow ledge, we held her tight, clinging to the bag. She could not get in. The door ramming and slamming shut! As it tried to close, it crashed back and forth, frenzied, trying to shut, but impossible to do so! Praying and hanging on, we rode like that to the next station! Stones and rocks reached up to her as she flew along! Arctic wind blew in her face as the train raced by. Rachel's body hung outside on the narrow ledge, held by us and the door until the train stopped. The door flew open, and gasping, she fell face down on the platform, so relieved. She rejoiced, exhausted, at last safe. Now to recover and never forget!

To travel to the camp in the forest far away, we assembled at the square waiting for the bus's arrival. In eagerness and excitement, when all arrived, we climbed aboard. Another new experience. Several hours later, we arrived in the woods in the middle of the forest, trees everywhere and a pretty lake just close by. We had a cabin with a heater, so we were cozy, but the others said they froze with no heating.

BUS TO THE CAMP MEETING

The camp meetings beyond expectation were wonderful. Before the meetings, the pastor had said, "We will do whatever the Holy Spirit wants and give Him space to move."

With no sermon, we allowed the Holy Spirit to draw us into intimacy during the worship as God's presence increased in the assembly.

The pastor's sister sitting well back in the meeting wept. I watched her with concern. "Call the people to repent, call the people to repentance," the Holy Spirit said.

"God is calling, God is speaking. Do you have sin in your life? It's time to repent," I cried. "Don't grieve, God with your lives, He wants clean, holy lives. Turn to Him, turn from your sin. You have wrong attitudes and are involved in wrong actions? Clean up your lives, the Lord is saying. Tell Him you are sorry and will change." I could hear loud sobbing throughout the large room.

About a third of those assembled knelt at the front in humility and repentance. Some were wailing, all were sobbing with deep weeping from their inner being. Such a sombre time. We all cried out to God as we reviewed our lives, confessing aloud wrong attitudes and actions, lack of devotion to Jesus and the word.

There had been an exceptional time of the presence of God during the worship with testimonies from the previous day. A child shared his experience of the Godhead, and as he did so, his face shone with the glory. God revealed Himself as three immense balls of fire to this ten-year-old boy whilst he lay on the floor under the power of God. Glory touched him and others in those meetings.

CHILD TOUCHED BY JESUS

"Don't grieve the Holy Spirit," I cried. Tears rolled down my cheeks. "He is here. He is grieving for you. He wants your entire lives. Turn to Him. Tell Him you're sorry. Confess your sin. Just as the coal touched Isaiah's lips and hurt him terribly, he changed. He cried out to God. We are unworthy. We are unworthy."

Some more came, some gathered with others, God moved amongst us to change lives. We were all changed. This was my first experience of such a move of God. Even as I write, I could feel the call and cry to repent. It stirred within me. This powerful movement of the Holy Spirit brought conviction, humility, and desire to change. Every meeting we sang that amazing song, "I'm running, I'm running, I'm running to the mercy seat where Jesus is coming! I'm running to the mercy seat," sung every night during the Pensacola Revival. It brought such a heavy, powerful presence of God.

A man who smoked asked for prayer, and Pastor Victor told him to stop smoking, throw the cigarettes away, and just stop. Addicted, he could not stop. He needed help from God. He came to the altar call, and after prayer, for about a metre all around him, a most foul smell pervaded the area as the unclean, foul spirit left him forever, releasing him to new found freedom.

"You came for the women with so many problems. They needed you," the pastor said.

Every night we ministered in powerful meetings of healing and deliverance. By day, we did amazing sightseeing as we enjoyed the splendor, the scenery, the palaces of Saint Petersburg! Such enjoyment and exhaustion as we walked through the extensive metro, caught trains, escaped robbers, and explored the Great Palace (since burnt down), the State Hermitage Museum, the Winter Palace, the Small Hermitage, the Old Hermitage, the New Hermitage, and the Hermitage Theatre—which used to be the palace of the Tsars. The magnificence of a bygone era, everywhere you looked, artwork and beauty. The walls, the ceilings, the floors, and the actual paintings and sculptures. We planned what to visit, so we missed nothing. They designated entire floors to particular people and their magnificent artwork. Almost too opulent to describe! So much to absorb. So little time to see it all! Whole floors, not just a few amazing paintings, but whole floors dedicated to Monet, Picasso, Van Gogh, amongst others! Unforgettable!

THE HERMITAGE

GREAT PALACE

At nights we ministered and watched the Lord touch to transform broken lives. Autumn, or fall, as Americans would say, with the magnificence of the trees in full incredible, breathtaking colour.

Many families suffered with tough relationships! They struggled with poverty, violence, abuse, and sickness. Men, heavy drinkers, put their marriages at risk. Shelves of vodka lined the walls in almost every home.

Jesus healed and delivered women from demonic powers. Ministry transformed them. God brought love and inner healing to those oppressed by shame and pain. They identified with stories of Jesus bringing freedom from pain in my life.

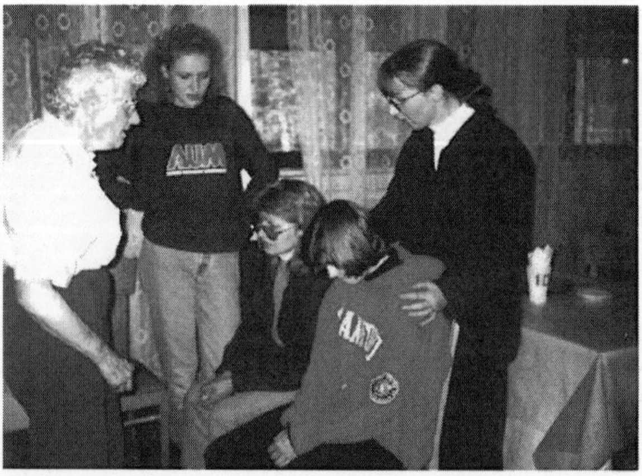

RACHEL AND ELISABETH WITH OLGA - PRAYING

"You are standing on a rock, looking across at unfamiliar world areas. In one direction is a land of harvest with lots of fruits. In another direction is a forest with trees stretching as far as you are looking at a land of trees!" He pointed as he said, "In the other direction is a desert, dusty, barren, a land of drought. The last direction is a land of rivers, much fertility, the harvest," the man prophesied.

We had baptised the new believers in the Baltic Sea. Those involved retreated to change their clothes. Inside the house, we celebrated the Lord's supper on this solemn and special occasion. There, in Russia, each person received prophetic words as they received the Lord's supper. My turn had come. And as I have visited nations, I have always remembered those words. Each time we drive in the United States and pass along highways lined with trees, I remember this prophetic word. Each time in Cuba, I remember the word: a land of rivers, much fertility, the harvest.

BALTIC SEA

Yet another night, with little sleep, as we had chugged, rattled, and shook for twelve hours on the train, Olga wide-eyed lay in a carriage, above a drunk man who snored and talked all night! This overnight train returned us to Helen's Moscow house after the tremendous time in Saint Petersburg. Here, we bade goodbye to Olga who travelled on to Vladimir.

No sooner had we arrived, and Helen said, "School starts today. We must visit the school."

Rachel, Elisabeth, and I arrived at the large junior school, where the assembly had begun. Helen spoke with the principal, who invited us to speak to the assembled children.

What a miracle, to speak at a Russian school on the outskirts of Moscow after the fall of communism! What an opportunity, a divine appointment without question! "This is an important new day for you. A special day for the school. It will affect the rest of your lives. This is the first school day of the new year. The first day of fresh developments, a fresh way of life, for new friends, for catching up. There is another new day, even more important to your future and life. That is the day when you give your life to Jesus Christ, when you ask Jesus to be your Lord and Savior!" I said.

Helen urged us to come with her to talk to the principal, who said, "Please come and speak with the classes? You are the only people to come here and speak! The first from New Zealand!" She invited us to visit classrooms in the school.

"It's the day when you are born again, when you ask Jesus to forgive your sin, to come into and take over your life!" I explained how to be born again! In the brief sessions, 125 children came to faith in Jesus Christ. When we realised there would be no one to disciple them, after the prayer of faith, I spent half of each session teaching on how to follow Jesus, how to hear His voice and do what He said. We returned to the house for brunch, elated at what God had done!

DENISE TEACHING THE CLASS

ARRIVAL IN BULGARIA PASTOR ELENKOV AND FANNY

They said they wished the people outside could hear, but they shut the door and later bolted it! In answer to prayer, they reopened it. As I spoke, noisy children came in and out. An old man rose and showed them out! A very violent man at the front rushed around the room and thumped people! Chaotic! It had been an interesting meeting at Ploutia, Bulgaria, outside the city in the very poor area where Roma people lived. The church in the middle of a large compound had no microphone.

The ministry time came, and the people crowded in from outside, pushing us further and further back and crowding around. They gazed at what happened, wanting to touch us. It soon became impossible to minister as it became dangerous. The leaders feared there would be a riot, and the meeting quickly closed. They locked and bolted the door!

People shouted and banged on the doors, trying to enter. They peered in the barred windows. The power of God had come with the near riot! The leaders evicted the entire group and shut the doors. They allowed only a few into the church at a time. A wonderful presence of God, as the Holy Spirit moved powerfully and prophetically. Gradually, the room filled as they admitted more and more people. Once again, as it became dangerous, we escaped to the apartment building close by, where we stayed the night with the pastor and his family.

On we travelled in Bulgaria, this five-nation trip. We were back in the little church where miracles had happened. The woman and the child she had sought to abort appeared. Glory to God! That same night a grandmother came to testify that her grandchild, crippled, deaf, and dumb, after prayer, healed of all conditions over the weeks that followed. She and the church were praising God for the change in their lives, the result of the ministry received.

DIMITROGRAD TEAM, MEETING THE PASTOR. HE CAME ON HIS BICYCLE WHEN WE ARRIVED FROM THE TRAIN

WOMAN HEALED TESTIFIED

What great excitement as the elderly pastor summoned us to the front of the tiny church and said, "Take photos, take photos."

Seeing our bewilderment, he called some ladies forwards. "These are those healed when you came last time," he said.

Chernogoronova, Bulgaria—miracles! The people shouted and pointed. A woman lay on the floor. I had anointed her with oil a few minutes before, and when we bent over, we could hardly believe what we saw, astounded to find the oil on her head in the sign of a cross red like blood. That morning at Parsdjeck, where we stayed the night, the pastor brought out his shirt to show us all that over his white shirt were twenty-four black crosses. Signs and wonders and miracles, as in the prophecy. In that trip in Bulgaria, the glory of God came.

That prophetic word and dream said signs, wonders, and miracles as great as Cuba!

Very excited, this Roma woman beamed at us as we entered the main office of the Church of God Bulgaria.

Pastor Elenkov appeared and told us, "God spoke to her, and in obedience to the dream by faith, she travelled to meet a woman in Sofia, where she would be healed of a brain tumour. She found the woman who invited her to a meeting where we ministered. That night, healed, she returned to her home."

We remembered a woman who seemed excited; she kept touching her head!

She visited the doctor who, puzzled by her newfound health, asked, "Where did you find the money to have surgery?"

She replied, "God healed me! I obeyed the dream."

As a result, her husband found faith in Jesus Christ. She asked the Lord to meet us as she longed to share what the Lord had done. After a month of travel throughout Bulgaria, we all arrived at the office at the same time! God told her where to go to find us. What timing! What a miracle! What a joyful reunion we indulged in as she shared her story. This daughter of the King acted on the promise of God. Obedience is always the key, obedience by the team, obedience by this precious lady!

That year in Starazagoro, we met Apostle Ivo, Gangka, and their small children Stefan and Rumen. We came to love them all. Someone waits on the other side of our obedience. After staying with them and ministering in their small church in the Roma ghetto, we gave them a small gift of US$100. Years later, we discovered this gift brought a turning point in their lives as they faced a desperate situation. For many years, our relationship with them became a focal point in our lives.

APOSTLE IVO AND FAMILY, STARAZAGORA

Bulgarian buses and trams were interesting and challenging, and we had to be ever alert for deception and attack! We stopped wearing money belts in front of our bodies as they attracted too much attention. Gangs of Roma people preyed on bus passengers, especially foreigners. People would fall down in supposed fits or sickness, and in the distraction, the others would rob people! The ticket purchased on entry to the tram needed clicked at exit. But we as foreigners did not know this! Halfway inside the bus, the passenger took and clicked the ticket! People who knew the system had their ticket clicked on the way on and off the tram or bus!

Because we did not get our tickets clicked, the inspector accused us of cheating by not paying fares. Pastor Elenkov and Rachel visited the police station to sort the problem as we were in trouble. He explained we did not know the process.

Again, signs, wonders, and miracles featured on this second trip to Bulgaria. We arrived at Parsdjick in the late afternoon that day.

After we unsuccessfully sought accommodation at the local hotel, we trudged with all our luggage over the stony rough paths in the area located to the Roma church. As the Spirit of the Lord moved upon the people, we had an amazing service, in which many found new faith in Jesus. Jesus baptised others in the Holy Spirit. After the service ended, we discovered that 80 percent of the people didn't understand a word. Yet they had translated our English into Bulgarian but the believers didn't understand the Bulgarian translation.

ELISABETH BEING PRAYED FOR

LIFE AND GLORY CHURCH, STARAZAGORO

LOVE BRIDGE CHILDREN

We said our goodbyes to Pastor Elenkov, gave away our Bulgarian leva, and pushed our bags into the airport to catch our flight to Frankfurt, on to Bangkok, and eventually to New Zealand. As we pushed the heavy carts, we noticed no one there! Startled, we looked around us; the counters empty, absolute silence everywhere! No one anywhere in the airport! Puzzled, we stood bewildered. Our flight was due out just after midnight, and it was now almost 10:00 p.m.! We could not understand it, why no activity, no people?

I said, "I'll look to see if I can find out what is happening?"

I walked into the departure hall. No one—not anywhere. I walked further. I noticed there was a Balkan office with a light on. I knocked on the door and explained our predicament!

The lady official looked at our passports and tickets and said, "Your plane flew at 12:05 this morning!"

Stunned, almost lost for words, "This morning!"

"Yes," she said. "Look, it says 12:15 a.m.! That is this morning!"

"What will we do?" I asked, recovering from the shock.

"We will put you on another flight, but it may be three weeks!" she said.

"Three weeks!" I said shocked. "Why three weeks?"

"Flights are difficult here! Come and visit me in down town tomorrow. I will see what I can do to help you!" she said.

"Our flight left this morning! We may have to wait three weeks for another!" I told the others in dismay.

"Three weeks!" exclaimed Elisabeth, horrified in unbelief! "Three weeks!" She found this difficult to comprehend!

With help from the lady official, we phoned Pastor Elenkov and returned to Fanny's house. Next morning we travelled to the city by bus, and when we arrived at the office, we met a group of Americans who told us Princess Diana had died! Shocked and affected, we were like the entire world. Everyone loved Princess Diana! After three days, with prayer around the world, we continued our journey to Frankfurt, Bangkok, Myanmar, and Nepal—five nations in ten weeks.

ROMA GHETTO OUTSIDE THE CITY

AN ORTHODOX CHURCH

A flight into Myanmar to stay at the Olympic Hotel Yangon near the main road, where we swam some days, but they wanted US$5 each time we swam! Protests followed each swim as we refused to pay. We found Pastor Tu's brother Pastor Lazum Lahtoi, a tour agent. Pastor Grace, his wife, and the family, Esther, Samuel, Sarah and Julianna, were to become our dear friends and part of our family, and we loved them instantly. Armed with Lahtoi's phone number, we contacted him, and he visited instantly. When we asked, "Where do you live?"

He said, "Very near and very far!"

We visited his apartment to meet his family in the nearby housing block next door to the hotel grounds, very near, but we rounded many corners, back and forth, very far! It took a long time to get there for somewhere so close, and now we understood his statement. Integral in working with us over the years, he set up meetings and conferences and made connections for us.

THE LAHTOI FAMILY-JULIANA, ESTHER, GRACE, LAHTOI AND SARAH [SAMUEL IS ABSENT]

SAMUEL PLAYING GUITAR IN THIS HOUSE MEETING, WITH ESTHER AND SARAH AND JULIANA[THE FRONT THREE GIRLS]

In obedience to the Lord, we visited a prominent Christian organisation in Yangon. With no information, we knocked on the door by faith. That visit became a pivotal part of relationships and ministry in Myanmar. We prayed for Pastor U Zin Hla and his family and the work of his teams to deliver gospel booklets to every home in Myanmar. We challenged him to a new walk with the Lord, to rise and pray 4:00 a.m. daily for four hours, then we left to visit others. Imagine three ladies told this leader of a ministry to do this! A pure-bred Burmese, descendant of the second convert from Adoniram Judson and cousin of Brother Ronnie, as a conservative Christian, he had little experience of the Holy Spirit. He said, "In nine years, I have seen little fruit from my ministry!"

ZIN HLA FAMILY

We travelled north to Mandalay on the train, a fun experience, like a bucking bronco shaking and rattling on rail lines built by the British 150 years earlier! Met by a Lisu man, we stayed at the Taungzalat Baptist Hotel for four days in downtown, close to everything.

We shared a basic little room with a double and one single bed, no air-con, three ladies with just a fan in this tropical place on the third floor up steep narrow stairs. Power, irregular, remained shut down ten to twenty hours each day, but we had torches.

This time, at the Taungzalat, set the scene for the future in Mandalay. We met a pastor on the narrow stairs, and as a result, an amazing outpouring of the Holy Spirit happened in a tiny room on the ground floor.

He asked us, "Where are you from?" And after some conversation, he said, "Let's go down to the foyer, and you can meet my friend."

When we reached the foyer, he and his friend said, "Please pray for us. We are pastors."

"Where can we go?" I asked.

"There's a little room just here," they said.

We no sooner filed into the little room with a table, chair, and window along the wall, then the presence and power of God came. Soon the men were on the floor, laughing, shrieking, crying. Two workers entered and were slain! The tiny room overflowed with people, and they laughed, cried, and shouted as God's presence filled them. We looked up, and trishaw men had come in from outside, their noses pressed against the glass, eyes wide open, amazed at what happened. We stepped out and asked them, "Would you like to come in?"

"No," they said as they shook their heads in refusal.

A young man appeared and stood by the shut door. I opened the door and asked him, "Would you like to come in?"

He stood against the door and said, "I follow Buddha, I've just come from Yangon."

"Jesus loves everyone," I said.

As I put out my hand, the pastor and I prayed for him, and he slid down the door to the floor where he looked up at us wide-eyed with amazement. He gave his life to Jesus, as one touch from God and it changes us. Never the same again. Jesus changed him.

YOUNG MAN, PASTOR NENG AND DENISE

"Please, let's have a revival meeting on Friday at 9:00 a.m. on the roof. There's a room up there we can use," the pastors requested.

"Let's do it!" we replied.

When we learn God's way, our faith grows. Faith does not require understanding to function. Those pioneers in Hebrews 11, their spirits received understanding from the Holy Spirit, and they acted. When we act by faith, our spirits receive insight from the Holy Spirit.

> Without faith, it is impossible to please God. Our faith pleases God.
>
> —Hebrews 11:6 ESV

> My righteous one will live by faith.
>
> —Hebrews 10:38 ESV

As we continue by faith, we please God. We moved by faith in Myanmar, prompted, activated, motivated, urged on by our convictions of the faithfulness of God.

For as we moved, recognising no impossibilities, we gained an intimacy of relationship. Like Abraham, who became the friend of God. As with Moses, who loved and showed an intimate relationship with God.

As we obeyed the Holy Spirit at every step, spoiling for action and possessed by a spirit of adventure, we explored new ground.

Friday came quickly, and with a sense of excitement, we climbed the stairs to the roof. Nine o'clock in the morning, for me, is always significant! Acts 2 speaks of an outpouring of the Holy Spirit at nine o'clock in the morning! Over forty people gathered, eager for God's touch; some travelled hundreds of miles. The young man from Yangon came, and he, along with many, in a glorious outpouring, was baptised in the Holy Spirit. The Spirit of Jesus changed them as after prayer, they were healed and released. Our relationship with one of these pastors has continued through the years, and we regularly minister at his church in the suburbs of Mandalay, where we have seen God move mightily.

God promised there would be signs, wonders, and miracles in the prophetic word given in 1990. Daily I declared this as I laid hands on the world map.

We flew on to Bangkok and a new territory, Nepal, for the last steps of the journey.

Earlier that year, at a New Zealand church, we noticed an Asian man at the back, listening carefully. Our friends told us about Moa, that he had come from Asia, that we needed to meet him. Afterwards, he came to ask, "Do you go to Nepal? You must come to Nepal!"

"No! I don't go there!" I replied. "It's been on my heart for three years, and I thought I would go there this year, but it's impossible," I said. "It's not one of the four corners of the earth."

"No," he replied, "but you are going to Myanmar, and it's only three hours from Bangkok. There is very little additional cost for you to go on to Nepal. I can open doors for you there. God told me today to come and ask you to come to Nepal." (The rest is history, spoken of in *Heavenly Kaleidoscope*.)

Prayer followed, and the three of us visited the training centre in Kathmandu, Nepal. Not knowing what we were going to, we thought we were ministering to women. This small centre attracted twenty-one evangelists, pastors, leaders from all over Nepal. Two could not read or write, but they could raise the dead and moved in miracles, signs, and wonders. Some of them lived in caves and the mountains high in this Himalayan region! At one stage, I thought, "Wow, we came here for this few people!" But what wrong thinking! That soon changed. If we reach leaders, we change the church and even the nation!

WALKING IN THE LOCAL AREA

TRAINING CENTER

NEPAL

During the ten days' teaching, four hours a day and ministry, we met our interpreter Dan and his young wife, Elisa, Nepalis from India, another divine appointment.

Each day, with no notes and the help of a concordance and Bible, I spoke on faith, vision, the anointing and fire of God, sharing miracles from New Zealand and places I had travelled in God's plan. What a final glorious day when many were baptised in the Holy Spirit. They came from darkness to light, from deliverance to freedom, as we ministered the power of the word in the Spirit's power. In an unforgettable, terrifying ride to Pokhara to see the mountains, on one of the world's most dangerous roads, trucks and buses hurtled frequently over cliffs as they played chicken with one another, and entire busloads of people died! We returned on Buddha Air to Kathmandu.

About an hour into the countryside on a tourist bus trip far into Nepal, we visited a power project at three levels, where engineers diverted the river. There, Elisabeth fell, hit her head, and lost her memory. Distracted, she did not notice a ledge and hurtled into a deep hole! Retrieved with help, her head bleeding, she did not know her own identity, where she was, or who we were! Gravely concerned, we returned to Pokhara to find a doctor. He trimmed her hair, treated her cuts, gave her a tetanus injection and antibiotics (this at the back blocks of dirty, filthy Nepal!), and reassured us that her memory should return in about a week. As a nurse, I had concerns about the bugs and risk of greater infection! Worried and concerned, we prayed. How could we take her back home with no memory? What would her unbelieving husband Don say? Constantly, day and night, she asked, "Who am I? Where am I? What am I doing here? Who are you?"

Patiently, day after day, multitudinous times, we replied, "Your name is Elisabeth, we are in Nepal on a mission trip, Don is your husband, you live in New Zealand."

By the time we came back to NZ a week later, her memory was restored. A glorious trip of answered prayer and changed atmospheres. Nepal finished, I never intended to return, but God had other plans. We only see the smaller picture, but God sees the whole. He knew the bigger plan, I only saw the immediate, but He looked at the ultimate.

> For I know the plans I have for you, declares the LORD, plans for welfare and not for evil, to give you a future and a hope.
>
> —Jeremiah 29:11 ESV

Just a foretaste, a glimpse into what God would do, keys to unlock a doorway through which we would enter, we never dreamt that this unlocked door would open to later ministry throughout Nepal. God wants to do beyond what we could ever imagine, ask, or think, beyond our wildest dreams.

After that trip, we travelled regularly to Asia as Myanmar lodged in my heart. Vision birthed in my life for a stronger relationship with God and for nations, to empower and strengthen Bible schools, believers, and leaders. If you change leaders, you ultimately transform thousands. The pioneers in Hebrews 11, men and women of vision, lived with faith and obedience in their hearts as their relationship with God led and guided them. When we think of Hebrews 11, we think this is the chapter about faith, but really, it's about people who showed all the characteristics of pioneers. They, as foot soldiers, groundbreakers, were pilgrims on earth.

> Now faith is the assurance of things hoped for, the conviction of things not seen.
>
> —Hebrews 11:1 ESV

> By faith we know that the word of God created the universe, so that what is seen was not made out of things that are visible.
>
> —Hebrews 11:3

Though he died, Abel's faith still speaks; our faith has to speak.

Returning to Myanmar in 1998, we saw some outstanding things happen. With a team of twelve from New Zealand, we were running late that day! We still had many visits! At lunchtime, we reached the Zin Hla home, where we planned to greet him, pray, and move on. He must have sensed our hurry as he pulled up some chairs and sat in the middle of the room! He stated firmly, "I am not moving from here until she prays for me!"

Resigned now that we would not leave quickly, we settled down for a lengthy visit.

It excited and awed the team to discover that on the previous visit, God talked to him and brought change to his family's life.

He announced he was not a pray-er, but when we stirred him about a deeper relationship with Jesus and spending more time with the Lord, God spoke to him through us and told him to rise every morning and pray for three to four hours! This unknown thing for him, he and his wife did it together. Every morning they rose at four o'clock to seek the face of God. Nothing much changed for two months except they prayed. Six weeks later, he travelled with others on a mission trip to Central Myanmar. At a crusade, for the first time in his life, he watched five thousand people come to know Jesus Christ and experienced thirty-eight amazing miracles! Nothing is impossible to our God! Prayer brings breakthrough.

TEAM IN BANGKOK WITH DOCTOR TU, DR THEIN HTAY AND PASTOR CHAWKEE

STREET MEETING

PASTOR KHAM

The military government forbade street meetings, especially for foreigners, but a believer died and needed the funeral. The believers shut the street, and we held a crusade! The entire street turned out for the worship and preaching. When we called them to come to Jesus to ask Him to be their Lord and Savior, many responded.

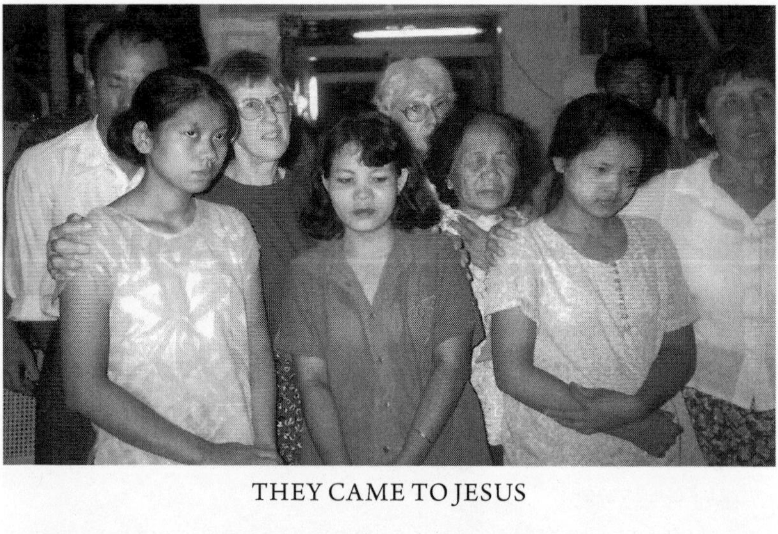

THEY CAME TO JESUS

EVANGELISM WHERE ALL CAME TO JESUS

After travel on the back of a truck to a remote Karen Village, we ministered to a house full of families, about eighty people. At the close of the meeting, after the challenge to give their lives to Jesus, all but one responded to be born again.

On one overnight bus trip with the team of ten, we stopped for the bathroom, then reboarded. As the bus pulled away to continue the journey, we noticed an empty seat and, in alarm, immediately missed a lady team member! We shouted to the bus driver who stopped the bus, and we ran back to search and rescue our lost friend, found asleep at the bathroom. After she took her medication at the journey's beginning, she fell asleep on the toilet!

Reader, you have no comprehension of what will happen if you will obey the voice of God. I could not have dreamt of all the amazing things God would do this past thirty years just because of simple obedience.

Multiple services the order of the day, Sunday with thirty services, the team in twos and threes travelled in many directions for an exceptionally busy day ministering to hundreds.

Quite a hotel with AC that rarely worked, a generator that kept failing, and black water when it ran from the pipes! Imagine a black shower! Challenges every day!

Dreams and visions feature our lives when we expect and live in the supernatural. Brother Niven experienced this as he joined the team after a dream about a green building and tablets that made the largest book in the world! Astounded, he watched a TV programme showing sights in Myanmar, and there were the tablets of his dream, and when we visited Mandalay, there, the green building!

Fascinating, challenging food. Most of the time really delicious, especially in Asia. You could eat almost anything, you just have to take care and look for the chilli. After a busy morning at the conference in the early days, my friend Elisabeth sat down at the table saying, "Goodie, goodie," and after the prayer of thanks, scooped many spoonfuls of red powder onto her food! Unfortunately, pure chilli! I'm not sure what she thought it could be, maybe spice or a vegetable? But after that, inedible!

On the last trip to Russia, Davi, a sound tech from Auckland, travelled. Stretched, extended, his worldview expanded beyond description.

He had never prophesied, and believing that we have all the gifts and just need to use them, I asked him to prophesy! "I can't do that!" he said.

"Yes, you can. I will pray for you, and you will prophesy," I replied.

And he did! Life changed for him, an ordinary believer who did not believe he could move in the power of the Holy Spirit until he reached Russia.

Attending a celebratory function, we drank a delicious preserved juice; safe, they claimed. On this boiling hot day, we consumed lots! Ministering in Suzdal the following day, as we counseled hour upon hour, I faced an impending disaster! The distant outside toilet stood alone at the end of a long path! On the ground outside lay a bowl for handwashing! The onset of diarrhea came, rapid and severe. Davi, at this stage, seemed unaffected! All day, every fifteen minutes, a new person or family came for prayer. Every fifteen minutes, I sprinted to that long drop! Too dramatic! No let up! Desperate, this developed into serious stuff! Dangerous dehydration loomed here in the back blocks of primitive Russia. I consumed buckets of liquid as I lost buckets of fluids and electrolytes! That night Davi started, and the family with whom he stayed became extremely concerned as he would not drink. Almost admitted to hospital, he finally realised the seriousness of the situation and cooperated. No one wants to go to a hospital in Russia. We knew hospitals to be terrible in the years when we visited! Wow, how we praised God for His deliverance when it all stopped!

When he returned to New Zealand, his life changed; he shared with our daughter that when people came into his presence, he knew what troubled them. And they manifested with demons!

CHAPTER 7

1998 God's Purpose Unlocked – Grandparents - Unlocking The USA – Cuba - Divine Appointments - Miami - 1999 Cuban Celebration - I Died – Venezuela – 2000-Myanmar Miracles - India – Morocco -Spain- Bulgaria -September 11 2001 – Turkey -Israel -Butterflies – The Himalayas - 2003 The Wedding

Kevin stubbed out his last cigarette after forty years' smoking, threw the packet never to smoke again, and we boarded the plane for our life of unexplained, unexpected adventures. Pioneers to steward the breakthrough glory. Imagine with only US $800 we left to travel the world for an entire year trusting God. With one connection in Miami and no idea of where to stay just an ongoing flight ticket for the year. Were we crazy, simple minded or people of faith? God is amazing. When we trust Him, He does far beyond anything we could ever imagine, ask, or think, beyond our wildest dreams. Imagine being over fifty years old, abandoning all, signing over your house to your children, and leaving with two bags and only $800 to follow your wife into the unknown. In our generation, this was not just unusual but almost unheard of! What normal man does that? Not knowing where you're going or who you would meet or what would happen. Kevin is a remarkable man who has done just that, obeyed God, done whatever He said. In doing so, he released me to do whatever God said and says. Remember, we are not natural, we are supernatural. Our spirit man lodged with Christ, seated with Him in heavenly places has a spiritual inheritance, and leaves a legacy! As citizens of heaven, our home in heaven, we act accordingly. With the faith of God we bring heaven to earth.

God spoke to Rachel, our daughter, and told her we would not be available, that we would be overseas when the children were growing. Sacrificially, she laid down relationships with us, help, support, family. All those things that everybody holds dear! To have grandparents right there, but we were absent, an expensive phone call away on the other side of the world! It costs everything to follow Jesus. He asks us for everything, not what we want, just what we willingly give. In our case and our family's case, their relationships with their grandparents or their own parents, the fact that we were at the other side of the world all the time, either in ministry in Asia or in ministry in the USA. Were we abnormal or what? We simply did what God said. That's what people did in the Bible. Kevin and I made a choice to live with a Biblical world view according to the word of God, and not conform to the culture.

As new grandparents we left our lives behind, everything we held dear and travelled to find a new life of ministry, of adventure, beyond our wildest imagination. When most people are preparing for retirement, we left all to follow Jesus. In fact, the family thought Kevin would never leave even until the day we flew. They were sure he would never get on the plane. The day before leaving, he flung open the wardrobe, took a huge rubbish bag, and said, "Well, I guess I better pack some stuff, get rid of the stuff!"

He threw armfuls of his stuff in the trash bag as we gasped wide-eyed in utter amazement!

"Salvation Army," he said. "That's where it's all going!"

And when we returned for Christmas a year later, the family thought he would never leave again! But he did! Pioneers, when they set their feet to the task, never look back!

> Faith motivated Abraham to obey God's call and leave the familiar to discover the territory he was destined to inherit from God.
>
> —Hebrews 11:8 TPT

So he left with only a promise, and without even knowing ahead of time where he was going, Abraham stepped out in faith.

As a man in the dark, Abraham followed the call of God by faith, not knowing where he was going. A property of faith is you cannot see the way. God is the guide to light the path before us. He didn't know where he was going. He left behind all the familiar. He trusted God and travelled in blind obedience when God said, "Get out." Faith is like a light in the dark. The inheritance was for his children, yet he had none, and that in itself was another huge step of faith. A pilgrim, he owned nothing and even had to buy land to bury his wife! That he should have a whole country promised to him and his seed, and yet had no seed given him.

> Although God gave him no parcel of land he could call his own, not even a footprint, yet he promised Abraham that he and his descendants would one day have it all. And even though as yet Abraham had no child . . .
>
> —Acts 7:5 TPT

> We travelled by faith as though in the dark, not knowing what to expect or where we were going, trusting God to look after us. Much of the time it was just like that.

Cuba, with signs, wonders, and miracles, could never be forgotten. Idalia waited for us in Guantanamo.

We ministered for seventy-two days with one hundred meetings and hardly slept in the same bed twice.

"You stayed in M for twenty minutes and B for three days . . . You visited . . . The car arrived in H . . . For a day, you visited . . .," they said, naming everywhere we visited and everything we had done since entry to Cuba a few days before, the people we had seen, and the minutes we were at each place.

"It's forbidden. You are staying in homes! Your tourist visa says you must stay in hotels or private rooms! You are in churches, you are driving in private cars, and we forbid this!" They examined our passports and entry visas. "How long are you staying?" they asked.

"Three months," we replied.

They laughed. "Impossible." They said, "You must go at the end of the month. We cannot renew your visas! Everything you do is illegal!"

This contingent—the immigration, the civil authorities, and the police—stood together as the house had few seats. We spotted them as they came in single file on the narrow path down the hill from the road. The previous night, the noisy, crowded house church meeting spilled across the field! We experienced a mighty move of the Spirit with the police station right there!

"Be careful, say as little as possible. Don't volunteer any fresh information. Tell them only what they know, only answer what they ask!" the senior pastor instructed us from the bedroom.

On a tourist visa, we preached and ministered in churches, travelled in private cars, stayed in church homes, every action forbidden in this restricted nation. They knew everything we had done, even where we had been, to the minute! We explained, "We have been coming for many years, are visiting many friends, and with no hotels, no taxis, we must stay here!"

After they warned us and left, we continued every activity. We renewed our visas in another city, and two months later, we left the nation.

We continued to do the crazy thing—obey God, not man! Heaven was touching earth in Cuba.

Pastors in the hills had no blankets, and the young couple suffered such pain in their legs because of the cold. The following year, we bought Mexican rugs to bless this couple, and when we arrived at the senior pastor's house in the hills, he commented on the rugs, and we told him they were for the couple we had previously stayed with. "They have no blankets!"

His comment was, "We have no blankets too!"

How bad did we feel!

One couple in another district, when we stayed in their house, gave us their bedroom to use. In the night, on a visit to the bathroom, Kevin discovered the entire family lying asleep in the kitchen on the concrete floor!

In a church house, where we stayed, the pig lived outside our bedroom, and at midnight, they washed the pig! An hour later, we slept! With the pig within five feet of the dining room, flies covered every surface. No matter what they did, flies! The most spotless pig you could ever see, but flies wherever you looked. Flies flew everywhere. Hundreds of flies on all surfaces: on tables, chairs, cupboards, everywhere. And when cooking, flies! The pastor and his wife were desperate. We bought them a ceiling fan, and what a transformation! Like magic! Like a miracle! No more flies!

After this amazing time in Cuba, with little money, we returned to Miami, and again, God faithfully gave us a house to stay, with Carlos, who became our friend, and money was thrust into our hands for our needs.

With ministry in Cuba and Mexico and around Miami, invited by new friends I travelled to Orlando for an Aglow conference and Toronto to Catch The Fire. As the year unfolded, the north began to unlock as we met people from Indiana who invited us there. So many new experiences: hammocks, staying at a resort in Mexico, gifts of new shoes, new clothes lavished upon us, riding horses in Cuba, the amazing Cuban celebration that instead of being illegal, for the first and only time, we were legal with religious visas. To say nothing of my death and healing in Cuba! And what of the visit to Venezuela to a persecuted church where we prayed at 4:00 a.m., midday, 4:00 p.m., and 8:00 p.m. and on the Sunday experienced a tremendous move of the Holy Spirit. All part of God's unfolding plan (written of in *Endless Safari* and *Heavenly Kaleidoscope*).

Again, we saw the provision of God and His faithfulness. The fares and all expenses met, we saw God bring change to many lives. Every week we ministered in churches, and always, God provided.

They pushed forward a small boy in a wheelchair for prayer. Each day we prayed and anointed him with oil. Fear in his eyes disappeared as the Lord brought His healing love and the peace of His presence. Several days later, the pastor called us. "The little boy you prayed for has never walked before, but today is walking strongly! God healed him."

Later we received a wonderful photo of this child walking, his face radiant with the joy and wonder of what God had done for him.

God met all our needs as we looked to Him for our total provision. After a marvelous ladies' meeting in Broward, where God brought His healing touch to many, a woman said to me, "I want you to come to my store."

With only one week before leaving for Bulgaria, I replied, "It's impossible!"

Insistent, she said, "I want you to come so I can bless you and your husband."

Finally, I got her to write the directions to the store and said we would try to come after returning from Bulgaria.

Lunch at the Rainforest, where we felt like we had been in a rainforest with sound effects accordingly! We walked into the mall to discover an enormous store, and there was Rosa! Kevin turned and asked me, "What are we doing here?"

I replied, "Rosa wants to bless us."

An amazing time followed, trying on lots of new clothes. Whilst this happened, Rosa showed Kevin through the racks of men's wear, holding up shirts for him to admire. "Do you like this one?" she asked.

"Well . . . yes," he replied.

Again and again, she held up a shirt. "What about this one?" she asked. "Well, don't you like any of them?"

"Of course," Kevin said, "but I can't buy them."

"What if they were a gift?" she asked.

"Well, that would be wonderful," Kevin replied.

How amazed we were, when, after an hour or two, we departed from the store with three bags full of fashionable clothes for Kevin and myself.

DENISE AND A NEW DRESS

A complicated year, as I suffered from several infections and difficulties, with no medical insurance! God is amazing. He sent a doctor I knew from Cuba. He opened up a clinic in Miami, where I visited a specialist who assisted, diagnosed, and treated the issue. God looked after me. Can you imagine specialist care, a minor operation in the USA, free? Later, on our return to New Zealand, when checked out by doctors, a clean bill of health.

All expenses paid, we visited Cuba. A time of glorious celebration. The Catholics had celebrated when the pope visited the previous year, and the evangelical church of Cuba asked for their celebration.

GOD LIVES IN CUBA TODAY. THE CHURCH IS VICTORIOUS IN CUBA TODAY.

Banners waving, the traffic ground to a stop, as the multitudes poured by, yet it was only 7:30 a.m. The bus stopped, and I eagerly swung out the door to photograph a sight I thought I would never see. People marched and waved banners in great joy as they sang songs of praise to Jesus. This was in Camaguey, Cuba, in 1999, where we saw over sixty thousand people gather in Revolution Plaza to celebrate Jesus. Young and old, small and tall, they all came, waving flags of Cuba and banners of the Cross. Wonderful banners, "JESUS LIVES," "GOD IS HERE," made from a variety of materials with vibrant colours; small ones, big ones, short ones, tall ones, all bringing the same message despite oppression, restriction, communism. GOD IS ALIVE.

The people poured across the park to stand in the tropical sun in demonstration of their faith in God. All those with invitations sat on plastic seats at the front, with umbrellas to shield them from the scorching sun (read more in *Endless Safari*).

CUBAN CELEBRATION WITH KEVIN AND IDALIA

THE VIDEO CAMERA WE TOOK

Though only there for a month, we were every day in new churches and visited a remote area of Cuba. "Whilst preaching, you died! You slid from the pulpit to the floor and died!" Idalia, our Cuban translator, told me later.

I asked, "What did you do? Did you take my pulse? Did you do any resuscitation?"

"No!" she replied. "We prayed! We laid you on a pew and prayed!"

"How long did I die for?" I asked.

"Three quarters of an hour," she said. "You had no pulse, no breathing! No sign of life! You died! We prayed! After all that time, suddenly, you sat up and asked us, 'Have you called the people to come to Jesus?' We said, 'No! We prayed!'"

Kevin, shell-shocked at what happened, did not speak of it for months. When I asked him, he told a similar story! I pondered this.

That day, I had suffered high fevers with degrees of delirium but attended the church to preach as expected. When I returned, resurrected and healed to the pulpit that night, I prayed for the sick and finished the service.

Not only raised from the dead, but also healed, *God's presence became heaven to me!*

The following year we returned about the same time, midsummer, the very hot season, and a high fever developed. We stopped travelling in the hot season, too hot for me. But none of us will die until the day God decides.

A call came from our friend Rosa. "Come with me to the Orlando International Aglow Conference and stay in my room, all expenses paid!"

***

In the crowded elevator travelling to our room a tall thin woman asked me "Where do you come from?"

I replied, "New Zealand."

She said, "There is a lady here beside me from New Zealand." She told me later, as she was tired and it was the end of the day. She did not want to talk to anyone. God spoke to her and told her, "Ask that small woman where she is from." In obedience, she did. If we love Him, we do what He says.

It was in that elevator I met Chris a New Zealander who lived in Montezuma, Indiana. We travelled up, down, up, and down, until alone in the elevator, we talked and talked.

A divine appointment to unfold in time. After a wonderful conference and return to Miami, I flew to Venezuela to minister.

Four amazing days and Sunday came quickly after a tremendous outreach the day before. About 1,500 people came to a great morning service where ministry lasted 'til 5:00 p.m. Individually, we prayed for hours for a long line of believers hungry and thirsty for the touch of God. Words of knowledge and wisdom flowed with people healed, set free, and repenting. So many waited for prayer, that we stopped praying, and I announced, "If you have sin in your life, kneel now, repent and get free! Don't waste our time!"

People asked the translator, "How come she knows so much about everyone?"

He replied, "It's the word of knowledge and wisdom. Get right before she prays!"

Finally, as we sat drinking tea and eating a snack before the last service, the pastor said, "What would happen if there were ten thousand? You could not pray for them individually like you did!"

CHURCH AT BARQUISIMETO OF 1500 BELIEVERS

OUTREACH

The next day I flew to Miami and on to Toronto to Catch The Fire Airport Church, with a wonderful group of ladies from the Florida Keys, for a tremendous conference and more divine appointments. There, I met Larry a pastor from Seymour, Indiana, who said, "Please come to Indiana."

The Lord stirred our pot to go north and minister. Florida, it appeared, only had a heart for Latin America!

After our return to New Zealand, we attended an Auckland Pastors Day. We noticed a group of ladies sitting behind us. One of them asked me, "Where do you go?"

I replied, "Myanmar, Thailand, Cuba, Venezuela, USA... oh, Bulgaria!"

"Bulgaria? I want to go there! When are you going again?" she asked.

That began our relationship with Nan and Marian, who both became an important part of our lives (read about her in *Heavenly Kaleidoscope*).

NAN [FAR RIGHT]A GLORY CARRIER. DENISE AND MARIAN

In the year 2000, what resulted in a Central Myanmar discipleship training centre astonished and astounded us as heaven touched earth. This was a season of adversity and regulation with persecution. A company of six from New Zealand, we ministered to a hundred conservative young people and forty orphaned children in a place of hunger and oppression. When we prayed for the youngsters on the platform, the Holy Spirit moved on them. For two hours, they howled and writhed on the floor. These young children, deeply touched, sobbed in His weighty presence. After the Lord visited the meeting leading to the programme's abandonment, outrageous glorious joy descended on them all, and for two more hours, they laughed as waves of shekinah glory filled them. One hundred students struck and saturated with the glory of God, undignified, rolled in the dirt, and spoke in heavenly languages, affected by heaven. Later, all were carried to their beds, and little sleep was had by all in the building as they laughed and cried the entire night.

Yet these children and youth encountered the glory in a fashion unfamiliar to all of us. When they testified, they told of spending time with Jesus, where they looked into the divine realm. Most experienced the overwhelming love of God and healing. Our first memory of a spectacular outpouring of glory. We asked ourselves, would we ever see this again?

THE TEAM IN MYANMAR

STUDENTS AT TRAINING

After arrival back in the USA from the trip to Myanmar, I opened an e-mail from Paul, who, after leaving us in Bangkok, had travelled on to the Himalayas. This e-mail startled me to see what it said. "Mum, you have to come to Silguri. I met a man who asked for you by name. They want you to do women's conferences!"

The man asked, "Do you know a woman in New Zealand, Denise Reid? Do you know her? She has a daughter, Rachel." The man was Pastor Dan.

Flabbergasted, Paul replied, "That's my mother and my sister!"

After travelling with the team in Myanmar, Paul continued on to North India and Nepal, where he met Dan, who asked for me by name! A Macedonian call, out of a billion people he met the one man who knew his mother! A man who had interpreted for us on the trip to Nepal in 1997! A man I thought I would never meet again! The Himalayas did not meet the criteria, the call to the four corners, but God clearly called. When I received this e-mail, "What a miracle!" I said.

E-mails are amazing communication, and we had one later that year from Myanmar from Lahtoi, saying, "The government has moved against the children's homes and taken the children you visited with in Meiktila. They put them in the prison!"

I wept shocked as the children we met and prayed for had experienced an amazing touch from the Lord.

After many weeks in the prison, the children said, "We don't worship gods of stone, we worship Jesus."

The officials said, "When you're here, you do what we say."

These precious children loved the Lord. Later they were transferred to the monastery, and we prayed they would continue to follow Jesus.

THE CHILDREN

Later that year, a team of four, friends from New Zealand travelled to spy out the land in North India. Each one said God instructed her to make the trip in obedience because of their love for Jesus. They were intimidated by a bomb scare when they arrived before me at Kolkata Airport. To travel to the train station, we clambered into two ancient yellow Morris Oxford taxis, one of which belched clouds of black smoke and looked like it might "die."

What an initiation to India. Chaos seemed to be normal! Crowds of rickshaws, cars, and animals battled for priority on streets with dirt and grime everywhere. After several near crashes, as other vehicles sought for our space, we finally arrived to get an overnight ticket north. "Here!" the driver stated, and he pointed left. Multitudes of people milled everywhere.

People gathered, pushing as we unloaded the luggage on to the pavement for two to stand guard. The ladies left behind surveyed the scene. Cars pulled up beside them every minute with people coming and going. "You will be safe here in this busy place," I reassured them. "We will try to come back soon!"

Jan and I made speedy progress across the road filled with people carrying all kinds of merchandise. We made it to the door and gasped at the crowds. The station reception area overflowed with people and animals. Crowds pushed against us! We clung to each other and tightly to our money as we pushed through to get to the many counters beckoning us. At only 7:30 p.m., when we returned to the other ladies who survived the abandonment, it felt like it took hours! A journey of endurance as we persevered to purchase tickets not as we desired but for the next morning. After going from counter to counter, floor to floor with so many problems, we said, "No wonder foreigners buy tickets in the town!"

Sitting on the floor between the aisles in the Miami Barnes & Noble store, I discovered somewhere to stay as I researched the book Lonely Planet.

In another old yellow taxi, we reached a street like nothing ever witnessed! Narrow, boisterous, and disreputable, with people everywhere. The filthiest street I had ever encountered, with garbage, excrement, pigs and rats that roamed and rummaged. What an environment! It shocked us to the core! Gingerly, we waded through it all, covered shoes, the answer!

Cheap! Clean! Safe! A Muslim hostel in Downtown Kolkata. With gigantic bolts, we locked our dingy dark rooms, breathed a sigh of relief, and collapsed into bed for a brief night's sleep. After the alarm buzzed at 4:00 a.m., I piled out of bed and found, to my great consternation, the money belt open and empty. Somehow all my hundred-dollar bills were spread across the entire room! It must have been open all the time! With a torch, I scooped it all up, threw on clothes, grabbed my bags to fall into the taxi with the others to return to the train station. Too early, we explored the dirty platform and watched the many activities as thousands of people arrived to catch their trains maneuvering past the sleeping beggars. With relief, we climbed on the train, which left on time at 6:30 a.m. Secure for at least twelve hours, we organised the bags and sat back, relaxed, and slept as we raced north.

"Coolie? Coolie?" the coolies asked when we arrived two hours late in the dark.

"No, no!" We shook our heads as we looked for our friends. No one! Later we discovered why. The e-mail sent from Bangkok had arrived okay. "We are coming on Wednesday." But which Wednesday? No date!

In consternation, we viewed the steep stairs at the end of the platform. How relieved we were when two coolies hastened to assist us. In amazement, we watched as they hoisted the many bags, layer upon layer, onto their heads. With incredible balance, they strolled ahead of us as though their cargo had no weight; we ran to follow them!

THE COOLIES

Siliguri at last. What did God have for us here? About ten o'clock that night, after checking out several very cheap hotels, we fell into an ever hard bed in a cockroach-free, clean, yet ever-cheap hotel. Aware that God had positioned us in His plan, we waited it's unfolding.

"It's very important to visit this sister. She has the power to open up the region!" Pastor Dan said.

The leader of the women's work shared. "Three weeks ago, my daughter had a dream. In the dream, hundreds of women held out their hands, and angels poured oil into their open hands. It released the anointing and power of God." She recognised the request of conferences for women as the plan of God.

I looked up at the sign on the clinic wall: "Do not ask the sex of your baby on ultrasound!" Why did they have such a sign? Because if the baby was a girl, the parents could abort the child! We discovered this sign on the trip to the medical clinic, after I collapsed at the meeting. To our dismay, I had developed shingles, but life travel, the ministry continued as normal! Despite severe pain, infection, and problems, nothing stops a pioneer, certainly not shingles! An adrenaline-punching trip with considerable adventure (written about in *Heavenly Kaleidoscope*). Because of that leader's vision, we returned the following year to hold women's conferences.

THE TEAM

After the first year in Miami (spoken of in *Endless Safari*), we recognised the need to travel north as people in Miami, Florida, seemed to only have a heart for Latin America and Cuba, but in the north and the east, people may have a heart for Asia or the world. The following year, after meeting the people in Toronto and Orlando, we travelled north on the Greyhound buses, twenty-eight hours to Indiana. What an exciting ordeal, I loved it with so many divine appointments. A memory unforgettable. The bus changed at Georgia. The new woman driver climbed aboard, turned on the speaker, and announced to our stunned amazement, "There will be no drugs, no alcohol, no sex on this bus! Any hanky-panky, I will put you off the bus!"

After ministry in the Rockville area, by divine appointment, we travelled to Seymour, Indiana, to visit Larry, the pastor I met in Toronto.

God is amazing. He's the orchestrator of divine appointments. We met Larry and Marlene and ministered in their church. They said, "We are just humble people, and you come all the way from New Zealand."

But, they became our family in America, accommodating us on each of our journeys to the area. In their living room, Larry asked, "You've been in Bulgaria, do you know a pastor there? He comes through and speaks here." I asked his name, but he did not know, and he said, "I have a letter from him in the study!"

On his return with the letter, we realised we knew the same man in Bulgaria. Another divine appointment! Christmases were wonderful. Treated as members of the family, they shared with us their family, fellowship, and food.

Because of ministry and relationships formed, Larry, Marlene, Donna, and Carl travelled with Elisabeth and me to Morocco and Spain. In the dream, I had heard a voice say "Morocco" and saw the word "SPAIN" in great big letters. On enquiry, I discovered Spain could be the doorway to Africa. We could travel to Morocco. Furnished with an e-mail for Madrid and the coast of Spain, we met in Malacca, and whilst waiting for our arrival, they visited a bull fight but could not stay long as it became too gruesome! There, we stayed at a YWAM Hostel and swam in the coldest water I've ever experienced, where the Mediterranean meets the Atlantic. After we crossed the Gibraltar Strait, we embarked on a prayer journey through Morocco, where we prayed, walked, and travelled miles, experiencing several divine appointments and catching interest from many spies. In Spain, Elisabeth and I stayed with missionaries, and the group from USA stayed in a hostel downtown, sleeping in bunk beds. Elisabeth and I travelled on by bus to minister in Madrid, whilst the others returned home to the USA. We were to minister to the Roma people who cancelled rapidly when they discovered Denise was a woman and not Dennis, a man! Ministry to the Roma in Europe could only happen in Bulgaria! God is amazing, to think He spoke in Cuba to this woman to go to the only nation in Europe where the Roma would receive a woman! We ministered in a great Spanish church in Madrid that graciously received us.

Elisabeth and I travelled on to Bulgaria, where we met Paul. Bulgaria beat it all! We always ate what people served as they went to great trouble to feed us, but this time it was the ultimate test, and sad to say, I failed! We stayed with a couple on the outskirts of the Roma ghetto, and our hostess told us she'd been cooking all day, she'd made a beautiful dish for us. We waited, curious to see what she had cooked, as she brought the green enamel covered dish. We lifted the lid, and to our horror, we saw little black, brown skewered things floating in a sea of black blood. Revolting sight! We were not hungry that day and ate only a minute amount of these pig's spleens, a great Bulgarian delicacy.

In a ghetto church in Sofia, after I spoke on what it means to be a pilgrim, a pioneer, I said, "Now Paul is going to prophesy over you!"

Paul, startled, with no warning of his ministry about to begin, said, "No, I'm not! I can't do that!"

After a brief altercation, Paul prophesied over each believer present to bring words powerful in encouragement, deliverance, and freedom. To prophesy should be as easy as speaking, and we don't struggle to do that!

I read Ruth Heflin's books, *Harvest Glory* and all her other books. I wanted so much to meet her, but she passed before we travelled and visited meetings at Ashland, Virginia, which opened the door to cause a significant change with a dynamic directional word.

"God woke me in the night. He spoke to me about you. God says He is giving you five new nations," she said.

In the meeting in Ashland, USA, the preacher called me out of the meeting. When she prayed, she knew nothing about me. God spoke of nations: North India, Nepal, and a closed nation high in the Himalayas. Lying on the floor I received a vision which featured an article read years earlier. Specifically, it showed me the pages of the magazine, with every detail of the nation: a Buddhist kingdom; a population of 180,000; illustrations of temples, dark without lighting; and accessible only by chopper or trekking! We searched everywhere for the name, but only two areas met the description. God is good. We had much confirmation. God positioned me to unlock the breakthrough He would do, the portals He wished to open, the glory He wanted to pour out, and the legacy for the Himalayan region.

> I give you power over all the power of the enemy, authority, to trample on snakes.
>
> —Luke 10:19 ESV

Because We have the faith of God, we have power from on high to overcome all the power of the enemy. The same faith Jesus had is in us. It's what we do with it.

Divine appointments, a group of women, End Time Hand Maidens we met in Ashland, travelled on a team to Myanmar. Some remain our friends today. To become End Time Hand Maidens (the Gwen Shaw movement), they each had to fast and pray for forty days. In these days, because of the restrictions and famine for the word of God, Bible delivery was paramount. Fay shared her thrill of when we prayed over the Bibles prior to wrapping them in brown paper to make them inconspicuous. She thought, "God, I want to do this more! This is so important!"

Some of the group declined to carry the Bibles; fear shuts so many people down! But Fay loaded her bag with precious cargo and experienced great delight to carry it all safely to the persecuted believers inside Myanmar.

We stayed in Mandalay in a questionable hotel to do a marvellous conference at the Paradise Centre close to a church. After the entire group sickened with vomiting and diarrhea, we discovered the hotel staff were giving us water from the fountain filled from the tap water. Polluted! Terribly polluted, you never clean your teeth or wash your toothbrush with Myanmar water. Fay, amongst the last to sicken, shared she only took some pills offered to enhance and speed up recovery, and when she reached Bangkok, she saw Burger King and raced to enjoy a welcome burger with no ill effects!

Into that hotel our precious brother Pastor Neng Kham Suam visited and on arrival in our room the Holy Spirit manifested. Everyone became drunk with the Holy Spirit as we laughed and laughed rolling on the beds.

Hungry for God's presence and fresh vision, we continued to visit Ashland.

AMERICAN AND NEW ZEALAND TEAM 2000-2001

Fay, Doris, and Dayle were amongst this group, and they would become an important part in our lives. Fay invited us to visit her at Staten Island, New York, and when she later moved to Tamaqua, Pennsylvania, we continued to visit her there. When God positions us, He plans the people. America opened, and we travelled now on a circuit to and from Florida.

"Quickly . . . Come and see . . . Quickly!" Fay called to us from inside her house in Pennsylvania.

At 9:00 a.m. On September eleven, the car packed tight with all our stuff, we were ready to leave for our appointment in New York. We had spent several days with Fay. Inside, we ran to see and hear the TV. We watched with horror the replay of the plane as it hit the first tower. In greater horror, we gasped when a plane hit the second tower! We had visited there just two days previously but declined to go up the towers, and now they were destroyed! The day unfolded as we watched the Pentagon hit, the Hudson River crash, and New York shut down! Just three hours away, we never made New York. Everything closed instantly!

Immediately, after September eleven 2001, the opportunity came to visit Israel and Turkey. After all, I had the dream; the dream involved Turkey. We had to go, and as Israel was so close, why not do both? After a trip to Bulgaria, we travelled on to Istanbul by train, which was another challenge, crossing the borders with the bags, changing trains. We visited Turkey several times and shared at a church in Istanbul; there when they announced that a group of Africans escaping to Europe drowned in the sea, as they did not swim; there too when, grieving, they announced that some young people baptised in the ocean all died instantly when snatched by a freak wave.

Istanbul had amazing tourist sites, as did the whole of Turkey. Unforgettable we went underground to the Basilica Cistern. This made an incredible impression as we saw pictures and historic evidence of early Christians in the area. We travelled extensively to the seven churches. Paul joined us for some of this. I loved Turkey. We made a memorable trip to the Gallipoli Peninsula and saw Anzac Cove. Mistakenly we by passed the modern highway and chose the old coast road, which fast deteriorated to become the old coast track, causing some anxiety as it became exceedingly narrow, like a goat track round cliffs and in a hired car! My only regret was we did not see the Florence Nightingale memorial.

BASILICA: CISTERN

KEVIN AND PAUL AT LUNCH AT PAMMUCALE

Impressed by Anzac Cove, where so many died, each year on Anzac Day, New Zealanders (and Australians) mark the anniversary of the Gallipoli landings of 25 April 1915. On that day, thousands of young men, far from their homes, stormed the beaches to die on the Gallipoli Peninsula in what is now Turkey. This entire peninsula is devoid of butterflies, birds, or life. What an impressive place, a place of death. The silence tangible. A memorial to tragedy. By the time the campaign ended, over 130,000 men had died; at least 87,000 Ottoman soldiers and 44,000 Allied soldiers, including over 8,700 Australians. Amongst the dead were 2,779 New

Zealanders, about a sixth of all those who had died on the peninsula. [The Gallipoli campaign - The Gallipoli campaign | NZ History, New ...]

There, at Ephesus during Ramadan when they had a grand commemoration, waking at 4:00 a.m. each day for its commencement with a ceremonial drum roll through the streets to waken the entire town, the entire city rose to breakfast before the fast began. A holiday, with celebration and parades the order of the day. On our enquiry, we discovered what they commemorated, this day was important as it was the day they pushed the British and Anzacs (New Zealanders and Australians) out of Gallipoli! They celebrated our demise!

ANZAC COVE

BLUE MOSQUE ISTANBUL

On to Israel, the fourth corner of the earth, Kevin and I flew, leaving Paul to return the car to Istanbul amidst many challenges—no road signs in English, horrendous traffic, finding his way—to catch his flight home. Whilst there, I realised how ill prepared I was as I should have researched the sites to understand and value more fully what we saw. We didn't hire a guide. We did this on the cheap. We stayed in a hostel found on the Internet, on the fourth floor and no elevator, with enormous bags. Samson rode again! Exploration of the old city and Jerusalem followed with visits to the garden tomb and the Gethsemane garden closed that day! McDonald's saved the day for food, expensive but cheaper there. And we watched as soldiers with their army-issue submachine guns just laid them beside the table whilst they ate food and picked them up to return to duty. All the time, we heard the firing, the planes, the bombings, and deaths. This just after September eleven. No tourists travelled! Never will I forget our visit to the memorial of the holocaust Yad Vashem and the impact of entry into the darkened hallway and auditorium with stars in the roof and photos of those who died around the walls, commemorating those who died. It was our dead day, so sombre, so sad, like nothing I had ever experienced!

Fay had given us the address of a woman who lived in Galilee, above the lake. With seven dogs, she took a break from the dogs and life and left us to hold the fort! We spent several days in beautiful Galilee above the lake and did the required sightseeing. Israel was special. To return has never been achieved in this busy life.

ISRAEL OLD CITY

Pioneers always bring breakthrough. God unlocked the keys to breakthrough with ideas for drama and instructions to do communion and foot washing everywhere we travel in the nations. God spoke to me before I visited India to hold the women's empowerment conferences, to use drama, communion, and foot washing as a strategy for breakthrough to steward His love and glory. In obedience to the Lord, we did all three and have seen breakthrough as lives opened to the Spirit of the Lord in a supernatural way.

Two important events followed. I read a book about the power of the butterfly. I visited the ballet and woke inspired to create dramas for conferences. The drama about the life cycle of the butterfly became an important introductory feature where we spoke of metamorphosis. Featuring 2 Corinthians 5: 17, that those who are in Christ are a new creation or species in Greek, those who are in Christ are a new species in God. God did a tremendous work in us to produce the glorious church.

> Therefore, if anyone is in Christ, he is a new creation.
> The old has passed away; behold, the new has come.
> —2 Corinthians 5:17 ESV

The fresh has come when we are ingrafted into Christ. The word "new" means no previous history, no former things, an original! You and I are an original new creation.

We are all familiar with the butterfly. How many of us have seen a beautiful butterfly fluttering around with all its colours? Envisage with me this prophetic drama of the butterfly which speaks of new life—the transformation in Christ.

First, we see the caterpillar; here he comes now. First, a caterpillar enters using any young men and team members. Dressed with a sheet, a cap and feelers, this caterpillar eats and eats. He is so hungry to grow fatter and fatter, for the purpose that is to come. It is a preparation for transformation. We are to eat and eat of the word of God to grow fat with the word: for the purpose He would fill and use us to reach out to a lost and dying world. The caterpillar speaks to us of the promise of things to come, a future and a hope, a vision for the future for a new life in Christ. When he is ready for the purpose for which born, he weaves and makes a cocoon to prepare for the transformation. We must all prepare—get ready—and have vision to see transformation.

The cocoons bound in crepe paper with wings and colourful scarves enter. These cocoons bound are getting ready for the new life; a transformation is taking place within them. Look here, the cocoons are coming now. [the cocoons enter] Look at them. They are bound. Prepared for the new life but still they remain bound! That's how we are without deliverance. Mark 16 speaks of setting new believers free, and we all need to be set free from ties that bind us. When we are born again, a transformation takes place within us, and we become a new creation. The old is gone, the new has come. But things can still bind us from the past, and we have to break out. We reap what we sow. Legally free at the cross the effects of the issues in life we have been involved in… go on and on.

The cocoons break out, but look at them—butterflies but their wings are weak and limp and useless. They are too weak to fly, and that's how we are without the baptism in the Holy Spirit. When we are baptised in the precious Holy Spirit, we break out into new life and freedom. Jesus fills us and releases in us the gifts of the Holy Spirit to strengthen and set us free.

The sun comes to dry their wings. The sun enters and brings the light of His glory. See, the Son of God has to come and shine the light of His glory upon us to fill us with the Holy Spirit and give us the gifts of the Holy Spirit. When we get baptised in the Holy Spirit filled with His glory, we can fly. They all rise to fly away with new purpose to a lost and dying world, to do new things, to go to unknown places, to carry the light of the glory of God everywhere they go. We receive new strength to do the works that Jesus did and greater. As we have done these dramas, God has moved in spectacular ways to touch the lives of those attending and some have come to faith in Jesus.

Oppressed people come dressed in gray, pushing, shoving, and fighting with labels declaring oppression, pain, shame, rebellion, strife, anger, and we declare the blood of Jesus. We discuss this, and in the name of Jesus, we declare freedom, showing the power there is in the name and blood of Jesus, and they flee.

Glory people dressed in gold enter waving golden streamers, wearing crowns. This illustrates they carry the glory, walk in glory, anointing, power, vision, favor, love, and miracles. They illustrate what it means to carry the glory.

Finally, God comes dressed in glory and brings prophetic words of vision and direction to those gathered. The people are so encouraged, empowered, and blessed by their involvement in what they have seen.

Powerfully, the Holy Spirit moves as creative drama speaks to people's spirits. They never forget what they have seen or the message behind it. The Lord knew that so many of the people to whom we minister would need this as their literacy skills are low and for the older people, nonexistent.

BUTTERFLIES IN COCOONS

GLORY TEAM

THE DEVIL VISITS

People love the drama, so simple but so direct. When the devil comes in the meetings dressed with horns and pitchfork, they clap and cheer! When the animals of the jungle visit and a hunter kills the monkey, they clap, laugh, and cheer! Imagine, do you ever see a conference leader going splat on the floor hit by a plastic hammer after doing crazy actions acting like a monkey? Unforgettable! Everybody loves it! We are fools for Jesus's sake.

In Bangkok, in 2002, prior to entry with the team to India, during a brief visit with Patricia Green, I devoured a book on her shelf, *Why not Women in Ministry* by David Hamilton and Loren Cunningham. What timing this was as it changed the ministry and women's lives in the region. I recognised the revelation in what I read. Our teams taught and still teach the materials across Asia. This book became the catalyst for changing lives and attitudes in those to whom we ministered through the years.

BAPTIST HOSTEL CALCUTTA

Entry to India complete, the team piled into the old yellow taxis and proceeded to the Baptist guest house where we slept the night and left early the next morning to catch the train! Arrival startled us. With all our bags, the entire group stood amidst the crowds.

GROUP UNLOADED FROM THE TAXIS
WAITING WITH THE BAGS

I proceeded inside the station where thousands of people milled to ask an officer to help us, as we could not proceed through the crowds, not with all those bags! He marched along swinging his cane, like a general to battle as I ran behind! He commanded coolies to assist, and delivered us to the platform of our train commanding, "Wait here 'til the train comes at 6:00 p.m.! And I will return!"

A night train. On a corner of the filthy platform, we sat, all twelve of us! Bags and all, we sat on newspapers in this smelly area previously used by squatters and homeless. June wandered off, and Marian rescued her! We would have lost her forever in this vast place! Robin kept opening her bag and giving away lipsticks, sweets, and small treats to the beggars! We attracted enormous attention just sitting there the entire day! Hours passed slowly as we watched the endless activity of thousands of people and multiple trains. Finally, at 6:00 p.m., the army major returned with his huge stride, swinging his walking stick, followed by many coolies who lifted all the bags to their heads and marched ahead of us into the train. Settled there, we sorted ourselves out to be shocked when a wail came from Robin in the next compartment. "I've been robbed! My bag is gone!"

Someone in the crush of the relocation stole her bag laid on the seat! Hastily, we alerted the army major. They wrote a report, but nothing could be done. The thief had long disappeared, and the train left full speed ahead for the north.

What a drama. Imagine losing your passport in India! After time in Siliguri, we sent Robin to Delhi for a new passport as she could proceed nowhere!

Foot washing astounded us. The moves of God, spectacular from the beginning, continue today.

At the Jaigaon border conference, on the first large team trip, women were sobbing loudly and wailing. They ran to clean their feet after we announced we would wash feet! The Lord showed us to do this unknown form of worship as a sign of humility. Astounded that foreigners would wash their feet, it broke the two hundred women! As the team washed and prayed for each lady, the water blackened and needed frequent changing! Neighbours and the entire street could hear the noise, the sobbing, the wailing, the shouting—such a holy time. Awed by what happened, we took no photos because of the outstanding presence of God.

After a team member washed her feet, a woman stuck tight, could not get off the chair. Whilst being prayed for, people fell in all directions, they lay on the floor as though slain for a long time whilst the Spirit of God touched, healed, and delivered them. Slip, slap, slosh! Absolutely no finesse! Even though we suggested to her she do it lovingly, gently, praying, no, no—slip, slap, slosh! And amazing, the ladies couldn't get out of the chairs afterwards. They stuck to the chairs after Brenda washed their feet. Such an amazing touch by God. We wanted her to teach on the blood of Jesus, the power of the blood, but she had never taught before. I asked Marian and Nan to help her—what a trial for them. They told her everything they could about how to do it, painstakingly taught her word for word on the blood of Jesus. They were despairing because she just couldn't seem to get it. So again, they helped her word for word and taught her word for word how to present the teaching of the blood of Jesus. We all held our breath when she got up to preach. It startled us as people came in off the street, people came to Jesus as an outstanding presence of God came. God takes the unlikely, the foolish, to do amazing things and always does beyond what we could ask or think.

FOOT WASHING

Lunchtime on the border, everyone retired to take a break. Yet we left behind a small group of ten children sprawled on the floor, under the power of the Holy Spirit. Kevin stayed with them as he wanted to find out what transpired. Children shared their experiences of the supernatural realm, how they glimpsed and spent time with Jesus, whilst a number saw the devil and demons and experienced the realms of hell. These encounters were like those shared in the book *Visions Beyond the Veil* by H. A. Baker. Over one hundred years ago, a group of children in Kunming, China, had experiences of heaven and hell. I pondered, could this happen more?

CHILDREN WHO HAD HEAVENLY ENCOUNTERS

We called them the clackers, this large group of tribal women who stood at the front of the Siliguri Conference and shouted in tongues through all the worship and even into the teaching! Such a disturbance in the meeting! They wouldn't stop even though we put our hands over their mouths to silence them! In desperation, we sought for another solution. The moment they started up en masse, we almost ran to pray for them so they fell down, and that stopped the problem! Every time they did it, we ran to pray for them! It took time, but they finally understood, and the behaviour stopped.

The meeting finished, and everyone left to return to the Karkavita hotel, except Marian and Aldwyn. As we had insufficient room in the vehicle, Kevin and Ian, who visited the city to shop, would come to get them. They waited and waited, but no one came. Finally, they said to the guys in charge at the church, "We need to get back. No one is coming!"

The guys in charge walked them to the main road, where, in a taxi, they returned to the hotel. On arrival, to their amazement, nobody had missed them! They concluded they could've waited there all night as nobody had missed them! And as for Ian and Kevin, well, they never even remembered to pick up the ladies.

Marian prayed, "Lord, I want to visit a really delightful house. There must be some pleasant houses in this wilderness of poverty."

Everywhere in North India, we had seen only very poor areas. After the team loaded into the van to go to a meeting, we stopped outside an enormous building with a gatehouse.

"Here we are," the leader said.

At the gate house outside the high sturdy brown wall, the guard opened the gate and led us through the grounds to the huge impressive door, which he flung open, and all ten of us filed in. The entire group entered, looking to the right at a beautiful shining stainless steel kitchen like one Marian said she had never seen. As we gazed at everything, we filed past the sumptuous lounge with the most beautiful swagged red velvet drapes hanging at enormous windows and the ornate furniture. In single file, all ten of us marched silently up the enormous staircase with ornately carved sides to an amazing balcony. When we reached the landing, we looked up, and our gaze reached a huge painting on the wall—Krishna. In horror, our leader said, "Let's get out of here . . . quick!"

What consternation, realising we were in the wrong place, in an unbeliever's house. We all turned like clockwork and hurriedly, silently, filed out. We walked back down the stairwell, past the kitchen, past the beautiful lounge, out the front door, across the path past the guardhouse, and filed back into the vehicle. In the van, we laughed and laughed! We had walked right through somebody's house there in North India with our shoes on, and nobody had stopped us. The guard man had let us in, all in answer to Marian's prayer. Isn't God amazing? He gives us not just what we want, not just what we need, but the cry of a heart!

In the evening, we visited the venue to pray for those attending, where with no power, no torches, they waited in the dark! Supernatural things happen when we pray. With the help of a small torch and no translator, we prayed for this group of about forty women who fell where they stood! Actually, they didn't fall! They fell as in a trance and squatted in a line like in frozen animation, joined to one another, the line of people squatting! Spectacular! I began to recognise my role and the teams role to steward the glory.

In Darjeeling, in a cold operatic theatre building with snow outside, a freezing day in this mountainous place, the glory fell, and the people fell, in a stack one on top of the other. Just amazing, as they didn't seem to get hurt, they were all bodies on top of one another, arms and legs hanging out everywhere as the power of God filled them, as the glory of God filled that miserable cold place. But when the glory comes, the fire comes, so no one remained cold.

We prayed our way through the thick fog and road works; we were two and a half hours up in the hills in another freezing place. We dried our washing with the hairdryer and filled hot water bottles with scalding water to wrap our smalls around them before we travelled to the meetings.

HIMALAYAS

Prepared for the colder temperatures, we drove along the Teesta through the steep incline, looking down on the magnificent scenes and river views, through the border and up, up, up to Namchi, on this trip to Sikkim. Houses three and four stories teetered on cliff edges. We braced ourselves for the intense cold at 4,300 feet. The hotel beckoned, and we piled out of the jeep and poured in. Upstairs, we checked the rooms, and there, we discovered a perfect room for the couples—dormitory beds with a line of single beds, about ten beds in all. After a call to the four married couples, we announced, "This is your room!" and awaited their reactions. We made our own fun on this trip!

Here at this church high on the hill, we prayed over pieces of paper believers put in a prayer bag on the table used for teaching. In obedience to instruction, we laid hands on the bag and prayed. We asked God to send His word, declared healing and deliverance to those involved. Nobody told us what the prayer requests said, but it was amazing. A poor broken woman with a tiny totally-disabled child put her prayer request on the table that day. When we returned a year later, the senior pastor showed us a photo and an article that had been in the local paper. There was the child totally healed, walking, talking entirely normal. How we rejoiced at this great miracle. It was here on a trip after lunch to the bathroom, I found a helper washing lunch dishes we used in the toilet! Little wonder many of the team were suffering vomiting and diarrhea!

Up on Thursday for two days in the intense cold at Gangtok, six thousand feet; coats, thermals, hats, gloves, snow on Kanchenjunga, 8,586 metres, the third highest mountain in the world, which we viewed from our bedroom window; wonderful days with tremendous breakthroughs. After a beautiful meal with the pastor and his family who shared, they rescued twenty-one abandoned boys and took them into their home. God moved powerfully every day with deliverance and healing. Jesus delivered many from smoking and alcohol addiction. How beautiful and angelic when a young woman danced freely in the Spirit with Jesus. When we washed one another's feet, they experienced an exceptional outpouring with significant power.

After we started ministering in the region, we encouraged the women to rise to the identity they have in Christ as carriers of the glory. To rule and reign alongside the men, in partnership with the men no longer subservient, no longer in competition. Together, serving Jesus, working together as one, loving and serving one another and the body of Christ as one, encouraging others to do what we do! Shortly after, we heard testimonies of ladies' teams going forth to evangelise in the villages.

The nations came to our family, and in 2003, whilst we were back in Auckland, it delighted us to be present when Paul and Kim, a Cambodian Chinese, married, with their first child Daniel born later that year, Rajana arrived in 2005; their family complete.

PAUL AND KIM'S WEDDING

Our niece Ruth travelled with us in 2003 or 2004. The team left to return home, but as we had a ticket out of India the following day, we visited a nearby Nepali church service in Kolkata and ministered in a tremendous Nepali service to several hundred Nepalis. Eighteen came to faith in Jesus Christ, and we delivered most of those present from demons and curses over their lives. With regret, we left our niece behind when we flew the next morning, but she braved her ticket problem and flew a few days later to join us in Bangkok.

NEPALIS IN KOLKOTTA

CHAPTER 8

Cuba – Dreams - Myanmar – Expelled – Nepal War -Escape From Nepal – A Base – Pathari.

Pastors live in poverty in Cuban rural districts. One home we visited far into the countryside, the married couple with a tiny child had nothing: a charcoal fire for outside cooking, a wooden table, no chairs, and a mattress that I would not have a dog sleep on! Straw in the twentieth century! No sheets, pillows, or blankets! Cuba is a tropical place but not at nights in the countryside! And think of the mosquitoes like homing pigeons and no nets! Some families had kerosene burners that were highly explosive and extremely dangerous! In many situations, there was no electricity, and they used oil wicks that puffed black soot smoke everywhere! Few had lanterns, and gradually, we provided some, first with kerosene lanterns then solar when they became available to assist them, as the government delighted to turn off the power when churches met!

Toilets were a challenge! Toilets and bathrooms were always a challenge and in every nation so different. Just a few examples of times experienced. The service ended, it being an amazing service at the church above a steep valley in the mountain. Needing to visit the bathroom, I asked the pastors, "Please, where is the bathroom?"

They instructed me, "You go down the steps right down to the bottom, and it's there on the left!"

Out into the darkness, I climbed down the steps, one flight then another, more and more steps, until finally I came to the landing where the long drop lived. I, a veteran traveller with only moonlight, pulled the latch on the frail stick door gingerly. The door creaked as it opened! In the dim moonlight, I could just see a hole! I stepped towards the hole, and suddenly, *waaaa . . . waaaaa . . . waaaaa . . .*

I screamed with shock! What a noise? What was it? A goat bleated loudly! Then I heard peals of raucous laughter coming down from the church. They were laughing and laughing and laughing because they knew of the goat tethered there, but I did not!

When I reached the bathroom in the field, a line of children sat on the fence watching. I climbed carefully over the wooden logs and visited there in full view of the line of children who wanted to see what this foreigner did here! They had never seen a foreigner before!

We laughed and laughed as we stood and gazed at this toilet! Built by a man, they're all built by men, but this one different! It was a joke! Built for the needs of a man, not for a lady. Yes, it had a small hole in the middle of an enormous square! How could a lady use this toilet? She had to clamber up three feet, poise on top, stand, and aim! We managed with difficulty! You can do anything for a limited time if you have to!

There were no toilets, just the bushes! In one visit far into the countryside, we stopped and waited for the service. Many hours, we waited sitting outside the house in the sun, eating food, resting, chatting; and there, a bathroom, just a concrete square with not even a curtain, and where did we go for the toilet? Into the bushes, but the bushes were one hundred yards away, and everybody looked! With nothing else to do, the entire group watched as you walked there. They laughed as you stayed there and chuckled as you returned. But necessities are necessities! You do what you have to do for as long as you need to do it, uncomplaining, happy, and gracious.

In another area, in a low-lying area close to the river with mud everywhere, we visited pastors with twins and another tiny child. With no toys, the babies and the tiny child played in the mud! They were entirely filthy, covered head to toe in mud! The entire area all around the house was thick mud!

Food is in such short supply, with bread, milk, essentials rationed and no red meat for anyone! The government owns all the cows; the farmers only have a right to the milk, not the meat! Every family has in their house a regular farmyard, turkeys, hens, pigeons, and doves; all farmed on the roof. Pigs are in padlocked cages inside or on the roof! Dogs guard them as thieves come across the roofs and drug the animals to steal them! With all the animals in the houses, rats commonly bring bubonic plague to the cities. Purified water is an essential as there is amoeba and *giardia* in the water.

No job was too menial, and that's how it should be. We stayed above the church, and downstairs was the bathroom, or should I say the toilets. They cleaned them out with a dirty rag. There was nothing else! No cleaning equipment, no chlorine, no solutions or soaps we take for granted, no mops or toilet brushes! The bathroom, the toilets were shocking, stinking, and in extremely poor condition! There was no water, just solid waste! After analysis of the situation, in the depths of my bag, I found some cloths and a small amount of chlorine. Clean toilets resulted! And I travelled back with a salmonella only found in the Caribbean!

During a visit with Fay, I had the dream. Dreams are so important in our lives as they can map out the path we are to follow. Simple dreams are clear, complicated dreams require interpretation, and this a complicated dream, and another one followed. Some of my dreams have taken one to two years to unfold and interpret. We were visiting the Blue Mountain Retreat Centre with Fay to hear a speaker. This man had a reputation for interpretation of dreams. I shared the complicated dream, which he interpreted. That night I had another complicated dream. I presented, telling my crazy dream about three bicycles and Dunedin, where I'd been born. How five people had to travel on three bicycles to a place called Shenandoah! Only I forgot to tell him the place, Shenandoah, and Kevin reminded me. Finally, I said, "Oh! The place . . . We're going to Shenandoah!"

It stunned him and the group with him because they all came from Shenandoah, in Virginia.

FAY

Great to keep in touch, but we never did. Busy people travelling, we did not visit Shenandoah as it was far off our known travel path! Because Fay kept stirring me to see this man, as a result, three years later, we visited him by appointment, again a divine appointment. Now he invited us to be part of his camp meeting and said that God had spoken to him that morning, regarding future involvement with us. Several months later, we returned to minister and have an amazing night, but just the beginning of many divine appointments. That night, still ministering at midnight, we watched in wonder as a three-year-old child spoke fluently in tongues for a full thirty minutes as he lay on the floor touched by the Holy Spirit. It was a sign and a wonder! We met a worship leader who introduced us to Wildwood, New Jersey, where we met our precious friends Bruce and his wife Gwen; they would change the course of our lives. Bruce listened to our stories and said, "I have to introduce you to some people. I'm involved in writing grants, helping people like you to access funding to enable those you work with in the nations."

As a result of this meeting Bruce took us to a significant meeting in Philadelphia, where we met an important woman, Nancy a funder of an evangelical organisation, and the rest is history. Because of meeting this amazing woman, she became our special friend. God is incredible! Over lunch, we discovered, to our total amazement, that she'd been to New Zealand, had met and received help from our senior pastor. We identified in so many ways, both her intercessor Barbara and I nurses, and though coming from entirely different worlds, we had so many things in common! As a result, she has funded conferences across the Himalayan region, funding more than $70,000 over these years, touching the lives of hundreds of thousands of people. A divine appointment, all because of a dream.

Pioneers listen to His voice and are careful to do what He says. They seek the purpose and plan of God. God is supernatural, and He wants to speak to us in dreams and visions. He wants to bring revelation of His word, but the key is not just listening, we also need to act. We should quiet our hearts to listen and carefully obey. Because we carefully listened and carefully obeyed, He positioned us for glory. He unlocked the door through which we entered, for He had spoken there would be no locked doors!

BARBARA, KEVIN AND NANCY

Fay wanted to introduce us to a man with a linen business from the church in Tamaqua. He had just married a young Bulgarian woman. Excited, we met to become friends, another divine appointment. They were to help us with ministry in the nations, and before her mother Rayna came to live with them, I visited with her in Bulgaria, where I ministered most years.

JAMES AND VASIL, DENISE AND RAYNA AND SASHKA.

It was about this time that we began to visit Doris in Newark New Jersey. We arrived late afternoon in18th Street after a long day's travel from Virginia in this our first visit to this area. Rainey and Doris were both desperate for us to minister somewhere that night and after a number of phone calls, jubilant they announced we would be at the Newark Tabernacle at 8pm! Obediently we presented at the huge old picture theatre in downtown Newark, for an awesome evening where God moved to touch and transform lives. The pastor sick was absent and an elder was in charge. He said they may contact us for Sunday's service if the pastor was still unwell. About midnight exhausted we climbed into bed only to be awakened by a helicopter landing in the street and the scream of police cars and ambulance! Strobe lights lit the street as Doris announced someone was murdered a few doors along!

Quite a street, the worst in Newark where prostitutes propositioned cars and people at 10am. With pit bulls behind tall steel fences and drug deals at street corners as I walked and prayed, Doris would pray for my safety.

Saturday night we said to Doris, well no service tomorrow! She laughed and said, this is New York they could phone any time up till midnight. Sure enough after 11pm the call came, "would we be available Sunday morning at 11am for their service. This began a long relationship with churches in this area as for many years we ministered in and around the city.

A powerful intercessor Doris remains our friend today, and we continue to keep in touch when we travel through Georgia where she now lives with her husband Cleve.

In 2003, we took an African-American team from Chicago, well trained by an apostle there, to minister in Yangon and Mandalay. They were an amazing group of young people, led by a powerful woman of faith. She trained them before arrival. They called me Mrs. Quickly, as with this sizeable group, constantly, I said "Quickly, quickly!" So hard to get all these people to hurry and not take all day to do things or go places! People said, "You can't take those black people there!"

But we did, and they were beautiful! They shook when they taught, they were so nervous as some were only fifteen and seventeen years old! But they taught and ministered so well, like pros. We visited their church and fellowshipped there on many visits to Chicago!

AFRICAN AMERICAN TEAM

When we arrived to visit the Zin Hla family and pray for him, his family, and his workers, it startled us to discover he had seen ten thousand find new life in Christ in crusades with many miracles, signs, and wonders. Each year he and his twenty workers attended our conferences, which equipped, empowered leaders and strengthened the churches in this severely-restricted nation. He testified our ministry changed his life. After prayer, Jesus filled them with the Holy Spirit, and they moved strongly in the gifts of the Holy Spirit. His workers saw signs, wonders, and miracles as they moved in healing, deliverance, boldness, the word of knowledge and the prophetic. Great miracles and deliverance happened wherever he went. As an apostolic, prophetic leader in the nation, he moved powerfully in prophetic intercession.

This man waited on the other side of our obedience. And we never dreamt what would happen because we obeyed the voice of God. Someone may wait for you to obey the Lord.

Such marvelous stories. When one leader visited a village, the people were crying. He enquired, "What is wrong?"

They said, "Our baby is dead! We must bury him!"

"Please don't bury the child," he said. "Let me pray."

After he prayed, God raised the child from the dead!

He shared, "A man with many demons came for deliverance. He owned several jade mines in the hills of Kachin State in the far north near the China border. Once very poor mines with hopeless production, but when he returned home, it overwhelmed him as the mines were full of incredible pure green jade. Now everything was pure jade, and he became rich with huge mines!

He said, "Even though I had only $30, I went to Myitkina to hold a crusade. I wanted to rent the city hall, but the officials would not allow! After they refused, I told them, 'I want to feed the poor! Do you want healthy workers or sick? We will pray for the sick.'"

After the officials consented, in offerings, he received sufficient money to feed hundreds of sick people, and miracles started: cripples walked, the blind could see, all costs were met; and they started with only $30!

A young woman who travelled with me said when I travelled to Myanmar, I smiled a special smile and came alive there! Can't you tell I love Myanmar?

PASTOR U ZIN HLA TESTIFYING

In the U.S.A. we attracted friends from New Zealand who had travelled with us previously to Myanmar. Pete and Ros stayed three months and travelled with us all over the East Coast and Florida and up to Toronto. It was a great time, but now we needed somewhere else to stay in Indiana, and we moved to new friends out by the Illinois border. We spent wonderful times with this couple, Donna and Kent, who introduced us to a church in a nearby city, where we still continue to minister. American people have been incredibly hospitable to these New Zealanders looking for beds along the many journeys.

Later others travelled, including my niece Ruth, who was a marvelous asset. Cuba continued to have a prominent place in our hearts. But after a prophet in Chicago who later travelled with us to Myanmar prophesied that I would lay down a baby in my life, life changed. As we were now visiting Asia at the times I would go to Cuba, I needed to find other times for Cuba, maybe the late spring or later summer! January-February became our times for the Himalayan region, cheapest then and the best time to travel.

Because we visited in homes, we met lots of people, so many amongst them with witchcraft idols on shelves; people suffered, oppressed by the devil. In one home lived a woman who suffered effects of a stroke. There, in that home, we encouraged her. After we prayed, laid hands on her, anointed her with oil, we explained how to exercise the areas of her body damaged by the stroke. After we showed her how to move her arm, to move her leg, to exercise, we explained the importance of speaking the word of God over her body. A few days later, she appeared at the church. Until then, she could not walk any distance, but now she walked to the church, which began the healing. This healing came by faith, existed by faith. By faith, she walked to the church; by faith, she moved, she trusted God, that God, true to His word, had healed and began an amazing work in her.

Because the Myanmar government moved against Christian children's homes, took all the orphans, and threw the precious children into the monasteries, Lahtoi moved his family from Yangon to Mandalay. We had an e-mail from our precious brother Lahtoi. As he wanted to set up a discipleship training centre for disadvantaged tribal young people, the e-mail from our precious brother said, "Sister, we want to set up a training centre to empower our peoples."

When we prayed, a supporter in New Zealand funded the building rental. Soon Lahtoi and Grace had twenty-four students living in a two-storeyed house near a tea shop and close to a church, where they involved us. Later, when we visited the training with two Americans, Jerry and Kitty, we had to hide in the back and bottom of the car with a rug over us so that the people at the corner tea shop did not spot us. They watched everyone who came and went from the neighbourhood, and few foreigners visited! Spies were everywhere. Since Lahtoi and Grace already had four children, it was obvious they would collect more! More came, we prayed, and shortly after, we asked the same supporter if she would fund a children's home to house the children gathered. They had a glorious vision for discipleship and for God to move in breakthrough. He collected around him young men who loved and served him and our ministry, Les Mu and La Win with their families, Zyee and Moses. Moses and Zyee lived and became an integral part of the family.

CHILDREN

It was during those years we visited Toronto Airport church with our newfound friends from Indiana. We traveled in their van, and sometimes by car. A time of divine appointments when we met a brother from Iowa who said—you guessed it—"Come to Iowa."

Ten hours to Iowa, where we ministered in a wonderful church there. During that weekend of ministry, we met new friends Brian, Julie, and their children and later stayed with them whenever we travelled to Des Moines. Brian travelled with us shortly after to Nepal and North India.

Every year we visited Iowa to see the church there and of course our friends Brian and Julie. It was there I had a severe attack of pain, high fevers and was in and out of consciousness for three days. A week later I visited a free clinic but they had no idea what could have caused the problem but in retrospect I believe it was the beginnings of the malaria. Iowa became a place where we suffered many attacks, with me choking on saliva as we drove round the city and Kevin having to pull over to help me breathe! Yet another time attending an eye specialist who was concerned a retina was detaching in my eye.

"What has happened to your passport? What's happened to this page? The page is missing," the stern United States immigration official spoke.

"This is a legal document!" Dayle tried to explain the missing page, but detained for an hour, she prayed.

Finally, in desperation, inspired, she said, "A crazy woman pushed me, grabbed it, and ripped the page out!" praying they accept her words.

They did, and years later, we laughed and laughed at how true that was!

Dayle had travelled in a group of five when we visited Hanoi North Vietnam. Immigration expelled three of the team! Caught carrying Bibles, the officials told them, "Bibles are worse than the worst drugs, the worst poison!"

Arrested, confined under police security in a hotel and expelled at 10:00 a.m.! I had phoned the US embassy at 10:00 a.m. and was told, "They are being expelled right now!"

My friend Eleanor and I had entered the night before, and when the others, who were on the plane with us, did not arrive, we became gravely concerned. On enquiry, they allowed me to visit with them for a few minutes to collect some belongings and the money they carried for the trip. We all carried the same literature, but God protected two of us and the Bibles we carried.

We were in the ladies' conference in a hotel in Ho Chi Minh City when I shared the scripture.

God whistles for you.

> He will raise a signal for nations far away, and whistle for them from the ends of the earth; and behold, quickly, speedily they come.
>
> —Isaiah 5:26 ESV

I took out my whistle and blew it loudly many times. The ladies grabbed their bags and belongings and fled! Startled, I called to them, "What's happening?"

When they realised I was just blowing the whistle to illustrate the points of the scripture, they said in relief, "The police, when they come, they blow their whistles, and everybody runs to escape. Otherwise, they'll be arrested! We thought the police had come!"

I never blew a whistle again in the Vietnam meetings.

After a Holy Spirit-empowered trip, we joined our friends in Thailand, who shared Vietnam expelled them, and on arrival in Thailand, the police waited and laughed when they examined their bags only to find Bibles. They were scared to find the police waiting at the airport, but it relieved them to be in a safe place free again!

After the trip, we needed to apply for visas for Myanmar, but there was a colossal problem! How could Dayle get a visa with a big expelled stamp on the passport page? We discussed the matter, and there seemed to be no answer. Then we realised there was only one answer: So a crazy woman grabbed the passport and ripped out the page! That crazy woman was me! Though Dayle passed through one embassy and five immigrations with border entry-exit points, no one noticed the page was missing until she travelled back home!

Would you do it? Do the crazy thing? Go to a nation carrying Bibles? Rip out a passport page?

We ministered in East Nepal during the civil war, when most groups stayed away, as Kathmandu and West Nepal were a sea of terror. Blood ran in the streets and forests. But not FCM and the teams. We continued to travel, and people continued to come. Nothing stops a pioneer.

Nothing could stop us! We knew that war raged and East Nepal was in disarray. Many others cancelled their trips, but we travelled regardless. Why should war stop the purpose of God?

Maoists hid in the forests, behind the trees and graves and shot at those who passed by. Nepal was at war with fighting and bombs all over the place. Strikes disturbed and devastated the nation. Burnt out cars lay by the roadsides. Bombs fell thirty miles from where we stayed, but never where we were, always before our arrival or after we left. God was watching over and protecting us. No other tourists were in the region!

In 2005, after our conference with hundreds of people in Dharan, they proclaimed a strike for the day we had to leave! Brian, our friend from the USA, needed to exit to return home, so we had no choice, we must travel—in the strike! They burnt strike breakers' cars; they chopped off drivers' heads. Prayer was the key. We hired two vehicles at great expense. The anxious drivers were sombre, fidgety, ready to get on the road, as we placed a sign (NZ Tourists) on the vehicle dashboards. New

Zealanders have favor in Nepal. Again, prayer was the key. Brian wrapped a shawl round his long blond hair as he sat between two elderly ladies in the vehicle. Purposely, we told him not to speak at all if they should stop us on the four-hour journey out to the border! As a US citizen, he was at risk of being ransomed if captured.

PAULINE PREPARING FOR THE RIDE

THE VEHICLE

At a town on the way, we veered to race through an imminent road block! Though they pushed a chopped tree to block the road, we slipped through with seconds to spare. A few seconds later, we could not have proceeded! Each of us praised God for His perfect timing!

Prayer took us past Maoists with guns, grenades, and bombs, hiding behind the tombs and trees in the forests, past the bombed cars. We were alone on the roads, but not alone as we had God! At the border, Indian TV waited for an interview of anyone leaving Nepal as no one exited! We refused as we wished to return! People saw angels taking us out.

During this time, we stayed with Mike and Charlotte, in the west of Indiana, and based there for a season, Kevin stayed with them whilst I was out of the country. One day Mike took us into the cornfields to the backside of his vast farm, down a long track into a remote area to visit an old house with holes in the floor and disrepair! He said if we wanted, we could stay and live there when in the United States. I retreated to the car as I could see no future in this idea— in the cornfields in Indiana, in the snow, no roads that you could speak of, no Internet, no neighbours, remote. How could this work? I turned it down without further thought. Why did we need a base anyway? God had called us to travel! And Indiana, with the severe winter weather, there was no further conversation. Much later, we discovered he planned to renovate it for us! Daily I walked and prayed to the covered bridge over a pretty river and to the river bottoms down the cornfields. One day Charlotte said, "I didn't want to frighten you but someone was murdered at the bridge and coyotes are in the bottom cornfields!"

Our friends in Pennsylvania offered us an apartment to locate from, and we turned it down as why would we want a base in a coal mining town in Pennsylvania? And did we really need a base?

Our friends back in Indiana looked at the sales of repossessed houses with the plan to purchase one for us to stay, but that failed too! Others in Tennessee offered and thought about purchasing somewhere for us to stay! But we didn't need a base. We travelled. Or did we?

We returned to Toronto! It was there Carol Arnott spoke on how someone offered her a horse! Why would she need a horse? She turned it down! Three times, they offered her a horse, but she lived in an enormous city, and what would she do with a horse, how to feed it, look after it? She kept turning it down, and then one day the Lord spoke to her. "If you can't accept the horse, how will you accept the other things I want to do for you?"

Stunned, the next time someone offered her a horse, she immediately accepted!

I turned to Kevin that day and said, “We missed it!”

“No!” he replied. “You missed it!”

I confessed, I missed it! I could not accept we needed a base and kept turning down the opportunities that God was offering. I failed to recognise the changing season, that Kevin needed a base! How easy it is to miss the plan of God, the changing seasons. I decided the next time anyone offered anything at all, I would take it! And we did!

Pathari, a place of destiny for so many. Undaunted when we had nowhere to stay, with all hotels in the area unsuitable for foreigners, and the conference the next morning. What to do? Do we cancel? No! Concerned where we would stay, we arrived at the church. The pastor showed us a large room above the church. Relieved, we all slept there. As soon as we settled at the church venue, the brothers hired ultra-thin mattresses, dirty well-used sheets, pillows, and grubby blankets, to sleep above the church with the mosquitoes! A walk to the downstairs Asian toilet, a bucket for the night, and a dip bucket shower. Rationed water as we could buy none because of the strike with no shops open, no cars on the roads. How we loved this adventure, eating on the church roof, washing in the bucket, it was a tremendous fun, a splendid experience.

JAMIE WASHING HER HAIR

During a wonderful first conference, we equipped and empowered three hundred ladies and fifty men. In an insignificant town, in this nation with restricted access, subjected to terror and war, God moved. Hungry men stared in the windows; brave ones sat at the back and hung on every word. Two women three years before had prayed. They asked the Lord to send this team for a conference, whilst they planned and prayed by faith, and their faith pleased God. With little money and few people travelling, I e-mailed. If we needed to cancel a conference, this was the one we must cancel! By the time they received the e-mail, God answered their cry. He spoke to an organisation in the USA to fund conferences in the region and two other persons to travel. The people who attended received transformation, deliverance, and empowerment, and wonderfully, Jesus filled them with the Holy Spirit. As one grandmother prayed, what a delight to watch the Lord restore an elderly lady's ear.

An older woman testified, "I came to the meetings with a huge liver tumour. On day 2, I visited the doctor who examined me and did an ultrasound. Today the tumour is gone! I'm healed! There is no sign of the tumour!" She beamed excitedly as she shared her fantastic news. That's the God we serve, the God of miracles. He delights to do miracles to heal the sick.

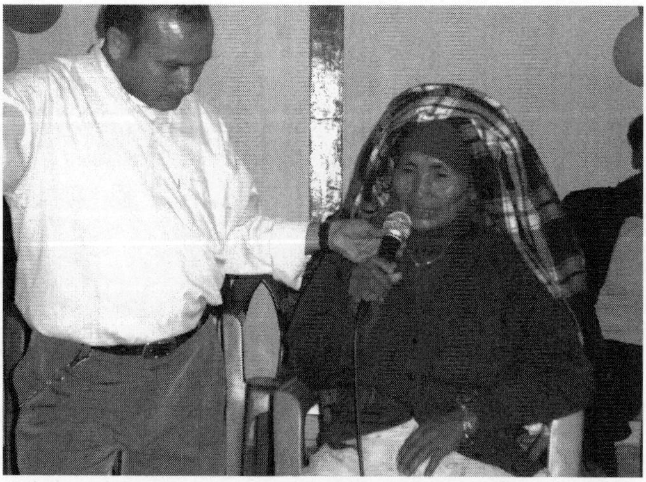

WOMAN HEALED OF LIVER CANCER

PATHARI NEPAL

We all loved Pathari. We had many visits there, and the people followed us around the district. They turned up at eight other conferences. Hotels in the area were horrendous, filthy. We couldn't stay in them. On later visits, they built a lovely room, in which several of us slept, with nice soft mattresses and mosquito nets—what a luxury.

Tim and Mony from NZ travelled that year. Mony shared the first few days she missed their three children then she had a dream and saw each child: Joshua, Peter, and Emily. She never missed them, again the entire mission's journey! It was smoggy weather. She had a chest infection and prayed, "Lord, I want some pleasant weather and blue sky."

In wedding season, they play loud music all night. We dread the weddings, but the wedding was next door to us. Rain came, knocked out the noise, and next morning a blue sky! God is so good.

TEAM

TIM AND MONY

The world says, "If I see it, I am convinced of it! If I don't see it, it's not real!" Reality is when I touch it, feel it, and see it! Faith says, "I see it by faith and believe I have it until I do! I believe I have it, and one day I will! I see the unseen!" As people of faith, we have a worldview of faith. We see the unseen and call it forth.

A pioneer is one who leads the way, who prepares the way for others to follow. They start, they open up, they forge ahead, they found, they break new ground; all because they see and call forth the unseen.

A pioneer has a quickening anointing that causes an acceleration of what God will do in His church. They draw a harvest of souls into the kingdom. When the Holy Spirit was poured out in Acts 2:41, He swept thousands into the kingdom.

Pioneers cause establishment of governing territorial churches across the nations, with captives liberated through deliverance prayer, set free to their purpose of freedom in Christ. That is what Jesus and the apostles did. They created a new blaze, a new trail of spiritual breakthrough. The apostles brought a great breakthrough in the spiritual realm wherever they travelled, bringing a pioneering anointing.

CHAPTER 9

Nepal - 2003 - 2006 - Myanmar - Cuba - Bulgaria- Vietnam Invitations - Malaysia - Intimacy

MAOIST SIGNS IN NEPAL

We continued to travel, and people continued to come. Nothing stops the pioneer. We all tried to ride in one vehicle as that way, we were all together! We sandwiched all the thin people in the back seat of the tiny van as we squashed to fit everyone in! All ten and twelve of us! Gangs of men intimidated us, bashing the vehicles, waving axes, spears, sticks and fiery torches at night, warning us of penalties if we drove in the strikes! Even in this tough season, the Lord led us. Strikes disturbed and devastated the nation.

War did not stop us! We knew Kathmandu had become a sea of terror and East Nepal in disarray. Many others cancelled their trips, but we travelled regardless. Why should war stop the purpose of God? This nation needed us!

PRAYER

PRAYING OVER THE MAPS

Military uniforms everywhere, Maoists hid in forests behind trees and graves. Nepal at war, bombs fell all over the place. Bombs fell thirty miles from where we stayed but never where we were. They fell before our arrival or after we left. God watched over and protected us. No other tourists were in the region!

The Nepalese Civil War (also known as the Maoist Conflict Maoist Revolution) was a fight between the Communist Party of Nepal and the government of Nepal from 1996 to 2006. The CPN-M launched the rebellion on 13 February 1996, with the stated purpose of overthrowing the Nepalese monarchy and establishing a people's republic. The royal massacre occurred on 1 June 2001, at a house on the grounds of the Narayanhiti Royal Palace, residence of the Nepalese monarchy. Nine members of the royal family were killed in a mass shooting during a reunion dinner of the royal family. It ended with the signing of the Comprehensive Peace Accord on 21 November 2006. Summary executions, massacres, characterised the conflict, purges, kidnapping, and other war crimes and crimes against humanity resulted in deaths of over seventeen thousand people, including civilians, insurgents, and army and police personnel, and internal displacement of hundreds of thousands of people of rural Nepal (Wikipedia). *"Prince blamed for Nepal massacre". BBC News. 14 June 2001. Archivedfrom the original on 7 January 2009. Retrieved 31 May 2009.*

Each year, from the USA, we visited nations, taking people from New Zealand and the USA. Kevin and I travelled together for seven years from 1998 until we returned to NZ after the religious visa exit for a year. During this year, we continued the ministry in Asia.

Once the Nepal war stopped, peace and calm returned to this war-torn nation. We were in Pathari, and an unfamiliar face appeared before the conference started. I greeted him, as Dan told me, the leader of Derek Prince Ministry, who provided thousands of books for our conferences! Pastor Gopalje smiled, greeted me, and we talked. At 11:00 a.m., the team waited for the people to arrive for the conference to start!

"This is East Nepal," he said. They will come about 2:00 or 3:00 or even 4:00 p.m.! It's different in Kathmandu," he said. "Come to my church and do a women's conference there."

I said, "We want the men to come too!"

He replied, "If you get the women, you will get the men!" He laughed and said, "No good man can stand against a wonderful woman! Come to Kathmandu!"

The following year, we travelled to Kathmandu and Pokhara.

PASTOR GOPALJE

BOOKS GOPALJE PROVIDED FOR THE CONFERENCES

NEPAL

WOMEN ARE THE LOWEST PAID AND GET ALL THE DONKEY WORK!

Before we could get Myanmar visas on line, we would go to the Myanmar embassy, in Bangkok, at 7:00 a.m. for a visa to enter the nation. As long as we arrived early, we had better attention. If you arrived later, you waited all day because crowds were there. We sat on the pavement until the embassy opened at 9:00 a.m., for two hours sucking car pollution when they stopped for the local school. Dayle presented to collect the passports that afternoon. But they would not give her my passport, saying I must attend myself to collect it!

With concern, the entire group came with me, on our way to catch the Myanmar flight. As I presented at the counter and presented the visa chit, the official looked stern, picked up the passport and said, "When did you enter Thailand? There is no passport stamp for entry into Thailand!" I froze on the spot!

By that time, a senior official standing behind him stepped forward. He recognised me from previous visits. He whispered through the counter, "Do you have another passport?"

Now I didn't know what to do or say, and my heart sank. Yet I wished the ground would swallow me up. Trusting God and whispering a silent prayer, I replied, "Yes, I do!"

"Do you have it with you?" he asked.

"Yes!" I said, pulling it from my bag.

"Come to the other counter," he requested.

I hurried there. Now we were alone! He took the passport and vanished for a minute. On his return, he asked, "In which passport would you like the stamp?"

After a sigh of relief, I replied the first . . . the first one, please."

Minutes later, the deed completed, the passport returned, I left the embassy ecstatic to join the group and fly to Myanmar.

What a beginning to a stunning day! On arrival in Yangon, we presented at immigration, and the official pulled out a piece of pink paper. He requested, "Come this way, please!"

I followed, anxious, wondering what could happen now.

Shown into a room where many officials lined the wall, the man at the desk told me to sit. I sat perplexed and asked, "What is the problem?"

"No problem." So polite as they smiled in reply.

But I heard footsteps and a familiar voice as my son Paul joined me. "This is my mother, I am travelling with her," he said.

"Do you have the baggage chits for your bags?" they asked. This meant they would uplift the bags and maybe send me back!

"No!" I said. "My friends have them. We are a group. I am the group leader. What is the problem?" I asked.

"What is the problem?" Paul asked.

But they made many phone calls and said nothing.

Finally a question came."Have you been involved in Christian orphan schooling?"

I reflected. The ministry involved me with orphans but not with schooling. "No!" I said carefully.

Frustrated, they asked again, "Never?"

I said, "Never!" I asked, "Where?

They replied, "Anywhere in Myanmar?"

I replied firmly, "No, never not anywhere!"

Now concerned, they made more calls and turning to me after the call ended. They said, "We are sorry for detaining you. You can go now!"

Paul and I hurried to retrieve our bags and join our praying group. What a relief. We praised God for the wisdom and favor God had given to deal with the situation. This trip, we took extreme care. This, a red flag, came as a clear warning: Be careful. They asked the wrong questions for them but the right questions for us. Of course, I had involvement with Christian orphans but not official Christian orphan schooling!

The previous year, our group had entered Myanmar across the Thai border at Mae Sai and visited a Chin church. Whilst having a wonderful time with orphans there, we picked up a spy. And they followed us from there through Mandalay to Taungyi, where we held a conference in an orphanage basement in the city. As several hundred from a nearby state attended, in order to enter Taungyi they signed in at the police station and stated their business. When all signed into the same police station, this alerted the police to the meetings, and they came to visit!

Whilst preaching, I felt an urgency to stop and pray. As the entire group knelt and prayed, police and immigration officers appeared outside. Our translator Rosemary and Pastor Lahtoi went to deal with the matter.

"These people are missionaries!" they said. "Look at all this stuff!" And they pointed to the table covered with drama materials which we used to enhance and illustrate the teachings.

"No," said Lahtoi, "those are our materials, they belong to us." So true as we had purchased a bag of materials given to them for conferences, churches, and meetings.

"You are holding meetings!" they said.

"No, we are praying!" declared Rosemary. "For many are sick and with demons, many who need help, and we are praying for them. Do you want people with demons causing problems? Don't you want these sick people healed?" she asked. "It's not a crime to pray."

Now they retreated, with no more problems, but we exited the meetings, and Lahtoi continued the afternoon alone. They visited the hotel to record and report our details, and I alone presented to reenter a year later.

ROSEMARY IN INDIA ON THE FAR RIGHT BESIDE THE TEAM. A MULTI NATIONAL TEAM

God looked after us all. They will expel none of us 'til the day God decides. Nothing thwarts God's purposes.

> Be strong and courageous. Do not fear or be in dread of them, for it is the LORD your God who goes with you. He will not leave you or forsake you. He protects, he guides, he hides us, and sets his angels guard over us.
>
> —Deuteronomy 31:6 ESV

> For he will command his angels concerning you to guard you in all your ways.
>
> —Psalm 91:11 ESV

When we ask, God acts on our behalf. He sets His angels to guard over us, to act on our behalf.

After days of ministry in Venezuela, Cuba we needed to return to Havana, and we should've caught a bus from Ciego, but to save money, the pastor wanted us to travel in the church bus with the others returning to Havana after the meetings. We missed the bus! Racing down the road at midnight, we caught up with the bus and signaled to the driver to stop! The back door opened, and it was driver to door, wall to wall with people! What could we do? We needed to reach Havana. They shoved the bags into the bus, and people shifted fractionally as we climbed into the crush! Kevin stood on one leg. That's all the space there was! The enormous bag allowed room for me to sink onto it, a leg on each side with the door slammed and locked behind us. Five hours later, on arrival in Havana, the door opened, and we spilled out!

How marvelous and different this trip to Bulgaria became. Unbelievers stood, peering through the windows during the service. Again and again, leaders chased them away. Kevin explained to the pastor. They are only a "pane of glass away from coming to Jesus." The pastor explained they could be intoxicated and disruptive from the bar right next door.

The following night, during the service, no one chased the onlookers away. When the altar call finished, although we were praying for people, only one had come to Jesus. Then three young men dressed in gang garb walked in. When we enquired what they wanted, it excited us to discover they wanted to give their lives to Jesus. Just the beginning. Thirteen came in from outside, and Jesus baptised all in the Holy Spirit!

One church I will remember forever. We entered the tiny dirt-floor room they had set apart as their church; the only seating a few thin, tired forms, leaning against the concrete walls., In the precious time we had with these believers, we shared a beautiful story of a woman healed, as the love and compassion of God poured into her when I hugged her in Cuba. To illustrate the story and to express the love of God, I asked a Roma lady to assist me, and as I shared the story, I hugged and hugged and hugged her. The tears rolled down her cheeks as the love of God poured into her. After this, we hugged every person present, and as the love of God poured forth, these precious people sobbed and sobbed. We are Jesus's hands and feet to pour out in love.

VIETNAM CONFERENCE

"This is just a request. It says they invite you," the senior pastor stated as he examined the pieces of paper. "When you receive an invitation, you can accept or decline! My advice is don't go! If you go, they will interview each of you individually. And you will incriminate yourselves and the others, then they will fine you $500. They will expel you. Is that what you want?"

Tired from a full day of ministry with the youth and an hour's travel each way across the city, we arrived at reception. Without a word, the hotel receptionist held out four official envelopes as she gave us our room keys.

In my room, we tore open the letters! They said, "We cordially invite you to attend the Immigration Department tomorrow at 8:30 a.m.!"

Pastor Meh came at once in response to a quick phone call. He shut the door, turned to us, and laughed as he explained. We accepted his advice.

We had finished the conference. A year before, on our visit, the team had arrived at the venue at 6:00 a.m. and left after 5:00 p.m. Police sat outside the church every day, from 8:30 a.m. to 4:00 pm, watching anyone who entered. This year the leaders laughed when we asked, "Do you want us to come early? The police know everything we do here!" We had gone at the usual meeting times with this result!

In case they came to check on us, we left early, returning late that evening. When they gave us our keys, another letter awaited! The final day, we left even earlier, returning later. Yet another letter waited. Anxious hotel staff awaited our return as immigration officials had visited the hotel many times, looking for us! They held out forms, insisting we sign, saying we received the letters! Praise God, we flew out the next morning without further problems, and I applied for a new passport!

God will always reveal His will to anyone who will do it. When we seek Him, God speaks to those who make time to listen.

After many visits to Vietnam to empower youth and churches, that season ended as those to whom we visited failed to understand the glory and power encounters shared. Vietnam, always a place of confrontation and challenge, the two-day youth conference was outstanding, with tremendous moves of the Holy Spirit.

As God is the God of miracles, we saw miracles of provision for we connected with the right people through divine appointments, dreams, and visions.

Every year we returned to Wildwood to minister and spend time with Bruce and Gwen. When Bruce heard our stories of the nations and the projects and Myanmar, he said to us, "You need funding, I can help you raise some money through grants!"

We worked day and night to produce applications. He took us to meetings, and we lived like in a whirlwind—amazing.

To support and empower the family and their initiatives, we applied and received several grants from a Presbyterean organisation to purchase a house for the family. With more support, and another small grant, we put a fence and another building on the property. Now they had a house for the training and the children. Despite that, what about food? We needed lots of food for fifteen children and twenty students plus the family.

Enabled through supporters, we raised funds to purchase ten acres of rice fields to produce rice to feed the family. By the time the family purchased oxen and buffalo to plow the fields, God provided a farmer family to farm the land. *If you teach people how to fish, they become empowered to be self-supporting.* Because Lahtoi and Grace were not farmers, as educated city folk, the village came to their aid. In a place full of snakes, planting rice in the flooded fields with no rubber boots, only God protected him.

THE HOUSE FOR THE FAMILY

TRAINING CENTER CHILDRENS HOUSE

When things go wrong, I know things will be good. Everything lost! My bag gone forever, lost by the airline! Never seen again. I had nothing, and we visited shops to buy clothes to wear!

I asked God for souls. As a missionary working across the nations over these years, thousands of lives were touched and changed, healed, and delivered, but at that time outside Cuba, few people had been born again. I said to the Lord before I travelled to minister to the Vietnamese in Malaysia, "Lord, give me souls. Lord, give me thirty souls."

And God did it. Thirty people in Malaysia born again of the Spirit of God, born anew in just a couple of services.

Now unfamiliar territory beckoned. A pioneer always takes unknown land. That's what we did on several trips to Malaysia. God spoke about crusades. Reaching the lost as the apostles did with signs, wonders, and miracles. In the new season, we planned to move into fresh territory, taking back souls from satan's domain, reclaiming the lost, those enslaved by demonic powers.

> Therefore, those who accepted and welcomed his message were baptized, and there were added that day about 3,000 souls.
>
> —Acts 2:41 ESV

Intimacy

During ministry in Vietnam, when a friend from Florida travelled, he wanted to teach on intimacy, and he did. He suggested, "You should teach on intimacy!"

We included it, and after that, we always did because it made so much impact and was so necessary. People are embarrassed by this love song, the greatest song written by Solomon who wrote of over one hundred songs.

"You can't teach that here, it's too Western! We don't talk about kissing. We don't kiss. We don't talk about intimacy. This is Asia!" Lahtoi exclaimed, his face reflected his embarrassment.

I replied, "The Bible does. The Bible has an entire book devoted to intimacy, the Song of Solomon. It has special verses dedicated to kissing!

It speaks of a love relationship with Jesus. The Jewish rabbis called it the kiss of God's Word!"

> Let him smother me with kisses—his Spirit-kiss divine. So kind are your caresses, I drink them in like the sweetest wine! Her desire is to be smothered by kisses, not just on the lips but all over!
>
> —Song of Songs 1:2 TPT
>
> And not just this verse, but many. It is specific about the kiss on the lips.
>
> Let him kiss me with the kisses of his mouth! For your love is better than wine . . .
>
> —Song of Songs 1:2 ESV

Not the casual kiss of a friend, this is the intimate kiss on the lips between a husband and his wife, the kiss of marriage, the kiss of promise, the kiss of I want more! Not the blown kiss, or the kiss on the hand, or the kiss on the cheek, but specifically the kiss upon the lips. Not a casual kiss but an intimate kiss, which creates a hunger for more! This is not Western. This is God's value for men and women, for marriage, God's value for relationships! This kiss is better than wine, better than the best wine. When wine is drunk, if it's superb wine, the desire is for more. You want to drink and drink and drink. You desire more. It's the same with the kiss! After that kiss, they lose control, walls come down.

No, we did not have an impasse! After we talked it through, discussed the teaching, and looked at the Bible, Pastor Lahtoi expressed willingness to translate. We taught the material everywhere and have done ever since at every conference and training held in Asia. It is extremely possible we are the only group that ever does, but whenever we do, God moves. Supernatural things happen: marriages change, healing comes, relationships deepen. When God shows us things, He moves to bring amazing revelation of His word.

CHAPTER 10

Love - 2003 - 2005 - Bulgaria - Myanmar Saffron Rebellion – Himalayas - USA - Family – Nargis 2008 - Jase Letter - Allentown -China - Tonga

> Until then, there are three things that remain: faith, hope, and love—yet love surpasses them all.
>
> —1 Corinthians 13:13 ESV

So above all else, let love be the beautiful prize for which you run.

It's all about love, learning to love.

> The love of God shed abroad in our hearts by the Holy Spirit not just to love God but to love people.
>
> —Romans 5:5 ESV

Yes, we ministered in nations, poured out in love, and saw God do amazing things. As we learnt to love, we learnt more of God's heart. As believers united as one with Jesus, we moved by faith and asked God to pour His love through us, and He did! As the hands and feet of Jesus, we move by faith to allow God to love people through us. We chose love. We choose to love!

He didn't need our words. A most wonderful move of love, as we were His hands and feet pouring out in love, the love of Jesus. So beautiful to see God's love in action. The more we poured out, the more He poured in. As we stewarded His love, He poured out more love.

> A new commandment I give to you, that you love one another: just as I have loved you, you also are to love one

> another. By this all people will know that you are my disciples, if you have love for one another.
>
> —John 13:34–35 ESV

We travelled all day to this place where the people waited five hours for us! Collected from the bus after the rugged journey, we raced to the ghetto church on the outskirts of the city! The crowded church had people standing all around the walls, eager for God to move. As these people had no water for washing or sanitation, the church was stuffy and smelly!

We shared, preached, and prayed for all. The entire group wanted prayer! But instead of just touching their heads, praying and anointing them with oil, I hugged each one and asked the Lord to pour His love into them through me! As I hugged, they slept in my arms; we laid them down, as though in trances, in deep sleep. God healed, delivered, and did amazing things in their lives. We knew nothing about them. But God did. It was a sign and a wonder, utterly beautiful!

The Rodophi mountains beckoned. We had never been there. We drove for hours through the beautiful mountains with quaint houses, round sharp bends, up and down hills until we finally reached our destination. The pastor shared of his persecution; people in the area hated them. They came with stones and broke their windows. Whilst we prepared for sleep that night, we experienced a loud noise in our room and a stone hurtled through, smashing the tightly-shut double-glazed window! Close to the border of Turkey, the people of another faith planted their religious buildings throughout the mountains in an aim to infiltrate the area. The aim really to annex this area of Bulgaria to the adjacent nation. An originally strong orthodox area changed with these religious buildings everywhere. Atmosphere changed as even with no ministers for that faith, the buildings declared change to the existing communities. Pentecostal churches viewed as a cult, anything other than orthodox regarded as a cult.

When we walked, a man came and said he would shoot Kevin if he came around this area again., the atmosphere became tense and scary, but we prayed for the sick, visited in homes, and encouraged those believers living in the area.

We stayed in a posh hotel near the ghetto, on the third floor in an elegant room with chandeliers. Everything was exquisite, the most beautiful place we had ever stayed in Bulgaria. Washing hung everywhere, from the chandeliers and across the windows in the enormous room. I'm sure no one had ever done that before, but we were missionaries and needed to dry our clothes! When we left, we rolled our bags to the steeply-curved stairwell! *Bump, bump, bump,* they crashed to the Bottom. Bags and walls after that, were never quite the same!

There were many tough times, as visits to the apostle became extremely challenging. We walked miles around the ghetto, visited homes, walked in mud, climbed hills, shared the gospel, and prayed for the sick. Until 1:00 and 2:00 a.m., we discussed endlessly, hour upon hour, round the table, theologically challenging stimulating questions about the apostolic and the kingdom. I always left stirred to read new books, study, and seek God more. I loved this family and regarded them as part of our family as they prayed faithfully for us and the ministry. I valued the prophetic words always brought in this place to edify and uplift me. I watched the two small boys grow up and marry and the parents become grandparents. I visited often as they were so much part of my life and the lives of our family. I will always remember the powerful impacting prophetic word brought by the apostle on one visit, that God had called four men to do what I do, but they had failed to respond. Then he called me as he looked at my heart and obedience. Another word came that like Maria Wood Worth Etter, I would see mighty things. I valued and treasured the times in this special place. There are some special places in life. This became one of those for me. Ministry was always great, but it was the people, how I loved them.

Trains were our way of life. We travelled on trains everywhere. It forged divine connections. We became experienced at jumping on and off with our enormous bags. When they bought a car life changed, we rode in style!

Another pastor, brother, shared he had started a system in the church to protect the young people. In his Roma area and all Roma areas, if a young man or any man wanted a girl, he kidnapped her, raped her, and hung the sheet out the window, showing the blood, and they married!

Now used goods, the family had no choice. To protect the girls once they reached puberty, he held a ceremony where they betrothed them to the young men in the church. It protected them from being stolen, and eventually, they married.

Trafficking is a genuine issue in Roma areas. With little money since communism fell and no work, women and children are trafficked through Europe, to Germany and Turkey, and throughout the world. In 2007, when Bulgaria joined the European Union, the borders opened, and people flowed all over Europe for a better life. This changed many Roma areas as families received finance from those earning in Europe.

We heard so many stories from my friend Patricia. She worked extensively with prostitution in Europe and at "Alabaster Jar," had rescued many Bulgarian Roma women in Berlin from prostitution! Families, extremely protective of their children, carefully watch to keep them safe! One pastor's wife shared after they stole her son, desperate, they searched and searched and prayed, and the Lord showed them where and how to rescue him.

PATRICIA AND DENISE IN BULGARIA

"We must be careful, the mayor will be present. It is the first time the church used the building. It's a trial run. Only a few will come as it's a new church."

After a two-hour journey through Balkan Mountains, all these comments filled our minds as we pulled up outside a concrete building surrounded by trees.

This place, alive with people; loud music reverberated through the entire building. We entered a large crowded hall, and on the stage were the church musicians, exuberantly worshipping. Almost bewildered by noise and people, we made our way to the front. Excitement in the air, we felt the presence of God and knew this would be a glorious night!

Twenty-five people poured to the front to give their lives to Jesus. The apostle led them in the prayer of repentance and prayed with each one for the baptism in the Holy Spirit. We ministered to crowds, and God moved mightily as we shared in this wonderful experience of the harvest. Late we arrived back at the church family's apartment, fell into bed contented to be in the plan of God, privileged to be part of the harvest in the earth.

Through these years I visited the borders of Myanmar Thailand to the refugee camps and Lahtoi and Graces eldest daughter as she and her husband had set up a work with children at Umphang. Returning to New Zealand with a list of treatments and symptoms I had when I became desperately sick in the border the Doctor looked at the list and said categorically 'malaria!' Take these pills for three days. I said to him how can you be so sure? His reply "you've tried everything else it has to be," and it was!

Exhausted for three weeks after the pills killed all symptoms! The beginning of many attacks of malaria.

In 2006, after Rachel had severe whooping cough, the devil attacked our family big time, and our grandchild became a failure to thrive, baby at only three months. The baby, unable to breastfeed because of the medications, had to be introduced to milk mixtures. But after many reactions allergies crippled the child, she became a challenge, unable to put on weight, unable to eat! On one return to visit, when we took breaks from the United States, I fed this child hour by hour, two to three hours at a time, to enlarge her stomach and assist weight gain. At five years, unable to walk because of weakness and weight loss, she needed a tiny child's pushchair! The paediatric specialist said we did an amazing job as with no hospital admissions and one of the worst New Zealand failure to thrive cases; we broke through by prayer and hard work to achieve, and though the allergies remain today, she lives normally and successfully manages the issues!

DAVID, RACHEL, NADIA, AARON, DENISE, KEVIN, AND OLIVER

> Be strong and courageous. Do not fear or be in dread of them, for it is the LORD your God who goes with you. He will not leave you or forsake you. He protects, he guides, he hides us, and sets his angels guard over us.
>
> —Deuteronomy 31:6 ESV

> For he will command his angels concerning you to guard you in all your ways.
>
> —Psalm 91:11 ESV

When we ask, God acts on our behalf. He sets His angels to guard over us, to act on our behalf.

An e-mail came from Rainy a woman in Los Alamos who found our website: fourcornersministries.com. She looked for a site, and when she spotted the Myanmar dress, she knew she needed to contact us. As a result, she travelled to Myanmar with a team from New Zealand. Her grandparents had lived in Myanmar, and her mother was born there. We kept contact, and after meeting her again at a conference, I visited Los Alamos, where she lived. There in Los Alamos, I met Rod and Eileen who became part of our lives. We have visited them several times, and they have been integral in much of the work we have done in the nations, assisted with the well and tank stand in Uganda, assisted with empowerment of the children and family in Myanmar, and the sewing and children's initiatives in India. God's divine appointments.

It was time to visit Myanmar, but this was a tough season. Nothing is too difficult for our God. Nothing is impossible to Him.

We visited a week after the Saffron Revolution, which made the world news. A terrible time of protests and peaceful civil disobedience, where thousands of monks, men, women, and children demonstrated and marched in September 2007 in Myanmar. The national military government removed subsidies on the prices of fuel which triggered the protests.

SAFFRON REBELLION

On 27-29 September, the junta security forces moved against the demonstrations and raided monasteries across the country to quell protests. They arrested at least two hundred monks in Yangon and five hundred more in the northeast. Simultaneously, the army raided four other monasteries in parts of Yangon and arrested several monks. Up to fifty thousand protesters took to the streets in Yangon. Protesters, bleeding from beatings by security forces, scattered and fled. They reported security forces preparing to use insect spray to crack down on protesters. Eyewitnesses said, "I saw fire engines and insect spray carrier trucks in downtown Yangon."

The BBC received unconfirmed reports that fire crews were ordered to fill their machines with insecticide.

Thousands demonstrated in the major cities and marched throughout the nation, and the military junta moved against them. Thousands died. Blood covered the monasteries, and many fled the country. People, afraid of violent reprisals from the army, still took to the streets.

An audio message from inside Myanmar said that crying crematorium workers claimed soldiers forced them to burn injured protesters and civilians to death in YaeWay crematorium on the outskirts of Yangon. The *Times Online* later reported that it was "widely accepted that the cremations began on the night of Friday, 28 September," but the reports of people being burnt alive were being "treated with extreme caution by independent observers and have not been verified." In Mandalay, non-monk prisoners were taken to a field, and a barber was asked to shave their heads so they could be dressed as monks and forced to create confusion and mistrust of real monks (Wikipedia).

SAFFRON REVOLUTION

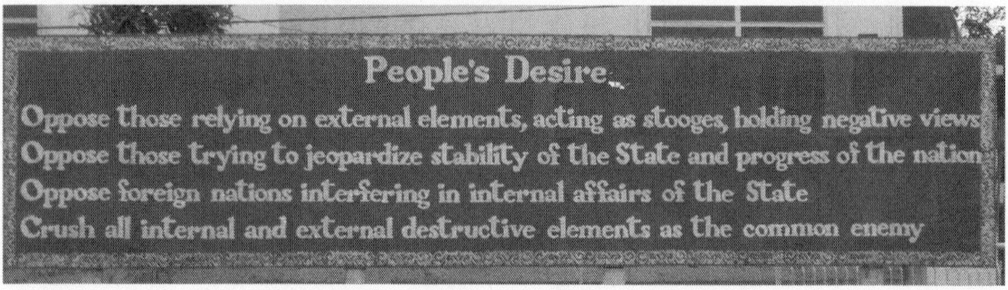

PROPAGANDA NOTICES WERE EVERYWHERE

I was taking a group to Myanmar! Could we even go with such unrest? Those intending to go were asking questions: How to get a visa? Could we go? Would it be safe?

My friends Pastors Murray and Julie in New Zealand had to apply to Australia, where they received their visas without problem. Coming from the USA, we had to do it in Bangkok!

Undaunted, with a young woman who travelled with me, we arrived at the embassy at 7:00 a.m. to be first in the line! What line? No one came. Whilst we sat outside on the concrete for two hours, we watched the world go by! No tour operators! Nobody! When the officials opened the entry gate at 9:00 a.m., they looked surprised to see us there.

We walked into the empty room where we sat and waited! And waited! With reluctance, finally, an official came to the desk. After he opened the counter with a bang, he announced, "No visas, no one can go to Yangon!"

I stood my ground and said strongly, "I need a visa! We must have visas. This is my family, we are travelling together. We must go, I have a group who have got visas from Australia, and I must meet them in Myanmar. They are flying through Singapore." This nonplussed the official. He went away to consult the senior man. He returned, saying, "Come tomorrow!" We retreated to pray.

Returning the following day, again they said, "No visas!"

Again, I insisted, "We must have visas, my friends are flying tomorrow to Singapore, and we must meet them in Yangon!"

Finally, later that day, after much consultation with higher authorities and prayer, they issued visas. Into Myanmar we flew in this divine appointment, to encourage believers suffering increased oppression. As the nation was tense, we held secret meetings and took extreme care.

PASTORS GRACE AND LAHTOI, RAMANDA, JULIE, RAINY, JOSEPHINE, HLA WIN, MURRAY, LES MU, MOSES AND DENISE

Buses caused excitement in the early days. They are great now, modern and efficient. Constantly breaking down, with dysfunctional and non-functional air con, one bus had the wall lined with plastic to stop the rain. Stranded on the highway, three of us waited for our third bus of the night in our trip to Yangon, but it failed to come for several hours. We laid mats down on the road and lay resting until the bus finally appeared.

Another trip was not without event when after all night on the bus, the bus halted at 5:00 a.m. in the countryside. All the men filed off the bus and went one way, the ladies the other. As the only foreigners, we had to think quickly, and with a Burmese *longey,* a long piece of fabric used as a skirt, in the middle of a field, two ladies held it up, and the rest squatted behind!

After ministry and a tremendous conference with the team in Northern Shan state in Lashio, students came to the training centre for the one-year course. Within a few weeks, four children got sick, Sarah became ill, and on investigation, we discovered all had contracted tuberculosis. Although they sent the students back, the children and Sarah required treatment. Until all recovered, this was a hard season, but then our precious friend Lahtoi contracted TB!

Most people on a US religious visa apply to become permanent residents during the season of five years, but in ignorance, we didn't know that. The religious visa expired, and we returned to New Zealand, but during that year of many challenges, we made the plan that we might pursue a green card on our return to the USA.

We returned to New Zealand in 2008, as we needed to spend a year out of the country before we could apply to return.

IN KOLKOTTA FAY, NAN, JACKIE, AND MARIAN CAME WITH A BROKEN ARM! NOTHING STOPPED HER

PAUL, AFTER HE ROLLED AROUND OUR FLOOR!

We heard the noise as he came up the stairs and along the passage; laughter preceded him. We opened the door to Paul who fell on our floor, to roll and laugh, and laugh. Tears fell down his cheeks as he tried to speak. Really, he was almost stupid. We managed to put together something about "angels on the path and the driver hiding in the bushes." Almost incoherent, we pieced it together as he told us what had happened. He and another leader had gone that night back to the pastor's house to pay the account for the conference. They left the driver with the van, as no one leaves vehicles unattended in India. After a great time with the pastor, when they discussed previous revivals in the area, they said goodbyes and stepped out onto the path. No sooner on the steep rough path than they began to laugh and fall down, as they became more and more drunk. Unable to walk, they rolled in the dirt! Finally, some time later, they managed to crawl to the top, laughing and crying. As they struggled to walk along the flat area, where cars parked, they reached the van, but to their dismay, there was no driver! Laughing, calling, looking, they could not find the driver. Alarmed now, where was the driver? From the bushes on the hillside, the driver emerged in answer to their calls and noise! Frightened, he said, "Three men walked by the van, and as I watched them, they disappeared . . . one moment there and the next moment gone! They just vanished!" Frightened, he added, "I hid in the bushes, it was so strange!"

Paul said, "Angels! Angels walked the path!"

THE TEAM IN THE HIMALAYAS

That year gold dust came on Pastor Sonny's head in the Darjeeling meetings. From the first visit to the region in the year 2000, the teams prayed across the borders and around the local area of the town every year. We travelled eight miles to the temple on the hill overlooking this Indian border town. Women from far inside this nation attended the conferences at the border, and children had heavenly experiences in the first conference. The contrast between both towns was striking! One clean, one filthy! On the Indian side, they cleaned and swept the street, burnt the rubbish every morning, but within thirty minutes, filthy again! Across the border, everything was absolutely clean, no rubbish, no dirt, pristine condition. The border closed to foreigners, and we discussed with a leader from the capital about the necessity of travel into the nation. I remember his words: "To light a fire, you must do it in the centre of the nation, not on the borders." In view of the vision in which I saw a nation of 188,000 people high in the Himalayas, a Buddhist kingdom with many dark Buddhist caverns, we had a responsibility.

Once the borders closed for foreigners, Nan and I travelled to the capital with a visa for two days. In the van, we climbed further and further back into the mountains, around the cliffs. Breathtaking scenery with mountains, glimpses of snow on distant peaks, roads cut through vertical cliffs with one-way drives in many places, with a stunning river gorge and amazing exotic houses. The architecture fascinated us. Leaving at 8:00 a.m. for the two borders, to exit and enter and a visa received. We arrived at 5:00 p.m., with only 152.8-kilometre journey, nine hours by road. Roads were bad; they blasted and bulldozed the cliffs as we travelled. Rocks fell all around us. Over time the roads improved, and a new steep dangerous highway along the cliffs opened, though recently, a vehicle fell to disaster. We visited, the house church family in the central city. To this a conservative religious church, we brought a new freedom in the Spirit. Over the years of ministry there, we have seen increased freedom as the God moved to refresh and renew lives.

We held a day of teaching with this very religious group, who were almost like Catholics in the way they prayed and worshipped, and flew the following morning to Bangkok. On that first visit, we washed the believer's feet, which was extremely powerful, bringing increased love and unity.

ROADS INTO A RESTRICTED NATION

SCENERY

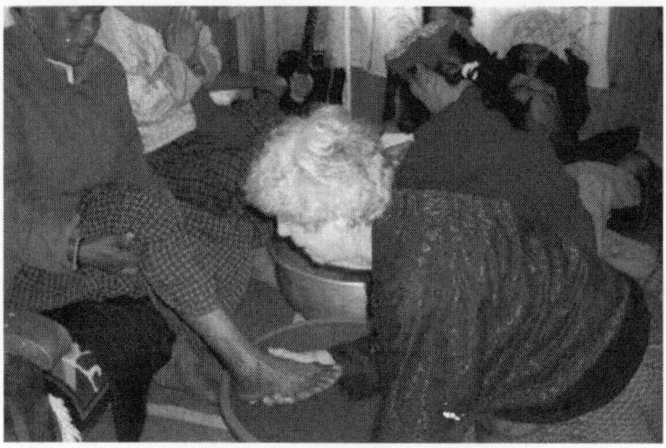

NAN FOOT WASHING

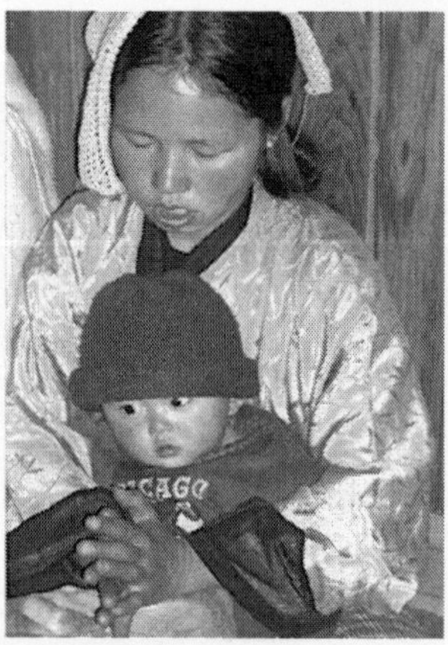

MOTHER AND CHILD

Luxury was the name of the game. After India and Nepal, it was like *the icing on the cake.* Top-notch hotels, wonderful food, we felt so blessed. It cost us dearly, but we loved it! What a challenge.

Though providential for the family, it became a year of monumental challenge and suffering as the devil sought to kill our family members. When I returned from India, we visited Paul and Kim and our grandchildren Daniel and Rachana. At only three a half years, she appeared white, like the white of a newspaper, the white of a painted wall. We discussed her condition. "She doesn't look good. You should take her to the doctor as she is crying all the time and unable to walk upstairs."

Easy to see she was anemic, but I never dreamt the problem! They had just returned from India a trip with me, and that day in church, the entire family dedicated themselves to reach peoples of another faith.

Next day, the family visited the doctor, who said, "I rarely do blood tests on children this young, but you've been in Asia and India, and so I'll do a blood test to check what's going on."

He did the blood test! The following day their phone rang!

"Bring the child immediately, she needs urgent care!"

Alarmed, they travelled to the hospital accident and emergency department. On arrival, with no explanation, they showed them immediately to a private isolation room in the children's cancer ward! We picked up the phone in shock to hear, "Rachana has leukemia!"

On one blood test, they confirmed the diagnosis! Severely affected, the time of challenge began an entirely new day.

The battle began, the fight for her life. Stunned with the news, we reeled from the shock. That day the hospital told Paul and Kim she had acute lymphatic leukemia, with no further diagnostic tests, not even a bone marrow or a lumbar puncture, they diagnosed on one blood test: this child, very sick, dying! The norm became weekly bone marrows, lumbar punctures, poor pain control, living in two places: hospital and home!

GRANDCHILDREN, RACHANA AND NADIA

Shocked, we prayed. The church prayed. We put out news asking for urgent prayer as believers around the world prayed. Paul took her to Australia against advice for healing prayer at Benny Hinn's meetings, but despite the pain and suffering, the treatments continued. Three and a half years later, doctors declared her cancer free. At every point, we declared and decreed healing. We declared and decreed the word of God.

That same year, our son-in-law Aaron, diagnosed with cancer, walked through the pain, the suffering of chemo and costly surgery. Kevin travelled with him each week for chemo in this extremely tough season, two family members fighting for their lives. We were so grateful to God for His timing as we were home just when support and love were so needed.

Such a difficult year, I thought maybe we are eligible for some government assistance. I attended an interview, but it was a group interview for work! Not seeking work, I was clearly in the wrong place! A supervisor approached me to ask me to follow her to a private room. She listened to my story of all the issues and said, "You need a sickness benefit!"

I said, "But I'm not sick!"

"Just fill out these forms and go to the doctor, and we will give you a sickness benefit!" she said, handing me some forms.

I visited the doctor, and sure enough, they paid us the benefit for the rest of our stay in New Zealand.

A year later, we returned to the USA, our visa renewed, and I called New Zealand to talk to Paul, who said he sat in the bathroom, and there was a lot of noise in the background.

I asked, "What's the noise?"

He replied, "I'm in the bathroom! Rachana is in the passage, she's throwing all the cutlery at the door, I retreated here for peace."

I could hear the screaming! I prayed.

Nargis hit the Myanmar Delta in 2008. My friend Marian and I travelled to encourage believers in the nation. Yangon was a sea of blue tarpaulins, for Nargis destroyed roofs across the city, and huge fallen trees lay everywhere, blocking roads, buildings destroyed! Heat intensified dramatically in Yangon because of the loss of the tree cover. Thousands died as the hurricane reached two hundred miles inland. We received horrible photos of hundreds of bodies in the trees and clogging the rivers. The Myanmar military government refused aid from nations and turned away ships carrying aid. The population of the nation decreased from 59 million to 51 million with no explanations! Christians had to buy back the aid given freely by other nations to assist those devastated by the disaster. We received reports that the government closed the roads to the delta, and no one could go there for two weeks. They left the people to die! It became an amazing time for the churches. In teams, they travelled to the delta, built buildings in which they stayed, rebuilding houses and giving aid in the process. After the first project, they realised, if they were smart, they would build bigger buildings and use them as halls for the community and evangelism. Whilst one team went to bring aid, another travelled later to rebuild. To appear disconnected, the second team came solely to do evangelism. Hundreds came to faith in Christ, as the government didn't help them; the nation's religion didn't help them, but Jesus did. We held a conference in Yangon with Nargis survivors where Jesus healed a man with HIV. In this special time, all these new believers who had lost everything needed encouragement, teaching, and prayer.

During our time in Mandalay, we rose and were getting ready for the day. I had showered and asked Marian about to enter the bathroom, "Did you lock the door?"

"Yes," she said, "it's secure!"

With that, she vanished to the shower. Sitting on the bed with a mirror, I examined my private parts as I had some problems with prickly heat. As I gazed down at these areas, the door burst open, and in came a Chinese man gazing at me! Shocked, he said, "So sorry! Sorry! Sorry! Sorry!" He shouted as he turned and retreated rapidly, closing the door quickly behind him!

I quickly pushed the lock on the offending door, and when Marian reappeared from the shower, she asked, "Who was that? What was that?"

We laughed and laughed at my embarrassment at being caught in such a position! After that, we took great care to ensure the door bolt really was locked and bolted!

MARIAN WITH SAMUEL AT THE TRIBAL CENTRE

Within a short time of our visit to the hospital to see Lahtoi, he became seriously ill, and shortly after, news came that he had passed to be with Jesus. Devastated, I wanted to travel to Myanmar. Friends said, "He's gone. Why go now? He's in heaven."

"You don't understand," I said. "I loved this man, and I love his family. I have to go!"

Three weeks later, Lyndsey and I left NZ for Bangkok, arriving there as the military closed the airport! We caught the last taxi.

2008 November 26 [Wikipedia] Thousands of overseas passengers were stranded at Thailand's main international airport today after all flights halted because of an invasion by anti-government protesters. The takeover of Bangkok's Suvarnabhumi Airport led to the cancellation of hundreds of flights and represented a dramatic escalation of the demonstrators' efforts to oust the government.

Bangkok, under siege, had many buildings burning. The city, like a war zone, had military and police everywhere. Roads barricaded, razor wire, police vans and trucks lined and blocked the street where we stayed. Tourists wept and sat on their bags on the streets, stranded and out of money.

Stranded in Bangkok for several days, we visited a tour agent near the Myanmar embassy, who offered to help us travel into Myanmar. He called us and said, "You can get to Yangon! The first flight out to Yangon is going 4:00 a.m. Wednesday. You must be at the king's statue beside the park at 4:00 a.m.! Come and pay for your tickets. Your visas are here. A bus will go from there to the military airport four hours away. Don't be late!"

Up at 3:00 a.m., following instructions, tickets in hand, with crowds of people and the mosquitoes, we waited in the dark for the bus and travelled four hours to the airport.

It was an incredible day, when in the tropical sun, they checked us in with paper and pen. No technology, no computers, none of that. Like a gala and market day, food, drinks, music, and people, lines of people, everywhere! We proceeded into a sticky hot building, where, again, we waited in lines for hours before eventually proceeding to a final room out of the stifling heat. Again, we waited, until eventually, they announced the flight, and relieved, we scrambled aboard for Yangon, arriving late that night; another flight to Mandalay the next morning. It only took us a week plus lots of prayer to get there.

We arrived at the training centre and climbed the stairs. Grace sat at the back of the long room. As she looked up, a faint smile flitted across her sombre face, and she said, "I knew you would come, you love us. You loved Lahtoi. I've been waiting to see you."

Tears rolled down our cheeks as we hugged and hugged, releasing our love for her and Jesus. We are the hands and feet of Jesus, bringing His love and mercy. Loving Jesus releases love in action.

It's not enough to do stuff. We are Jesus's hands and feet to pour out His love wherever we go.

What would we do without our precious brother and friend? God always has the plan.

My friend Jase wrote, "We sat on the roof praying, beating the drum. At the gate is a group of people waving flaming torches, shouting, with axes, weapons, and knives. We prayed and worshipped 24/7. In a neighbouring village, believers heard the drum and shouted, 'Jesus!' When the attackers heard the shout, they dropped their weapons and fled."

The e-mail, incredibly descriptive, sent out throughout the world, alerted Christians everywhere to pray. I know I prayed, my heart touched by the plight of my friends in the heavenly compound. Christians were being attacked and murdered, families fled to the jungles, children experienced indescribable terror throughout the region.

They estimated that over 395 churches, 5,600 homes, and 13 educational institutes were set on fire, demolished, or vandalized during the attacks, and over 90 killed (largely Christians) and 18,000 injured, with 54,000 displaced. Another report said that around 11,000 people still lived in relief camps as of October 2008. Some tribals even fled away to border districts in neighbouring states, and it affected 310 villages. Not one hundred years ago or the early church, but this century!

The 2008 anti-Christian riots were remembered as the worst instance of Christian persecution in India's modern history. In August, Kandhamal's Christians were wrongly accused of assassinating a local Hindu leader. This sparked off three months of anti-Christian violence, in which mobs of Hindu radicals attacked village after village in Kandhamal, targeting Christians.

When the violence finally ended, over 100 Christians had died; radicals destroyed over 1,400 Christian homes and displaced 56,000 believers. To date, many of the Christian victims of the 2008 anti-Christian riots have received little to no justice from the local court system (03/04/2019, India, (International Christian Concern).

Meanwhile, in the USA, Allentown, Pennsylvania, a Spanish church, opened up where we formed long-term friendships. At a Saturday morning breakfast meeting of doughnuts, coffee, yoghurt, and fruit, after speaking, we showed video of powerful moves of God in the nations. The Holy Spirit moved powerfully on the people who lay swimming on the carpet as God touched and revealed Himself to them. Spanish people who couldn't swim, how ridiculous, but there they were, and they said they were swimming, too amazing! As we declared and decreed God is here, Jesus is here, angels are here, the water of refreshing, renewing, reviving of the Holy Spirit flowed all over them. As we sought and released more of His presence, He came. One man said he had no plan to attend, but God stirred him to do so. God touched him. There were many testimonies to God's supernatural power. The next day everybody waited, excited, expectant that God would move. With two services, one ran into the other, and the services lasted until three in the afternoon. A wonderful day and a tremendous time of God moving, with people on the floor crying out to God, all blasted by the Holy Spirit. A woman came forwards and said she had severe pain on her leg with a major leg and spinal problem, and that day God healed her. Leadership asked us if we would stay on, but it seemed impossible as we had other meetings booked. It's difficult to rebook cancelled meetings! Sometimes we do the right thing at the right time, and sometimes we miss it. This time perhaps, looking back, I think we missed it! It's easy to be in the plan of God, to be in the purpose of God, to be hearing from God, to see Him move and just miss His timing. In reluctance, we moved on, but the following year, I returned to spend time there and stayed with a woman in the church who extended hospitality.

The people came hungry for God to the many meetings. Three weeks, we stayed as God moved to bring powerful repentance.

Vanessa, broken and weeping, testified, "I walked on the body of Jesus, and as I stepped, the blood seeped out from His wounded body! Every step I took, the blood oozed out, and He said to me, 'Please don't wound me with your words!'"

A ten-year-old boy came with a bag of his playthings, Spiderman suit and various precious stuff he had collected over years. He laid them at the front and said, "I saw Jesus, and He told me I don't need these things anymore!"

A leading elder said, she stood at the back and watched all the emotional responses and said to herself they are Spanish, so emotional! But she found herself at the front, repenting of her pride of position and place!

The young people, as they walked down the nearby streets, saw chains breaking off the people they passed.

Kevin reminded me of the music group all being blasted by Holy Spirit, unable to play any worship lying on the floor under Holy Spirit power, as waves of glory filled the church.

An unforgettable, powerful move of God.

PASTORS JAY AND MARGIE, ALLENTOWN

HEALING

CHURCH ALLENTOWN

We stayed in the countryside on a special site, a secret Bible school for believers, but when we drove there, it was during daylight. With little security, we climbed in broad daylight on the roof to see the neighbourhood, and they could see us! The entire neighbourhood knew of our presence! They saw us drive in and drive out; they could see us walk through the property. After our visit, persecution broke out, and they had to close that Bible school! We could have travelled in and out by night, not viewed the world from the roof or walked the property by day, but these were matters outside of our control. A beautiful time, but when we presented to fly out, after giving my passport to Dayle, though we searched her and my bags, we could not find it! With enormous airport stress, where we unpacked bags on the street, they flew without me, stranded in China with no passport and the embassy thousands of miles away at Beijing! I couldn't return to the hotel, no passport, thankfully, the believers accommodated me. Three days passed before I could fly. When the team returned to Bangkok, they searched the bags, and there, in the back, obscured under the lining, the passport had slipped! Fortunately, our connections in Bangkok arranged delivery to return the passport to me, and three days later, I flew to Bangkok. What stress! Losing your passport is no fun!

CHINA

CHINA TEAM

I returned alone to New Zealand to see family because Kevin could not fly as he still underwent the unsuccessful process for the green card. God never intended for us to live in America, only minister there. Confused at the process, a senior pastor sensed my confusion and said, "Kevin needs to come. I need to see him to talk to him."

We arranged for Kevin to fly down, and we spent some time with this special man who spoke often into both our lives. He shared with me after he spoke with us. He asked, "Did God speak to Kevin?"

And I said, "Yes."

He asked, "Why do you think God gave you a grace to travel and didn't give Kevin the same grace?"

I replied, "I don't know! I have often asked that question."

He said, "Maybe He doesn't mean for Kevin to travel? Now it's time for him to do what God has told him to do, and you to carry on!"

Stunned, I accepted this, and when people asked, "Why doesn't Kevin travel?"

I replied, "God told him not to!"

This stopped all discussion, as what can anyone say in reply to God told me? After that, I travelled alone, whilst he stayed and prayed, a challenge because for years, I always had people with me, and now I would travel alone. But not alone as God was with me, and believers always met and spent time with me.

My dear friends Murray and Julie who so often opened their home and the church to us in Pauanui travelled several times to Myanmar, which they loved. Julie loved the family, and at her River Day, which she started many years earlier, where I ministered, they took up an offering every month to bless Pastor Grace and the children. She loved and sowed into the ministry, and stirred and created vision as she brought before the ladies the needs of the family there, until she passed to heaven after a brain hemorrhage. We miss her. They travelled often with great sacrifice. Well, I remember that they had to wear flip-flops as shoes would not go onto their feet! With feet so swollen, they had difficulty walking! They were there when we experienced a significant move in Myitkina of the joy of the Lord. Where there is great love, there is the release of great joy. They were lovers of God and lovers of people, loving and serving Myanmar with all their hearts!

MURRAY AND JULIE

Kevin stayed in an older mobile home based in the Florida Keys for the season, whilst I travelled in and out to New Zealand and to nations. After immigration rejected the green card, we continued with a tourist visa, travelling to and from New Zealand. The RV functioned until we settled in Indiana.

A woman knocked on the door. We were in Auckland, and she said, "I am a Tongan, a pastor. Will you come to Tonga?"

I refused, saying, "I don't do Tonga!"

But she persisted and kept bothering me. As a result, we visited Tonga, not once but three times, taking three teams. After a glorious evening of sharing, drama, and ministry, in which we experienced a tremendous move of the Spirit of God, in an outpouring of the Holy Spirit, about eight people experienced heaven. They saw Jesus and talked to Him for about an hour and a half and were still seeing Him when we returned to our accommodation. When we prophesied, God moved very powerfully, and the pastor's wife wailed. One leader's wife saw Jesus carrying a lamb, and another met Jesus, and He commissioned her. A young man wailed as he knelt on the floor. He wept and wailed and appeared to have an encounter with God. Like in a trance, there in body but absent, we could not rouse him. In amazement, we watched for over an hour. It continued for over three hours long into the night. The pastor told us the next morning he had a heavenly encounter, saw Jesus, and visited the heavenly realm. We ministered for a season in many Tongan churches around Auckland. In everything, there are seasons.

TONGA TEAM

CHAPTER 11

2010-2015 - Stewarding The Glory - Myanmar - Himalayas - Cuba - Robbed - The House - Nepal - Bangladesh - USA - Heavenly Experiences -Miracles -Signs And Wonders -Cuba Disaster -The Dream Unfolds -Long Island -Supernatural

It's not enough to do stuff. Everybody does that! They go with their programme and do it. We travel with God's programme and do what the leaders want. We are Jesus's hands and feet, lovers of God and lovers of people, to pour out His love wherever we go.

What would we do without our precious brother and friend? We depended on him, my precious friend, so much. I missed him dreadfully. For three years after his passing, I could not speak of him without tears rolling down my cheeks! But God always has the plan, even when we cannot see it.

I learnt to love his son Toi San Aw Samuel, a skilled graphic artist with a good job, who lived in Yangon and avoided me. He would appear to greet me at the trip's end. Backslidden, the Lord dealt with him after he moved to Mandalay to assist the family. He came with nothing, a history, long hair, an earring, but his heart changed. The Lord did a work on his life in answer to believing prayers. He abandoned all, a successful career in graphics to follow Jesus.

> The Lord says, I will deliver the children of the righteous.
> —Proverbs 11:21 KJV

God promises to look after our children. We experienced it with Paul; now God did it again. He positioned Samuel for His plan and future purpose as He does for each of us. When the rest of the family learnt English, he resisted, and now he became the translator! I think God has a tremendous sense of humor. This pastor's son, resistant to ministry, did a master's degree in divinity, became involved in ministry, organised conferences and church meetings, and today runs a successful business, married with three small children.

SAMUEL AND FAMILY

I opened the e-mail, and my eyes filled with tears as I read with horror the assault upon a sister and prominent family whom I knew well in the nation of Cuba. The secretary in the church, only sister of a dear brother, leader of many churches in the nation, murdered, abused, strangled in her own home. Her body discovered when she failed to appear at the evening service. Worse came. This grieving family faced her two small children being orphaned as shortly after this terrible event, police arrested her husband and incarcerated him for life for the murder of his wife.

What a privilege to visit the pastor and his family some time later and see his victory in the face of such suffering! His church had grown to over five thousand in less than six months, and they had eleven thousand new converts in their movement in eighteen months!

"We have revival!" he said, beaming from ear to ear. He had shared with me on an earlier visit stories of revival in the nation.

***

We attracted so many people to travel with us. A maverick, a colourful man full of fun who made us laugh and laugh. Amongst ourselves, we called him johnababu, a man full of fun, always the life of the party!

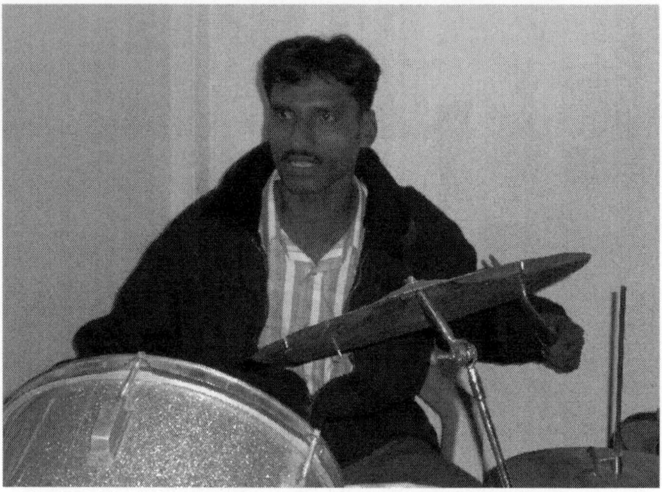

OUR AMAZING FRIEND PASTOR JOHN BABU

He came to us numerous times and introduced many pastors and leaders to us as he sought to empower them. When he visited, we laughed a lot and enjoyed the fun he created. We loved his wife, who travelled several times with him. We visited his work in the south twice and became involved with him in several crusades and conferences. Arriving at midnight from long flights into Bangalore, he met us, and there began our new adventure, always ever challenging. Without warning, involved in baptisms, he asked us to give the candidates their new names, and in total surprise, we watched as when baptised, they immersed under the water, not once but three times, on video, impressive. At the pastor's conference, we watched a team member wash an older pastor's feet. The pastor cried as he testified Jesus came and washed his feet!

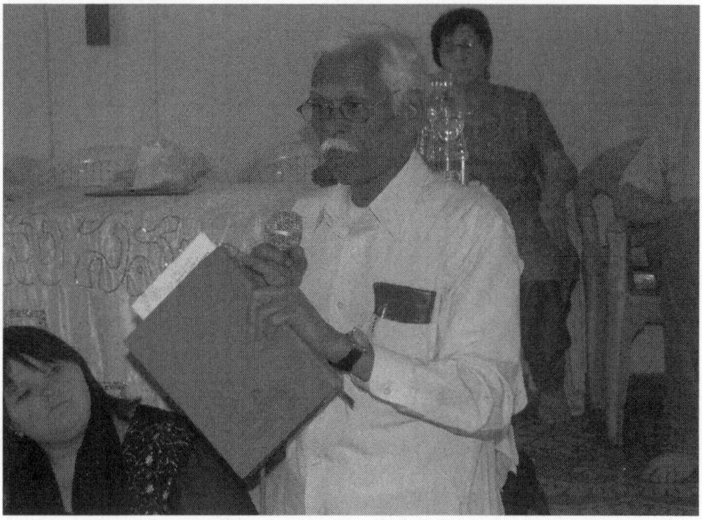

OLDER PASTOR WHO SAW JESUS WASHING HIS FEET.

At another conference, in shock they announced, that morning radical believers of another faith had burst into a home and murdered a pastor in the area. That night we had to travel to a resort at midnight up in a freezing place. Unimpressed, we arrived in the cold and were astonished to find few blankets, no bathrooms, and sinks without taps or plumbing! After many arduous experiences, we no longer visited his area and encouraged him to visit us.

We met Pastor Rathnababu in 2010 in Siliguri, when he came with our brother *johnababu*, who introduced many leaders to us. He only spoke Telegu but understood some English. He could not do any teaching and still cannot at our conferences but is amazing at praying, doing drama, and anything that needs doing.

Twelve years is a long time. His church grew after his first visit, from being a conservative, ordinary church of three hundred people to over three thousand people hungry for the Holy Spirit with over 120 churches associated.

PASTOR RATHANABABU AND MERE

In 2011, in Sikkim, high in the Himalayas, an area historically resistant to the Holy Spirit, the entire group screamed and yelled. This shocked us! On a return visit, after an amazing move of God the year before, when we were all sick, the glory, the fire of God, fell like in Isaiah 6, where the fiery coal touched Isaiah's lips. The Lord touched the entire group of men, women, and children. When the fire fell, the women said that it burnt them from the inside out, and they felt clean inside. A young man testified; he repented of secret sin and expressed that the fire changed his life. Children screamed and writhed as they lay on the floor. The Holy Spirit blasted the entire conference, and they all lay on the floor, some kicking and screaming as the fire touched them. People noticed lightning flashing in the room and fire on our heads brought by fiery angels. Angels came in the room, and Jesus walked amongst us. The glory fell again and again. We continued in His presence, calling down more and more fire. As we persevered in His presence, waves of glory came. We learnt to recognise and steward levels and waves of the glory. As the glory lifted, we called down more glory and pressed in for more. We learnt the more we seek, the more He comes.

SIKKIM

Sobs and wails preceded her as she returned to our room! We heard the noise as she came along the street, up the stairs, and into the passage. In horror and dismay, we tried to discover what had happened as she tore at her long black hair, pulling it out in lumps and scratching her face as the tears poured down her cheeks! Rosemary returned from the phone booth; she had gone to call her family in Myanmar as she had heard nothing since the beginning of the trip. Finally, she wailed, “He’s dead! He’s dead! My father died a week ago! No one could contact me!”

Shocked and appalled, we gazed in horror! Impossible to get her out, stuck inside East Nepal with no possibility of leaving, she had to continue with us to the end of the trip several weeks later! What a trip.

In the Itahari-Damak areas, after we challenged the people to rethink many cultural issues in the light of God’s value for women, we had a spectacular move of God.

Jesus’s relationship with women is expressed so clearly in Genesis 1:26-28 ESV:

> Then God said, "Let us make man in our image, after our likeness. And let them have dominion over the fish of the sea and over the birds of the heavens and over the livestock and over all the earth and over every creeping thing that creeps on the earth." So God created man in his own image, in the image of God he created him; male and female, he created them. And God blessed them. And God said to them, "Be fruitful and multiply and fill the earth and subdue it, and have dominion over the fish of the sea and over the birds of the heavens and over every living thing that moves on the earth."

Notice here in this passage, God spoke to them. He did not give the instructions only to the man, but He gave it to them together. Instructed by God to rule and reign and have dominion, they were to carry the glory. They would be fruitful through intimacy with each other and God, multiply, build a family, fill and subdue the earth. He commanded them, both the man and the woman together. God's intent that together as one, they would love and serve each other and God.

The foot washing brought wave after wave of glory and fire. Repeatedly by faith, we moved forwards to expect and declare that waves of glory were there, that Jesus walked in the meeting, to declare some of you are seeing Jesus, Jesus is kissing and hugging you. After having their feet washed, the entire group lined up for prayer, and God hit the children as they wept, shook, and screamed. Many experienced Jesus, caught glimpses of angels, and gazed on the glory. Someone had an open vision of Jesus, and others shared they experienced His presence. Jesus came and hugged people. The sight of an enormous ball of fire overwhelmed one man as he wept, overcome with God's presence. A woman, who had lots of revelation, watched Jesus holding a huge fiery scepter. Jesus took so many to their mansions, with amazing houses in heaven and beautiful green pastures. Those touched by the Lord glimpsed fire on the heads of everyone as in the book of Acts, a flame for every head. Glorious lights came on team members' heads. A small girl rode a horse, with three other horses, white, black, and gold. In a staircase vision, some people were walking easily up the stairs, and some were crawling. So many magnificent testimonies. We could not wait for them all! We travelled on, overwhelmed at all God did and showed us. Every day more revelations and encounters happened as we stewarded His glory.

ITAHARI

The war over, with soldiers everywhere, we travelled to Kathmandu and on to Pokhara in West Nepal. There, we experienced a tremendous move of God: A lady visited heaven for the first time. Unforgettable, I watched astounded at what God did. Amidst 150 people, the Lord moved on her as she knelt right in front of me. Glory covered her face as she talked, hugged, and kissed someone. But no one was there, just me watching. Tear drops fell as her face glowed with glory and wonder. She seemed to be in a trancelike state, unaware of anything happening around her. Eventually, she woke and gazed around her. The translator informed me, "She's been with Jesus . . . He hugged and kissed her . . . He told her the secrets of heaven . . . He took her to a garden with flowers . . . He gave her the flowers." Then he urged me, "Why don't you get her to give away the flowers?"

Beyond logic, beyond reason, I obeyed and called the people to come. Logic says, how could you give away what is not on earth, only in heaven? Anyway, we did it, called the people, and they all came for prayer to receive flowers from heaven! Entirely wonderful! Before she even prayed for them, God moved on 140 ladies who came hungry for the touch of God, shaking, weeping, falling down. That assisted my journey to steward to unlock the heavenly encounters, every step a new one as I learnt to steward Holy Spirit waves of glory in our conferences. Learnt to declare and decree by faith that angels were in the meeting and Jesus was walking amongst us.

THE ENCOUNTER

After a powerful time of ministry, a woman, married to a man of another faith, came and shared. When she arrived home from the meetings, he asked her, "Who do you love? Me or Jesus?"

Carefully, she replied, "I love you and Jesus!"

Again, he asked her, "Who do you love, me or Jesus?"

She said, "I love you and Jesus."

He then said, "If I get a can of kerosene and make it look like suicide, I will pour it over you and light a match! Who will you love? Me or Jesus and kerosene?"

She courageously replied, "I choose Jesus and kerosene!"

We prayed for this courageous lady who loved Jesus enough to die for him.

During this time, Dan learnt his brother was dying. We had to proceed on to another nation and into Bangladesh without Dan as his brother Benjamin was in Siliguri ill, dying and required him to return speedily to visit him briefly to say goodbye!

In Kathmandu many experienced heaven and several visited hell. A leader from YWAM writhed for a long time on the floor releasing loud groans and wails. Later he testified from the platform, "I saw my whole village taken to a cliff edge, men, women and children all pushed over the steep cliff falling into hell. Women with babies hurtling into the fires which leapt up to consume them. Little children, the entire group of people. I saw the smoke, I saw the flames. The flesh burnt from their bones. The stench was horrible! Then they were pushed out of the fire and flesh returned to their bones. It happened again and again, as they went through the fires, and over the cliffs. it was perpetual! I saw their skeletons it was so terrible. He wept as he shared, overwhelmed at what he had seen. He cried out, "we must reach the lost, they were all lost we must reach the lost!"

Later that same year, in a severely-persecuted area near Guantanamo, where we have visited for many years in a tremendous time of ministry, we were gobsmacked at what happened. God is amazing. We experienced the greatest move of God we had ever seen in the region. We had seen miracles, signs, and wonders before, with people falling on the streets when we prayed, people slain beside rivers when we prayed. God was moving in power, but this was very different! I believe, as we learn to steward and carry the glory, we take the presence and outpouring wherever we go. After what happened in the Himalayas earlier, I carried it to this remote area of Cuba! Because of the restrictions, always, we finished early in this persecuted church in a strongly-demonic communist area, but not that night. We finished everything about eleven o'clock. What excitement at what God did! Unbelievers crowded into the house church; crowds gathered all around the property and overflowed into the road! Unlike previous visits, when we came in secret, the pastor had announced our visit! A close relative had died that day, and his wife grieved. After preaching, prophecy, and prayer for healing, incredible, we experienced move after move, wave upon wave of the Holy Spirit. They removed most seats to allow room for people to pray, and as more fell, the more seats were removed. People wept in the prayer line, and they fell down, many at a time, in lines. The Lord touched so many, and Jesus revealed Himself too many as they lay slain for a long time. God's glorious presence became so heavy as believers and unbelievers experienced and shared of His touch.

THE 8-YEAR-OLD WHO ENCOUNTERED JESUS

The pastor's niece, a small eight-year-old girl, wept and wept as she lay slain on the platform for a long time. Suddenly, she sat up and spoke loudly. She spoke of experiencing heaven and spoke to the people from the Lord. She called the people to repent and worship for about twenty minutes! She wept as she called out. Again and again, she said the angels were around her, Jesus wept there beside her, and she pleaded with the congregation to get out and evangelise to reach the lost. This encounter unforgettable, exceptional, she preached from heaven and called everybody to a greater relationship with Jesus. The church dumbfounded, everyone present watched her encounter with amazed wonder at what God did. Before this night, no one in this church had ever encountered Jesus, and no one they knew of had ever seen angels or gone to heaven in this way! No person had ever preached as this child did. We experienced a sign and a wonder! Supernatural encounters were unlocked.

In another small church of forty persons, over two hundred came! God always takes me by surprise. About thirty to forty came to faith in Jesus, many of them children. The pastors must have advertised our presence, which is rarely done as usually we just appear and nobody knows we are coming! This affords protection for us and the church. Crowds came; the church with no room overflowed onto the street. We prayed for so many for healing. With no room for ministry, we prayed for people in their seats! God touched them all with many baptised in the Holy Spirit.

In the principal church at a children's meeting, a small boy visited heaven. After prayer, he lay slain for a long time, and when he awoke, he shared, "In my experience, a huge ladder appeared to reach up to the heaven. Angels were going up and down like in Genesis 28, where Jacob noticed the ladder to heaven. An angel took me up the ladder and at the top, showed me heaven. Jesus had a white cloak, and He welcomed me. As I looked down from the heaven, on the other side of the ladder, below were the fires of hell and demons screaming."

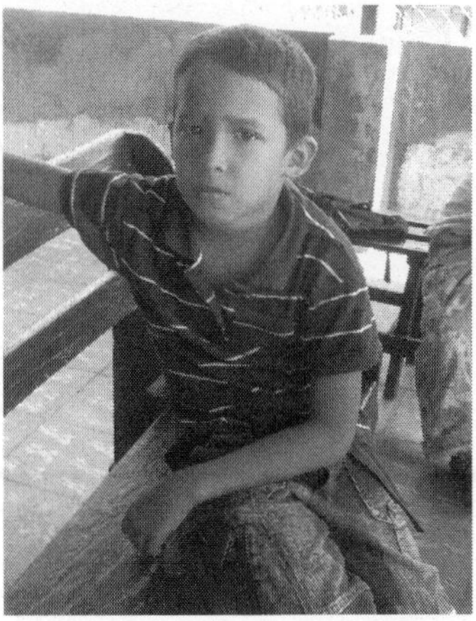

THE BOY WHO SAW HEAVEN AND HELL

As Kevin viewed the many videos that came back from the trips. He asked me, 'How can you say some of you will go to heaven, Jesus is here, He's walking in the meeting, He's here, He's touching you now, He's kissing you. You're receiving flowers from heaven. You don't go to heaven!"

What a problem or was it? I pondered this and replied, "I am declaring and decreeing, proclaiming by faith."

As a result, and because we needed to validate what was happening around us. I read books listened to podcasts, by Patricia King, Bill Johnson, Kris Valloton, Heidi Baker, and researched early revivals all of which validated declaration and faith. That I could not declare from an earthly position but because my spirit man is seated with Christ in heavenly places I could declare from my position in Christ as a new creation.

No toilets. Just filth everywhere. The sides of the roads were atrocious. You took extreme care where you placed your feet! The homes with beastly long drops and Asian toilets spotlessly clean, but what difficulty balancing with all the Indian clothes pulled up and down. But in Bulgaria, the worst bathrooms I've ever found, they were just awful, and at one home, the short drop abhorrent as you had to lift your clothes and stand extra carefully to aim because the liquid lay close to the surface, and with the splash, your clothes quickly contaminated, but you do all this for Jesus, smiling, happy, it's just part of the deal! If you come home with bugs, after treatment, they're soon gone! Every difficulty is minimal as when we visit, we have a choice to leave when we choose. They live there all the time. For them, there is no escape! We can escape and return to luxury, a flushing toilet, clean running water, a shower that works, scalding water in abundance, pure clear running water we can drink! But it's worth it all to experience the peace the presence of God brings, to encounter the glory of God, to watch Him change lives and transform people. Would we have it any other way? Absolutely not!

In Myanmar, 2011, a man shared how he travelled to the gates of heaven, and in front of the beautiful, immense, golden pearl gate stood an ugly black thing (a demon) that tried to stop him entering. An angel came and chased it away. Another appeared, and angels chased it away.

When in heaven with Jesus and the angels, he glanced over to the side and in horror, looked upon an immense black hole with raging fires. Whilst with Jesus, He gave him an inviting red and green fruit, which he eagerly bit into, crisp and crunchy, with juice that welled out and ran down his chin, like he had never tasted before, like an extra special exotic apple words could not describe. There, on a beautiful table, a small, costly, ornate gold-lined box sat covered with bands of gold and many red, green, and purple gems. During this time, a woman visited heaven encountered Jesus, and He took her to a garden, where He gave her multicoloured roses and armfuls of beautiful golden daisies like the sun in all its brilliance.

We visited Chitwan Park, West Nepal, in 2012 as a highlight of the trip. As we rarely had time for any sightseeing and caught the sights as we raced by, it thrilled us. But we watched the usual things—elephants, snakes, crocodiles—for the other animals like rhino and tigers slept that day. If you go in the middle of the day, you won't find them.

There, we had another tremendous conference in a big church built by the Koreans. Koreans have planted and supported churches all across Asia. Several hundred believers attended. Jesus touched many and changed their lives. There were many wonderful testimonies shared. I include some of them here:

A boy worshipper shared he asked for a flower from heaven and prayed. He chose a flower with a most beautiful fragrance and put it carefully in his pocket. God told him, "You have to give away the fragrance to the others." A man warring in the Spirit rebuked demons.

A young girl, in an encounter with the Lord, went up many stairs and passed through an area where she found a magnificent, enormous, ornate building. As she had never seen a palace, she was hesitant to call it that. The translator named it a palace! Whilst with the Lord, she saw many other children wearing white dresses dancing and playing. When she came down the stairs with Jesus, He told her, "I will wait for you." There, she watched as many boys overwhelmed by a brilliant white light repented in God's presence.

Another girl travelled to heaven, where myriads of beautiful butterflies of all colours flew everywhere with many small brilliantly-coloured birds. Jesus took her to an amazing garden laid out in squares, with different varieties of flowers in each square, everything perfectly colour-coordinated. He gave her armfuls of beautiful flowers. Other children cried out to God for the flowers. A young woman experienced the fire and repented as an enormous ball of fire came towards her. It covered her and brought tremendous peace like she had never before encountered. Afterwards, many young men repented and glimpsed the Lord. It was here that the older woman wept and wept after a heavenly experience. Concerned, I asked her what happened. She said she was in heaven with Jesus, and He took her to a beautiful street paved with gold, and amazing houses lined the street. She, a village woman, had never seen houses like it. They went into a house and walked all through it, and Jesus told her, "This is your house!" She was so happy and ran through the house, looked out the windows, and examined everything, and then He said, "Now you have to go back!" She was weeping because she wanted to stay there with Jesus.

After worship, about forty people came for more ministry. What an exceptional day with a fantastic breakthrough. Because of the foot washing, an outstanding presence of God came to touch and change those to whom we ministered.

THREE GIRLS WHO HAD HEAVENLY ENCOUNTERS AND SAW JESUS.

In winter in Kathmandu, on 20 January 2012, we experienced freezing and cloudy weather. With enormous cost for all these conferences, we always go in winter as it is the cheapest season! Tourists visit in summer. When rain clears the horrendous pollution, you catch glimpses of the magnificent mountains. On the outskirts of the city, in a smaller conference because of the rain and cold, fewer people attended. A team from all over India travelled, gathered by our friend *johnababu*. Often the teams were like the league of nations as few people spoke English and some had no common language. Translation became difficult with misunderstandings rather common.

Many journeyed to heaven. God moved tremendously. Gopalje's wife Gangka and I prayed for a young woman, who jumped up and down, grabbed us by the necks in a fierce grip, and kissed and kissed and kissed us all over the face. She shouted in English, "I've got a daddy! I've got a daddy!"

As she became more and more excited, her face glowed. Later she spoke at the front, testifying of her transformation, that she experienced heaven, where Jesus kissed her and gave her flowers. Though she spoke no English, she spoke in English and shared she had a fantastic revelation of God as a Father. The love of God transformed her.

THE YOUNG WOMAN

Testimonies are delightful and encouraging as we hear what happened in individuals' lives. They release power to believe and a greater level of expectation for God to move. I never tire of hearing testimonies as they release more faith and power for more wonderful things to happen.

People get so fired up when they hear God has done great miracles, signs, wonders. It encourages us all to press in more and be hungry for God. God blesses as He recognises hunger.

One lady visited a large exquisite mansion, with a peaceful atmosphere, where nearby there were rivers, gardens, flowers, and many brilliantly-coloured birds flew close by. She shared the birds came so close you could almost touch them, and when they sat on her shoulders, she could hear their songs, and she understood them! Jesus touched a woman, and her body became beautifully warm and comfortable. Angels drew one lady up a magnificent staircase, step by step, as they lead her by the hand. At the top were spectacular coloured flowers and hundreds of singing birds like nightingales. Jesus gave her flowers. In a series of very detailed visions, the Lord showed her the heavenly realms. She travelled in a heavenly bubble, through which she had an amazing view.

Many people received exquisite flowers, like none they had ever seen before, from Jesus. There followed much deliverance. After freedom, they worshipped with exuberance. God is amazing. They (maybe the angels) dressed a man in white robes, and he walked with Jesus.

A girl who journeyed to heaven three years before at Gopalje's church shared that it became a turning point in her life, and hungry to read the word, she now attended Bible school. After a woman slithered across the floor like a snake, we delivered her.

Whilst several people laughed, and I encouraged others to release the joy, the fire fell, and three women were burning up, shouting and shaking, touched by the Lord. When the fire hit, one lady involved in witchcraft gave ear-piercing screams, but the fire brought purity to cleanse and free her. The pastor and a leader received life-changing prophetic words from the team.

Sherry had a word for a woman about a swirling wind that took her up to heaven, Psalm 23:5 and Psalm 91:11-16, that she would encounter God at the banquet table. She watched her walking down the street with her enemies in entire protection. The woman said that she looked into the heavenly realm in a vision, a swirling wind took her up to heaven, and Jesus gave her a flower.

SHERRY AND DENISE

We first visited Pastor Rathnababu and his family in 2012 in Kakinada. After a wonderful evening and ministry, the suffering began when the radicals beat two ladies walking away from the church. They had built a shrine close to the church, and no amount of protest by the believers made any difference, they would not remove it. The pastor spent much time with the police trying to sort it. Shortly after we left, arrested on false charges, he spent a week in prison! Six months later, his son Madhu answered a call for help at the gate at 2:00 a.m. Once he undid the padlock, men burst in and beat him around the head and chest until he lost consciousness. After hearing his screams for help, the family rushed to his aid, but too late as he died! They prayed and prayed, cried out to God, and rushed him to the hospital! On the way, God touched him, healed him, and told him He had a plan for him to work in ministry, to be a pastor. Healed, resurrected, and restored, he now works in the church and has three small churches. Several of his family members have travelled with us around the nation and Nepal as members of our teams as we seek to empower leaders to catch the fire and passion for what God does to release God's breakthrough vision.

MADHU AND FAMILY

Realities, bad things happen to God's people. What a shock! A visit to the office safe in Mandalay, I opened the bag stored there for safekeeping to discover amidst the envelopes, someone had removed money from the middle of each envelope in a way to avoid notice. The management took no responsibility, and the police even less, as we could not claim or report money undeclared on entry to the nation!

The sign said, "Sunrise Hotel," but that's about the time you slept! In this place, noise. Temples and festivals all night, psychedelic lights flashing outside the windows, AC that didn't work, no scalding water as they turned it off at the mains every night! Power dysfunctional. So many problems. Every arrival in the fifteen years, I stayed there. I sorted the issues, hour upon hour, for those who travelled with me. Perry and Shona were in a pleasant room by the elevator. I arrived to check on them, and there they were, uncomplaining, sweltering at 40-plus degrees, with hand fans and no power! Lights in the ceiling that flickered on and off all night. I engaged two men hotel workers for hours each visit sorting and fixing the issues: paper over the lights, cardboard and blankets over the windows, fixing the hot water, turning it on in the office, which controlled it, changing AC filters black with old age! A challenge, until one day, I had enough! Enough is enough! A phone call to Samuel, and I moved out thirty minutes later. Anywhere must be better!

This time to a new Chinese hotel with no soft beds! All the beds hard like sleeping on the concrete, until after searching every hotel room on multiple floors, to my relief, I found a soft mattress on a small trundler bed! What hilarity came when the staff dismantled my room and installed this bed, but what relief when I slept on it!

After all the years of travel in 2012, a man robbed me and in a Christian hostel! After I returned to Bangkok from the ministry throughout the Himalayas, I collected Lyndsey from the airport as she arrived to travel with me to Myanmar. We had several days to relax in Bangkok, and two days later, I asked the receptionist for access to the safe to get money. There, I made an appalling discovery. On examination, someone had opened the bag of money locked in the safe, and I found a large sum missing! Thousands of dollars missing!

Shocked and alarmed, I retreated to the bathroom and privacy with the bag, to examine my discovery. But no mistake! A major amount missing! Every year I left the money for Myanmar in the safe as I carried too much money for safety in India and other nations! I checked my iPad for the amounts and dates to be sure and to show proof of its existence! Horrified, I announced it all to the manager, and it appalled him! When we visited the police, they laughed and said, "What rotten security!"

The hostel needed to change it. We notified the board president of the guest house. This shocked her! For light relief and to break the stress, Lyndsey and I visited McDonald's to have a drink and food, so concerned, horrified to find thousands of dollars gone! Not a few hundred, but thousands of dollars! Exhausted, we returned to fall into bed traumatized.

We woke unable to forget our ever-present drama. Distraction necessary. We visited the movies to enjoy the *Iron Lady*; it broke the stress. We did trivial things to kill the time: walked, looked in the markets, ate at pleasant restaurants. All the time, we prayed God would somehow overrule and we would have a miracle. After another day out on the town, visiting the mall, riding the canal, sightseeing, and eating, we arrived back at the guest house about 6:00 p.m.—and they found the thief. The manager awaited.

We travelled with him and the board president to the ancient first Presbyterian church in Bangkok, where we met the culprit! He apologised to us, and we forgave him! We prayed for him. Happy and relieved, we took solace in ice cream and returned to the guest house by a beautiful boat. The board took full responsibility to repay the money and sorted the details concerning the reparation. By my return trip, they had already installed a new safety deposit system. As Christians on our request for mercy, the board allowed the man to keep his job but away from security factors affecting guests. Relieved, we flew to Myanmar the next day.

We needed a house for a changing season, we needed a base as we travelled from A to B to C to D all over the East Coast to Florida, Georgia, Tennessee, Iowa, Oklahoma, Nebraska, New Mexico, even California and Indiana. This became very taxing as we travelled thousands of miles, and we needed somewhere where we could just hang out, put books on a stand, put stuff, just take time-out in between travel. Our friend Larry in Indiana said, "I've got just the place . . . We visited to look"

Remember the horse and what I said, "The next thing offered, I will accept!" A wreck but at only $12,000, we took it! Our friend fixed the roof, pumped the six foot of water out of the cellar, and now the job of renovation. A house with many broken windows, the neighbours thought the city would bulldoze it as the pigeons lived there; they called it the bird house! God doesn't ask us to do the possible. He reveals the impossible and asks us to do what is possible, and He does the rest. This two-storeyed house, God's provision for our need.

Whilst we stayed rent free in another house provided by a gracious friend, Kevin restored that house with the help of people who came from nowhere, some on work experience from the prison at weekends. People came, painted, cleaned walls, put up curtains, washed, and scrubbed. They amazed us. Others gave us kitchen furniture and renewed the kitchen. The firm came and replaced windows throughout, and the entire place revived. When we moved into this ministry house, friends came from Chicago for the opening, which we so appreciated.

THE HOUSE

Mandalay began the special times when we visited a Chin family who rescued children. They had eighteen children, nine of them new. Six came from the Wa tribe known for their head-hunting and drug-trading. They had rescued these boys from being child soldiers by the rebel army or Burmese military. Their tribe opposed the gospel. The Wa tribe is a warring tribe and were again in that season fighting the military. All the tribal armies were fighting the Burmese army with guerilla warfare like that done in Vietnam. The Shan, Karen, Kachin, Karenni, Wa, and Rhakine, all with their tribal armies fighting the injustices and oppression of the Burmese military. They recognised they could not win by open warfare but by ambush and stealth with snipers.

BOY SOLDIERS

As always, a beautiful evening. The children expressed their excitement and pleasure when we celebrated a special birthday for Jesus with crowns for each child as we identified their special identities as children of the King. Each colour spoke of their identity in Christ: blue for the Holy Spirit and His presence with them, gold for carrying the glory, green for growing to be like Jesus, red for the power of the blood of Jesus, and purple for royalty. We gave them balloons, small goodies, and cake. They sang for us, and we prayed for them, and as always, the Holy Spirit touched them all as they lay slain under God's power.

CHILDREN AND THEIR CROWNS

Many times we visited the children's homes secretly or held birthday parties for them in our hotel bedroom or the hotel dining room upstairs. It was forbidden for foreigners to visit children's homes as the military government said there were no children's homes. These were times when we took extreme care to protect the families and ourselves as tourists forbidden to do so many things.

Samuel said it cost US$450 a month for the family to live! He expressed concern regarding raising the money. The family serious about prayer, Grace rose at 4:00 a.m. daily to pray. They needed money and food and shared they had no money, yet Grace sent them to buy groceries at the market whilst they all prayed. Zyee left first. He reached the market with no money and came back with an enormous bag full of all kinds of food, vegetables, rice, noodles, fruits! He met people everywhere who gave him the entire amount.

Moses hopped on the bike and drove to the fields, which they own. There, the workers gave him food in abundance, bags of beans, onions, garlic, and greens. He came back loaded with food to feed the children. Samuel met friends in the village, and without telling them the need, they gave him an extensive amount of things they needed for the fifteen children. Sarah prayed that someone would come to the house. She attended a meeting, and whilst gone, a friend brought Grace a basket of corn. Julianna, their youngest sister, came from Yangon and gave them some money for a week. God looked after them, provided more than they could have asked or imagined. He is faithful to answer when we call upon Him. Faith always releases power from God, always releases the supernatural.

During this trip, we visited an orphanage our special friend started and prayed for the lady in charge who had severe crippling pain in her legs and could not walk; in front of us, she rose, healed from the couch on which she had laid for weeks. What poverty, with twelve children and one small child had died of appendicitis because of unavailability of medical service. Our hearts were rejoicing at the healing but broken by the circumstances.

Later in 2012, we ministered at a pastors and leaders Chin conference in Kalaymyo, where three hundred attended from the Believers Church. Sister Shirley, who translated for us, shared they had never had pastors and leaders meetings with such a powerful presence of God.

CONFERENCE KALAY

BISHOP CK NOCHUMM

After many years of being unable to visit the Paradise Centre because of the restrictions we entered a new season where not only could we visit the church but their children's home which they built illegally on a piece of land on the city outskirts. The government told them they had to destroy the building as it was on a rice field and illegal. They pleaded with officials who relented when they said, "there are forty five children here…where will they go?" With little support they trusted God.

There in Mandalay at the 5:00 p.m. service, God broke out. One lady in a heavenly experience spoke in fluent English for thirty minutes, though she could not speak or understand English. In heaven, she watched many people worshipping and dancing like David danced before the Lord. As she spoke of David dancing, she danced in a Burmese cultural way, speaking the entire time. She laughed, spoke in tongues (as in a trance), walked around with her eyes shut, nearly falling down. All this a sign and a wonder. There were many levels on the platform, and we positioned ourselves to stop her falling. When I reflected on this, I could only reach the conclusion that we failed to understand that Jesus led her and stayed with her. He kept her safe, and she did not need our protection. She said Jesus showed her the way with His arms outreached, pointing, leading her on.

This experience changed her; her face glowed, and her eyes shone. She joined us to pray for the twenty drug addicts who needed deliverance and imparted the glory to them.

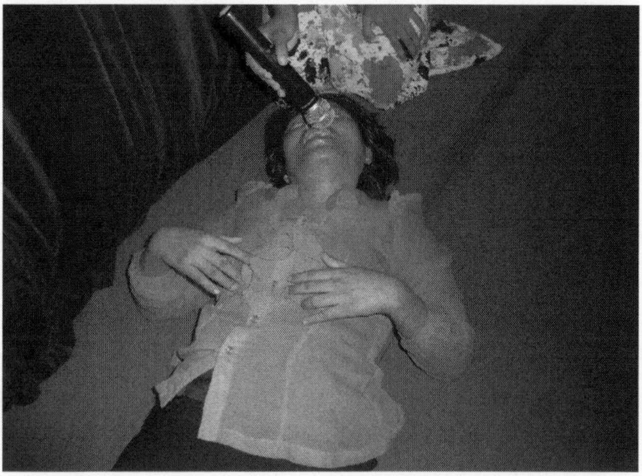

THE WOMAN WHO ENCOUNTERED HEAVEN

Jesus transformed one man before our eyes, and he had a revelation of his sin gone.

After all the men ran round the building, we prayed over them to be filled with the Holy Spirit. One other woman, in a heavenly experience, prophesied, telling the men they were stubborn and needed to repent.

She then grabbed the woman watching over her, and together, they rolled, lying on the floor, praying, and laughing as God touched and changed them.

Another woman with a history of involvement in witchcraft received ministry, and her life changed as Jesus transformed her. She too had a glory experience as God moved in power.

Issues prevailed in Nepal in 2013. On 6 January, Sunday, leaving Kathmandu, with our packed bags ready, after an early breakfast, at 7:00 a.m., the drama began! Fay lost her passport, and though we searched again and again, we couldn't find it. So stressful. Can you imagine? Have you ever lost your passport and in a foreign country? To lose a passport is undesirable! After much prayer, Elisa found the passport.

We left for Hetauda in the west, arriving there in the late afternoon. And more drama, as the hotel, inadequate with pleasant rooms, had no hot water—and Marian and I could not share a tiny narrow single bed! After much ado and a changed room, Dan came with us to talk with the owner. The manager, now more cooperative, offered us buckets of boiling water so we could take a bath! We settled in to share, pray, and wash one another's feet.

Confusion operates everywhere in this entire region! It's a spirit, and it attacks constantly everywhere. On 18 January 2013, Friday, we all rose early after a tremendous time. We were ready to go, and whilst the vehicles loaded, we ate breakfast. At 9:00 a.m., we left for the border, and there, a huge drama. We presented our passports to exit, but Fay had no entry visa! After much issue, the official informed us we must pay a huge fine, US$1,000, or five years in prison. We all prayed and asked Jesus and the official to help us. After some time passed, he asked me to go to a private room where we talked. He said if I gave him US$200, he would fix the problem. We paid the money and got out of there. He gave her the visa and stamped her passport for entry and exit all at the same time. What a lesson—check passports on entry. The official said that had the authorities discovered it, there would have been a catastrophic time. He told us she must travel back to Kathmandu to sort it! We had a miracle.

When we thought about it later, we remembered Marian and I entered Kathmandu together, and Fay had come later, on another flight. She said confusion reigned on entry, and she paid the money but never checked the stamp! They took the money and did not stamp her passport! We had been in many hotels and surrendered the passports, but no one noticed the missing entry visa! Such drama on Fay's last journey. Some weeks after that trip, we visited her in Whangarei, where diagnosed with a brain tumour, she died within weeks. We miss her. A precious, faithful, passionate follower of Jesus who loved and served the Himalayan region and those we love there.

FAY AND MARIAN.

17 January 2013, Thursday, Birtamod, Nepal

Such a noisy, filthy, dusty place, we woke early and left to travel thirty minutes to the venue. On arrival, we heard lovely worship as those who slept overnight worshipped before breakfast. What a glorious morning. Many had come a very long way, walking and busing through the mountains, and we finished early to allow their return home in daylight. After we distributed the Derek Prince books, over sixteen people shared of supernatural experiences of seeing Jesus, angels, and brilliant lights.

2013, Sikkim

Every day fantastic. We visited the church, where we experienced, two years in a row, an outpouring of fire. In the evening, in the cold and dark, we climbed down the mountain to a house meeting. A very steep and long climb with masses of paths and steep steps. How we groaned at the thought of the upwards journey! But what a great meeting. They squashed the house full of people. We prophesied over many. Numerous unbelievers came with seven or eight, finding faith in Jesus. Because years ago, Sikkim, with its capital of Gangtok, turned its back on the Holy Spirit, there have been difficulties since with ministry in the area.

The door opened to Bangladesh in 2011, and for three years, we ministered into a Bible school in Dhaka, the capital. On the flight path after the Himalayas, we stopped off in this city polluted by smoke, vehicles, and industry. When we presented at immigration, they gave our bearded friend immediate attention as now we were in a place where they honored men as they told us, "Angels lived in the beard!"

The college vehicle awaited us. We drove through this city like so many other cities in the region, but we only saw the road to and from the airport! They showed us a building where a clothing factory burnt down, where the entire shift of women burnt to death as they locked the doors to the upstairs floors after the shift began! Those precious ladies had no way of escape when the fire broke out! We arrived at enormous gates, which opened and shut until we left again. Our only sightseeing in Dhaka done!

COLLEGE

STUDENTS

Some members of the team, used to independence and freedom, found having to stay locked in the grounds restricting. In Bulgaria and Cuba, the leaders stopped visiting foreigners from leaving the compounds to roam and explore! In the ghettos in Bulgaria, too dangerous for foreigners to travel alone! Every trip to Dhaka became special. In this conservative college, God had appointments. Was it worth it? The sleepless nights, with pillows over our heads to escape the endless noise from celebrations in the area, the restrictions! Even when delayed because of my cancelled flight from Bangkok, I arrived a day late to miss the graduation at which they scheduled me to speak!

At two thirty, after a day of teaching, all students wanted prayer. Just one problem: a timing miscalculation! I should have allowed an hour or more. It's often impossible to calculate or even expect what God will do! How can we ever know what God will do? Quite wonderful, the way God moved. As we prayed for thirteen of the students, they knelt for prayer as we asked the Holy Spirit to fill them, and Jesus healed one young man with a leg problem. They laid hands on one another as they ministered for the first time in this way, so beautiful and special. It took ages. Then the girl in the middle on the floor cried and groaned. As others cried, a man behind the group groaned and wept. It became very noisy, and one other woman standing with her hands on someone was baptised by Jesus in the Holy Spirit. She spoke strongly in a heavenly language and screamed. The presence of God touched many, and as we were past 3:00 p.m., I asked the translator if I could use ten more minutes.

Other students and staff lifted the girl from the ground and did not know what to do as she seemed asleep, as though in a trance, touched by God. Bewildered that she would not wake up, they tried to give her water and honey as they thought she had fainted! They had never seen such things! She recovered after some time, but it puzzled them.

In the evening, I showed the students a video from the iPad. Excited and hungry, they wanted to understand more about God's supernatural ways. After a great time of devotions, we said goodbyes. Later the girl spoke to me, saying she had felt fire deep down right inside, in her heart, which seemed on fire. This supernatural experience changed her.

In 2013, we were once again in Yangon, visiting precious friends. What a wonderful time we had with Brother Zin Hla. After he shared about how God moved, we joined the family for lunch, and he took time to prophesy over Samuel and me. He spoke of how glory, increasing glory, and more and more increasing glory, and a mantle of shimmering white glory covered me. Such a prophetic, powerful intercessor, a leader in the nation, my special friend.

A young woman travelled with us from Indiana for several years. She became a blessing in the nations, such a blessing to us, but one day she felt to leave, time for her to move on. We missed her, but the day she finished, I visited the church just a block away, and a brother came by to talk to me whilst I worked on the Internet. He said, "You were in my vision!"

I replied, "Gary, what did you see?"

He said, "A circle, and you and I were in the circle. These people in the circle were standing strong, immovable, holding hands, but you and I were falling out under the power of the Holy Spirit. The power of the Holy Spirit touched only the two of us. It means that not all will go with you!"

I said, "That's amazing, Gary, because that's just for me! Ramanda is leaving, she's no longer going with us . . . not all will go with us!"

That's been so true of many people who have travelled with us; they've travelled for a season and then no more. But we carry on because nothing is impossible to God. We have the DNA of God, we have the DNA of a family of believers, servants, and lovers of God, and we must do what God has ordained, love people and be His hands and feet. Placed within us is that seed of faith, that seed of mission, that seed of commitment to His purpose and His plan, that DNA. Nothing can change it as we run with purpose, passion and vision to His plan.

GARY IN THE CENTRE WITH THE GROUP IN VIETNAM.

Supernatural encounters.

Divine encounters are always part of my life. Through a divine encounter, I travelled to two churches in Fort Wayne, Indiana. My Kachin brother Pastor Tu in Bangkok suggested to me I visit to minister there as they needed me. He opened the door to do so. Over ten thousand Myanmar people live in Fort Wayne, most of whom belong to another faith.

The pastor's children looked after me as the parents were absent. I travelled from Des Moines, ten hours driving and through Chicago, scary for me, a New Zealand driver, not experienced on US roads! Even with a GPS, which told me without warning to cross four lanes and exit left in all the traffic! Challenging and scary, I survived the journey without incident or accident! Happy to get there, the elder visited to instruct me regarding the service. On the Sunday morning, the elder led the amazing service where so many responded. When time came for the altar call, I invited the people to receive Jesus as their Lord and Savior. The first response came from the elder, and then the entire congregation gave their lives to Jesus. I guess it astounded me that all these Myanmar people had never been born again, and that day the entire group found a relationship with Jesus. They were religious but had no relationship. Afterwards, we called the people for healing, and crowds came, but as the next service waited to begin, they showed us into the back room, where we continued until I prayed for all. What a fantastic faith- and power-filled day. The sad thing with services like this, they never invited us back, and when I visited Bangkok, my friend Mr. Tu said to me, "Have you been back?" and I said, "They never invited me!"

On the journey to Seymour, the car broke down! Stranded on the road on the busiest highway in Indiana, alone! Frightened and challenged, a minister I had planned to meet came by and rescued me! Triple A came to tow the vehicle back to Seymour, and I drove back with them in the cab of the enormous tow truck! My life is full of adventure.

At first, it seemed God opened up Myanmar churches across the United States as we met a brother in Florida, another in Nebraska and San Francisco, where we ministered. We met the Tulsa folk we knew from Myanmar. During a special time in Tulsa, Oklahoma, I visited a Myanmar church, and there, a tremendous service followed when the Holy Spirit broke out. I stood in amazement and watched as three girls just flew across the room. On the floor, they rolled so fast, whizzing backwards and forwards, backwards and forwards, as God touched them with power. The pastor and I stood to stop, heads smashing on the pillars. A spectacular event, everybody watching, but the atmosphere became horrible! This my first time in this church, I became a little alarmed at what happened. I called the worshippers to sing the blood of Jesus, to play a worship song, to change the atmosphere because we are atmosphere changers as we don't have to live with the wrong atmosphere. People were just looking wide-eyed in amazement at what happened in front of them! Oh, thank you, Jesus, for changing the atmosphere. I lay down beside one girl to stop her rolling and stroked her long black disheveled hair as she just lay there in my arms. She opened her eyes, stunned that she lay in my arms. Tears were everywhere as they rolled down her face. Her big black eyes looked up at me. I asked her what happened; she told me huge black cords held her arms and legs as she was held above hell; the demons below shrieked and pulled her down; the fires roared with blazing ferocity upwards; the smoke swirled all around her! It terrified her until Jesus came and scooped her up in His arms and clasped her. He lifted her up to heaven. Her life changed, her face became radiant, and her eyes glowed. Church people told me two years later, when I returned, that it transformed her life. Nobody had ever seen such an experience. A very spectacular move of God. I believe, when I stopped her rolling and changed the atmosphere with songs about the blood of Jesus, Jesus came and rescued her.

Portals are interesting things. Have you heard of portals? Openings between heaven and earth, like a doorway through which angels and people can come and go. I believe, after a portal opened in the Himalayan region, Cuba and other places opened up as we travelled, releasing God's glory. Where there is great demonic activity, there is great angelic activity. We have seen great angelic activity, exceptional heavenly activity, and phenomenal demonic activity all across the region.

When we experience signs and wonders, angelic visitation and heavenly experiences we carry them to other meetings, districts and regions which is what happened in Cuba.

After Cuba I was invited to a ladies retreat in Florida with Pure Heart Christian Fellowship. There we had a most beautiful experience when my friend Sylvia stirred by the Holy Spirit bought 100 roses. After I shared the beautiful stories of the child in Cuba and the lady in Nepal who received flowers from heaven: while everyone prayed we put roses into the arms of every lady present.

FLOWERS FROM HEAVEN

The Shenandoah dream that opened up Wildwood, opened up a Presbyterian foundation to fund the provision of a house in Myanmar and the building of a Discipleship Training Centre on the property and purchase, all with a goal that our family there would be self supporting. Such memorable moments occurred because of that dream. It was at Wildwood that we met our Apostle friend from Washington DC where we ministered in her church and rehabilitation Centre just two blocks from the Whitehouse. When we visited the men's rehab centre we saw many delivered and set free. It was like being on the mission field all over again. No AC and not as hot! No power! A foretaste of the Africa that was to later unfold and again because of dreams. We were in our room at one of her special conferences, next door to a group of French speaking Africans from the German, Belgium borders when we heard the drums and prayer! On investigation we discovered they were beating the tables, chairs and walls as they worshipped Jesus in this special place.

After a never to forget episode when driving round the DC beltway we pulled in to an exit as our friend was suffering what appeared to be a heart attack. Everything happened quickly, a paramedic appeared out of nowhere, the ambulance arrived and we followed it siren screaming to the hospital where she was admitted. Such drama! About the same time we met and received an invitation to minister in Long Island at her mother's church.

We visited Long Island to minister in an amazing impacting service always to be memorable! Everyone wore white except the three of us the only white faces in this African American 1pm service.

Standing in the worship I was startled to receive a vision of the movie mini-series Roots. In this movie in the particular scene, I saw that day Kizzy the young woman who had learned to read and write was sold to another slave owner. There in the little room that she was taken the slave owner came in and asked her to pull off his boots. She pulled them off and then he raped her. Stunned that this was unfolding before my eyes there in this worship time. I agonized over what to do with this vision!

I stood there thinking, "what do I do with this? What do I do Lord? We are the only white faces in this church how do I handle this? So sensitive!" Then I remembered how Rachel had told me that week she had watched the William Wilberforce movie about the slave trade...

The Worship ended and I walked to the pulpit to preach, but I never preached that day as God moved so powerfully in the hours that followed.

I shared, "A few minutes ago I had a vision" and I repeated what I had seen and how my daughter had watched the movie about abolition of the slave trade.

I looked down at the people and said, "I'm not sure what this is saying but I believe this vision speaks to us of how Kizzy's virginity was stolen, her future as a young woman stolen, her slavery to a system, her loss of freedom. She suffered abandonment and rejection.. all speaking of her identity in God and as a person stolen...

I-am not an American but I am of British origin, and as such I need to repent for what was done to Africans as a people by my fore-bearers."

Ramada the young woman accompanying us stepped forward to say, "I am an American and need to repent on behalf of Americans."

We knelt on the floor and repented then all the women lined up and we hugged and prayed for them all. So powerful as everybody wept and we saw God's love and forgiveness poured out.

Then as we finished suddenly aware of the men I stood there and said, "Men! You are not abandoned...from you was taken your freedom, your responsibility for family, a eunuch spirit came upon and over the men and over you as their descendants as they were, and you are effectively robbed of your future and hope. There has been loss of identity, loss of manhood, loss of who you are as sons of the King.

I broke the spirits and powers operating and Kevin hugged and prayed for each man present. Such a powerful and wonderful day.

In Sikkim in 2014, at a little blue church on the hill above Rangpo, we began a wonderful conference for about 150 people. We stayed up another steep hill in the power station accommodation above the river. An exceptional time. After prayer, Jesus baptised most of those who attended in the Holy Spirit. What a tremendous move on the children who experienced outstanding supernatural encounters. They wept and wailed, touched by the Lord. One child, when Jesus came to her, said He took her to a beautiful garden with a table in the centre beside a stream of crystal-clear pure water. The water gleamed with translucent colours as it danced in a small fountain. Another child saw a brilliant white light like in Habakkuk 3:4, "the brightness of the Lord's glory," unexplainable in its brilliance. A man repented after being touched when a huge angel, all glorious in gleaming white, came and told him he must repent. Few in the church had ever had visions or dreams; no one had ever before seen angels, Jesus, or had a heavenly experience. They knew little of such scriptural or experiential supernatural activity. As the conference closed, a leader and Dan called all those with suicidal tendencies to come to the front. A great crowd responded with much chaos and confusion! After a call for order, we declared, renounced, repented, proclaimed the name of Jesus, the blood of Jesus. We told the demons to go, broke the confusion, and the people were free. In this spectacular day, God touched Dan to set him free from burdens carried.

> And the good news [the Gospel] must first be preached to all nations.
>
> —Mark 13:10 ESV

As we stayed at filthy places in Nepal, sanitiser became essential as were wipes impregnated with chlorine. Cleaning hotel rooms and toilets became an essential part of our lives in our many and varied accommodation. Birtamod, where we stayed, no exception, when in 2014, we travelled to Mangalbare in the Jhapa District. We experienced great meetings, where many received visitations from Jesus. Those attending said they journeyed as if they travelled on an aeroplane to heaven. They arrived in gardens with flowers, with brilliant colours and varieties of flowers never seen. A man with a golden crown led Elisa's mother, then she travelled, going up, up, up, and flying. When she woke from the experience, she thought she remained there! Surprised, she discovered she had returned to be with us! Another lady said she sat with the angels and Jesus in glorious golden splendor in heaven, with white shimmering light all over them. Then Jesus took her to a beautiful garden with flowers, where children, in glistening gossamer, glorious clothes, played.

In 2014, in West Nepal, at Nawala Parasi, we experienced the Spirit of God amongst those in the conference. At nights, we wished for sleep and would have liked to kill the dogs that barked all night!

> The LORD is my strength and my defense; he has become my salvation.
>
> —Psalm 118:14 ESV

After a journey of an hour beside the river through the beautiful countryside, we had an exceptional service. In the morning, there were significant words of knowledge, and God moved in power. At this very demonised place, we saw two very extraordinary demonic manifestations. Unfortunately, we had some mismanagement as not everything always goes smoothly. Demons must bow at the name of Jesus, but it is often a titanic battle until they do! A word came about purple and the colour purple, remembering the movie which featured abuse! Abuse, violence, rape. Many wanted prayer for healing and deliverance. As we prayed for healing of memories and hurts, many cried as God's love touched them. We watched them set free and come into glorious, newfound joy. Once again, we were Jesus's hands and feet, bringing and sharing His ever-present love. Because of the horrible thick morning mist and cold, the room stayed dank and a dark until the sun came out to fill the room with brightness and warmth. Each night we travelled twenty-five kilometres back to our dubious accommodation, stopping halfway for dinner in a pleasant restaurant where we cleaned the tables before eating.

A young man who spoke only Nepali and his tribal language lay on the floor, shouting in English, "I love you, Jesus! I love you, Jesus!"

After we ministered on intimacy, the move of God became exceptional with a significant move of the spirit led by Pastor Sur, a psalmist who led worship. During this time, there developed tremendous demonic manifestations. A young lady came to the platform. She squeezed and hugged Dan again and again. At first, we thought she showed love, and then it changed as she choked him! After this episode and prayer, she returned to stand on the platform and struggled with me, pulling on my dress and clothes. This small thin lady gained superman strength and picked me up and bodily threw me off the platform, not once but twice! I flew, hurtling through the air, landing in the lap of a woman sitting praying down below amongst the people. As I landed in the lady's lap, she gasped and gasped and braced herself with the shock of recovery from my forceful arrival. After the attacks, the men took that girl outside, and they prayed with her until freedom came.

The power of the testimony is so tremendous. Do you have a testimony, testimonies? Many experienced Jesus walking in the meeting and gazed upon Him in the heavenly realm in all the glorious beauty. Glorious in beauty, just as it says in the Bible. They encountered heaven, shared revelations of God's love, told us of the brilliantly-coloured flowers and beautiful flowing rivers, some of which flowed up hills, and when they swam in them, they never sank, absolute buoyancy.

One young woman, who moved around and prayed for people, found herself in heaven where Jesus gave her flowers. As though in a trance, she moved around in front of us, touching and praying over people, touching her head and kissing someone, but no one there. She shared Jesus came, and He hugged and kissed her. A man sobbed and sobbed after he encountered heaven, where he received amazing revelations. Jesus gave him flowers, and Jesus took him to show him the gardens, all laid out in total beauty.

When we pressed in and kept on pressing in declaring and decreeing by faith, God established what we declared. I found that when we stopped or got tired the moves finished. Yes, we had a great move but he was showing me and the teams that we could have more, indeed we could have as much as we pressed in for.

MINISTRY OF THE HOLY SPIRIT

In 2014, in nearby Hetauda, West Nepal, with Marian and Amber, God came, and we received many testimonies. A young woman, who had seen Jesus many times and sighted lots of demons, came to faith in Jesus. Another lady testified to going to heaven. An older man visited a dark jungle where Jesus came, and everything became bright with luminescent light. Jesus talked with him about so many Bible principles, especially His love for him and others. One lady glimpsed a person wearing bright clothes. As she travelled to heaven, she sat with Jesus, and He showed her many areas in heaven: the crystal lake and vast fields with beautiful animals she had never seen.

Another lady, shaking and crying, touched by the Lord, saw many things in the heavens; an angel gave her many scriptures for preaching, and she met with Jesus. As in the scriptures, in Revelation 18 and Mathew 22:37-39 ESV,

> And he said to him, You shall love the Lord your God with all your heart and with all your soul and with all your mind. This is the great and first commandment. And a second is like it: You shall love your neighbor as yourself.

So many testified to healings. The pastor who had nine orphans said it thrilled him as—what a great breakthrough.

AMBER PRAYED TO HAVE AN ELEPHANT RIDE AND GOD BROUGHT AN ELEPHANT. SUDDENLY AS WE RODE ALONG THE ROAD THERE WAS A BEAUTIFULLY DECORATED ELEPHANT.

In West Nepal, near Pokhara, God did amazing things at a church where few men attended the conference because they work in the Arab world for family survival.

"What did you learn?" the Pastor asked an older lady.

Inspired by the teaching, excited, she talked all the time about what she heard. When she told him in considerable detail what she learnt. He was amazed! She remembered every day's teaching in detail! He knew from Sunday's services that by the time each service ended, she had always forgotten everything said from the pulpit! Inspiration and revelation of the Spirit is needed to understand the word of God (1 Corinthians 2:13-14).

Back to North India, for three days of a most amazing miracle time, to a conference near Bagdogra, in the tea garden area close to Siliguri. Tea plantations cover North India and Nepal. Five churches attended, and approximately 150 came from as far as Jaigaon four hours travel. We experienced significant moves of God, with inspirational testimonies. Many demons, many miracles. Just like in Jesus's day. Everywhere he went he moved in deliverance and healing. A significant move of healing and deliverance! Excited, the man wouldn't stop talking. Three languages operated, and he talked and talked! Like the man in the Bible at the Gadarenes in Mark 5. He said he sat on a rock outside his house and ripped his body with stones, unable to talk, demonised. Healed and delivered during the meetings, we did not even know he had those problems! A young woman testified she thought she could never be of use to God, and Jesus changed her. She testified, this lady in green, vibrant as she shared, "I prayed, 'Lord, if You are Lord, talk to me, speak to me. I want to talk to You.' He started talking, and I saw the open heaven and huge angels. The angel of the Lord spoke to me and said, 'I baptise you in the Holy Spirit. Now pray in tongues and pray for those who want the Holy Spirit to fill them.' Yesterday, when I came here, at my house lay my mother, sick and semi-paralysed. She could not move her leg or her arm, and I prayed for her. When I returned home, Jesus healed my mother. Now she can move her arm and leg, no longer paralysed!"

DEMONISED MAN HEALED

WOMAN TOUCHED BY GOD

A young woman, a believer, whose husband left her because of her faith, had suffered much. We prayed, asked Jesus to pour His love and heal. A wonderful time, God did such phenomenal miracles in a tea garden with the Advari, a despised people group.

Mountains, we can never get enough of the majestic Himalayan range, Everest nearby. We travelled through mountains to a restricted nation. I just love the mountains! As the nation of my vision called, we drove into the capital for three days' ministry. By road along the steep cliffs, gazing up as snow peeked through voluminous clouds, we stopped to wait whilst they blasted on the rugged rough roads: rocks fell in front of us, boulders all around, to bring new improved roads, and out by plane to Bangkok for journey's end.

Another year, we had a glorious fire tunnel, where everyone walked through, and we prayed for them all. Blasted by the Holy Spirit, we saw greater breakthrough and glorious freedom.

A young woman lay on the floor in a coma all of day 1 and again on day 2 of our meetings. They took her in and out and prayed over her constantly. At the close of the conference, she was in the back room when Tim, the senior pastor, came to ask us to pray for her. We entered the back room where she lay in a demonic stupor. With some effort, we stood her up, held her forcibly, and woke her forcibly. Together, Marian and I commanded the demonic powers to leave her alone and get off her. After some declarations by us and by her, she acknowledged and confessed Jesus as Lord in her life and experienced freedom. The following year, she testified to complete freedom and her walk with Jesus.

THE GIRL SET FREE TESTIFYING

This was a marvelous time when the people were filled and empowered as Jesus baptised many in the Holy Spirit. God moved on a small girl, and twice, she experienced the heavenly realm. So frightened, she saw Jesus, and He told her, "Don't fear, don't be frightened, I love you." Tears rolled on her cheeks as Pastor Dan hugged her, and he shared how the Lord touched her.

After years of waiting, restricted, persecuted Karen State Myanmar opened to foreigners. We spent a night of travel to arrive close by Hpa An but could not cross the river as police shut the bridge 'til morning! In the pitch-black, we left the bus and travelled on motorbikes to a believer's home, where the floor, our bed, welcomed us. Everywhere we saw signs of poverty and degradation. Alcohol, drugs, tuberculosis, HIV, and AIDS, all rife in this area deprived of help for years, a war zone forbidden to foreigners. Signs said 80 percent of people suffered from TB! Suffering the bread of the church in this isolated, difficult region. At war since the British left the nation in 1948, despite the peace treaty of 2015 to which fifteen invited ethnic groups attended but only seven signed. This failed to bring peace to the warring ethnic armies (Wikipedia, "Myanmar's Nationwide Ceasefire Agreement").

We questioned the value as we had travelled so far to this our second smaller conference at Hpa An, but they shared many thrilling testimonies.

KAREN STATE CHURCH AT HPA AAN

Healed from a heart problem, arthritis, discouragement, hopelessness, rejection and exhaustion, Ching shared, "I wanted to abandon full-time ministry alongside my husband, the pastor of Mercy Church. After twenty years of ministry, Denise brought a prophetic word that brought life change and healing to my life that God healed and gave success. Denise told me in a prophecy that a big strong wall protected me, and God would keep me safe from all the enemies as the angels watched over and protected. You don't need to fight the enemy, you will have victory. Denise called to the elders of the church to take part with the pastor and feed and minister to the people. From that time, the leaders and elders have worked with us. She advised me to declare every day I am victorious and healed. Later, healed in the ministry, we had a double blessing. Before, in my life, I had decided to never to do ministry again. After that prayer, it exalted God in my life, they ordained me as a minister in my AG church. By the grace of God, God sent Denise to give us His peace and joy. That's why I am testifying today if anyone feels like me and wants to abandon ministry, stand victorious in the word of God."

She brought her daughter to show us scars on the girl's neck millimetres from the jugular vein.

THE PASTOR WITH HIS FAMILY. CHINEE HIS WIFE. THE TALLEST GIRL IS THE ONE WHOSE THROAT WAS SLIT.

We asked, "What happened?"

They told us, "A man cut the power to the house, broke into the girls' bedroom, and attacked our daughter with a knife and cut her throat! With blood everywhere, she gurgled her need for help, and her sister awoke us. We rushed her to hospital to save her life! We are so grateful to God for the warning you gave us that God had put a wall of protection around us."

La Htawlu shared, "I attended the three-day conference. The last day evening, I had amazing visions, and the Lord touched me. Denise prayed for me, and I fell down and felt the love of God. In a vision, I arrived at heaven's gates, Jesus welcomed me and hugged me, and I felt the deep love of Jesus. Jesus knelt beside God and prayed for the people. I also saw Jesus die on the cross and felt His great love for people and experienced the ultimate love of Jesus that cannot be received from people. As I stayed there in the presence, I visited paradise—the place the believer goes. There were so many believers and martyrs with their crowns and Adoniram Judson [the great missionary] with his crown."

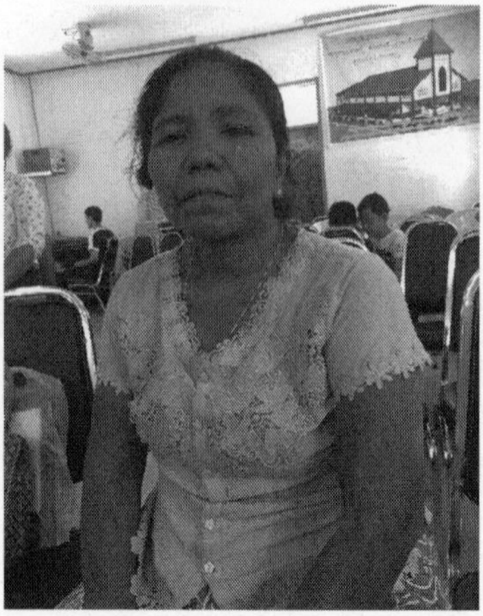

HEALED OF BLEEDING FOR 12 YEARS. SHE HAD A HEAVENLY EXPERIENCE

Sick and unable to work, oppressed and rejected by my family, my father told me, "You will always be a failure!" shared Yadanaphaw. "I live in the army base in Myangalay. Today I felt freedom and the love of God. I am delivered from all my past. Denise told me just speak in faith, then I said hallelujah and received a heavenly language, my tongue moved very fast. I spoke in faith. I received deliverance and the love of God."

"For ten years, I suffered with pain and a discharge of blood, which was very bad. My husband is a Christian, I was baptised and became a nominal Christian. After I arrived in Karen State, Denise Reid and the team came to Karen State. They prayed with me, and I was healed. That's why I came to know the true God and became more interested in God.

Until now I have been finding the grace of God and feeling a lot of grace from God. I was crying when I raised my hands to invite the Holy Spirit in.

I saw like the gate of a church and all the floor was decorated with golden plate, and it was like I climbed up to heaven at that time Jesus was wearing a beautiful dress. His face too glorious, I cannot look at His face. He was greeting me, and I was holding the Bible.

After waiting years to visit Kayah State in 2014, we travelled to a persecuted area isolated by the military. In the book *Land beyond Evil*, it featured the suffering and atrocities of the peoples in this area. As the military did not want the world to know about the atrocities, the government closed the region. Police checked our entry and exit and followed us everywhere.

Since independence in 1948, the Burmese military have oppressed the Karenni with forced labor, land confiscation without compensation, involuntary relocation, torture, arbitrary executions, sexual violence, and other violations of the rights of Karenni— all contributed to a dire situation for the small population of Kayah State, with widespread malnutrition, poor health, and lack of education opportunities.

Karenni resistance to Burmese authorities brought years of a bitter war as has the in-fighting between Karenni factions. Many peace treaties failed. The situation of Karenni worsened and displaced almost a third of the population in the region, with about twenty thousand fleeing to Thailand. Some reports suggested that the military destroyed over 2,500 villages and forced their inhabitants to relocate.

Ongoing offensives, since 2002 by the Burmese military, cleared villagers in the Karenni-Karen border areas and relocated them under military junta control.

In 2011, with dam constructions on the Salween River, the military flooded villages, planted thousands of land mines, and displaced over twelve thousand people. Local communities were subjected to forced labor, sexual violence, extrajudicial killings, and prioritised water scheduling leading to crop destruction. They ordered people off their lands with little compensation. About 80 percent of the local population still has no access to electricity (World Directory of Minorities and indigenous Peoples www:/ minorityrights.org).

For years, we wanted to visit this restricted region of great suffering and extreme hardship as many students came to the Mandalay training from the area. We knew Holy Spirit's fire to have fallen because of the suffering.

> The blood of the martyrs is the seed of the church. [Tertullian.]

Even though we had two seats each, the day on the ugly bus from Yangon was no fun. The pastor greeted us on arrival in Loikaw Kayah

State. This small city isolated and pretty with a river, lake, and hydro project nearby. The church within walking distance from our simple accommodation housed our conference. The pastor and his wife visited the Taunggyi Conference and remembered Kevin travelling in 2000.

LOIKAW CHURCH SAMUEL, MOSES AND DENISE

At the smaller conference, we had a joyful reunion with some of our old friends, former students from the training, and families that had moved back to the area after our precious brother Lahtoi had died.

What a tremendous move of God after I taught of clean hands and pure hearts based on Psalm 24. Jesus appeared to many ladies multiple times as waves of glory rose and fell. We sought God and released the glory. I learnt to declare, "Jesus is here. He's touching you now. He's kissing you, putting His arms around you. Angels are here. There are waves of glory here."

When we seek God and press in, the glory keeps coming and the Holy Spirit keeps moving. When we settle complacent that God has moved and stop seeking, then everything finishes. We can have as much as we seek! One woman received the fire, but a leader thought it was demons, and we removed them as they caused a disruption! Afterwards, when she shared, we discovered the fire touched her. She shook and screamed, burning up as the fire cleansed her.

As always, the dramas touched and entertained those attending. At night, the teaching featured intimacy, and the Lord touched four women with substantial power. One had a revelation from the Holy Spirit about her life. Jesus came to the others; with one crying and crying for ages (like a trance), when she woke, she shared she talked to Jesus, visited heaven, where she met with crowds of angels. She explained she saw the three, Father, Son, and Holy Spirit, and glory everywhere. She sat beside a crystal river, and Jesus took her to a most beautiful garden where He gave her fragrant, colourful flowers. The presence of God overwhelmed her.

Another girl, broken with travail and weeping, said Jesus came and told her He had taken away her sin, that her entire family, unbelievers, would all come to know Him.

The last girl touched by God (as in a trance), first at the front, then in the pew, came forwards, laughing, falling down. She shared Jesus hugged and held her like a baby in his arms. He kissed her and lifted her up to heaven. There, she walked alongside the beautiful river of revelation with lots of trees, with much fruit, with many people receiving the fruits. She saw the Godhead and lots of glory. Jesus told her He loved her. That night another girl saw the angels, she said it was all exquisite, and there she observed a magnificent tiger (she looked at the head of the tiger, like a Bengali tiger) looking up at the angels. Another saw huge white cliffs and many saw trees as in jungles.

Life, full of adventure, challenged and changed us. Visionaries are single-minded, purpose-driven, focused on the long-term goals. Myanmar just part of God's bigger picture, but how I loved it. God's plan released as His glory poured out wherever we travelled.

We have had so many powerful moves of God in Myitkina, Kachin State, the place of much suffering. A war zone for many years, the junta fighting restricted areas around the city to foreigners. The government sold the rights of the river to the Chinese. The people fought to stop a dam being built on the river, flooding ten thousand people's land. There are many refugee camps in the area and across the China border with thousands of refugees who have lost everything. Soldiers subject the region to forced labor, fighting, and war! The military burn the people's homes, rape the women, take the men in forced labour, and destroy the wells and fields! Families shared of living in houses in a valley, and when the warring factions shot across the valley, they hid in the cellar as the bullets ripped through their house and walls!

Shaking, they laughed, cried, wept, and even sobbed as God touched them, and many spoke of the presence of angels. One man became powerful when we prayed for him. He became like a great terracotta Chinese warrior. Doing movements like a powerful, immense man. A seraphim touched him, and he said fire was everywhere. I have seen nothing like it. His actions and walk so invincible! A girl became demonised and attracted all the attention just when God did great things. We had to call the people back to focus on Jesus. Great waves of glory came again. A mighty anointing evident. I prayed for almost all the people, and they were, as in trances, in my arms. Many children visited with Jesus in heaven, and Jesus told a woman the church must preach to the lost and drug addicts. Pastor Grace visited with Jesus. Children spoke of the blood of Jesus and many angels surrounded by glorious light. Moses brought a tremendous presence of God as he worshipped during the time.

In Yangon, we had a wonderful ladies' conference at Gospel for Asia, and some women so touched by Jesus lay on the floor under God's power for a long time. One lady got up to testify. She carried her water bottle, and she cried. Overcome by His presence as she tried to stand in the pulpit, I supported her. She said, "I sat at the table with Jesus. He looked in my eyes and told me He loved me. He said, 'Take a drink of the wine, the wine of the Lord,' and He held up the goblet for me to drink . . . I drank with Jesus."

She held up her water as tears rolled down her face as she shook and shared of her transforming experience with the Lord.

"And He said to me, 'Drink, drink the best wine, the wine of My love.'"

Wonderful what God did.

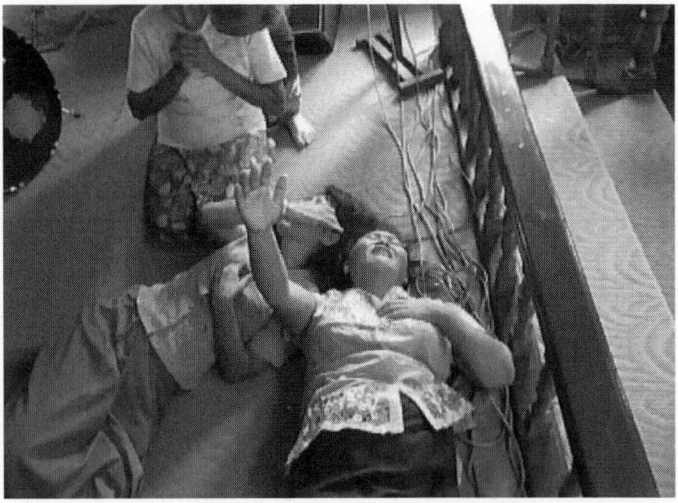

THE WOMEN TOUCHED BY JESUS

Again, in Myitkina, in the conference, day and night, we experienced the glory. With many healings and baptisms, astounded, we watched as heaven visited us. So many experienced the heavenly realm. A woman danced with Jesus for a long time. Two young men touched by the Lord were like in trances. One left us and was gone for about an hour whilst he danced, sang, rode a white horse, doing all the actions of riding a horse. Everything stopped whilst we watched. He preached from heaven, talked and walked with Jesus, and acted out all the things he saw in heaven. He told us he was firing bombs at the devil, and before our eyes, we saw him pull a pin out of what appeared to be a hand grenade and fling it! When he returned to us, he testified of being with Jesus, fighting a war with devil and seeing the monkeys and elephants in heaven worshipping Jesus.

After the hurricane in 2015, which hit the east of Cuba, a Miami Aid organisation asked me to travel for a week to assess damage. On entry, the officials at immigration were difficult, questioning where I would go, and I wondered why. They seemed concerned at my proposed destination. No one met me, and with little Spanish, I found a taxi at the back of the car park that would take me. On the road, we stopped at a checkpoint, a line of demarcation. Asked to get down, we walked through disinfectant, and they washed the car wheels with disinfectant.

I pondered, in all my visits, they had never done this. There appeared to be a problem. After three hours, we arrived in Guantanamo to discover bubonic plague, black plague caused by rats, leptospirosis, and cholera. No surprise the hospitals were full! But the churches prayed, and they had a zero incidence; no believer died and few sickened!

One pastor shared an angel saved their roof in the storm's height! Deafening wind roared, and pounding rain woke them, and they prayed, convinced the roof would lift any minute. As they watched the roof lifted, the wind caught the corners, and it seemed about to fly away, but heavy feet moved across the tin. The roof rippled, and they heard the thunder as something heavy walked above them! They said they felt such a presence of God. The roof shuddered and lifted in waves as winds captured and tried to peel it back, as the hurricane stormed. The heavy presence on the roof refused to allow it to yield! That roof immovable!

The car bomb. That year, we hired a car! We always use other believers' cars, or they find some car that an unbeliever rents to us. We travelled around the countryside and city to visit pastors, who, devastated by the hurricane, lived in desperation with destroyed houses and little food. Some slept on wet moldy beds, wet for three weeks, unable to dry them! Houses destroyed had walls lined with plastic! In one desperate situation, we visited an entirely destroyed church, no water, no power, the entire family slept in one room with no water or sanitation, just a concrete pad remained! Destroyed by the hurricane. Unlike Western nations, there is no insurance and no aid and never any government assistance.

We travelled to the countryside to visit some churches in the hills. Several hours from the city, we needed gas in the tank, yet with no gas station, we could not buy gas. When they opened the boot of the car, I looked into the back, and there, a plastic tank with no lid, and the gasoline! In amazement, I looked again, no metal tank, just an open plastic container swishing gas, and gas swished back and forth in the back of the car, in the plastic, with no lid. I thought, "Wow, this is a bomb!" and I laughed. "We'd driven in a bomb for a week!" Only the protection and the prayers of God's people saved us that week from the potential bomb.

One night a lady a church worker came to share. With a lump in the esophagus and another lump in her throat, she received prayer. Cancer!

That night she awoke, and the Lord told her He operated on her throat, inside and outside. The next day she visited the doctor, and the ultrasound showed the lumps gone, and where they had been, there were two fine scars. God operated on her throat after we prayed!

She shared that many years before, about 1993, Pastor Osias and Apostle Alipio baptised 120 new believers in the church, that I prophesied over them all that they would all be workers, pastors, and missionaries, and today everyone of them is in full-time service.

ALIPIO BAPTISM

Adias, our friend's uncle, shared how many years before he had a peptic ulcer and suffered badly with pain and problems. After he received prayer, the next day, when he went to the bathroom, he passed a ball of fatty substance and became well. In the Guantanamo district during the time of ministry, I spoke on loving Jesus, loving one another, serving one another in love, and during the ministry time, I called couples to come for prayer. When instructed to look in each other's eyes and express love for each other, I asked them, "When did you last give your wife flowers? When did you last tell her you loved her?" The married couples stood in front of each other and took each other in their arms and looked in each other's eyes and confessed their love for each other. I was so touched when one man stood there and sang to his wife a beautiful love song. Precious ministry moments!

As we sought to empower families and churches to break the poverty cycle, we started goat and sheep projects. These were, to some degrees, successful. In one area, as there were lots of wild dogs, this resulted in the loss of some animals. Survival of the goats appeared better than the sheep, as they were more hardy for the region's terrain. To provide much needed water, we built a water tank in an extreme desert area! In another area, to assist the families, we bought pregnant pigs, one for the pastor and another for the church, so they could raise the piglets and sell them, keep one, and start again. So important, not just to visit and do wonderful ministry but to leave a legacy, to change the situation. In love, we served them as Jesus's hands and feet; we brought mercy and love. We endeavored to bring transformation, not just spiritually but also physically.

On a visit to Villorio after almost ten years, I met the young woman who at eight years of age saw Jesus and preached from heaven. She said she prayed for ten years asking the Lord that she could please meet me again and the very night I was at the church she felt urged to travel from the city. She said, "I was in the principal church Sunday when I saw a great light, I tried to move away from it but could not! It was God. I saw two hands in front of me and I heard a voice that said, 'revival is coming! Tell my people!' On her request I showed her the video of when she saw Jesus. She wept and said she could never forget it was so wonderful! That night she spent most of the meeting weeping as Jesus came again to touch and reveal himself to her. He told her again she must speak and tell the people Revival is coming!

DELILAH THE GIRL WHO SAW JESUS
AND SPOKE FROM HEAVEN.

After prayer a young man deaf and dumb left the meeting only to return speaking!

Forbidden to preach with only a tourist visa, we stood in the pulpit alongside the pastor testifying (but really preaching) unless in a safe place. The Guantanamo senior pastor sent us to a house church in the downtown main street. We arrived at 9:00 a.m. for an action-packed service, with windows open, crowds of people inside and out, and tremendous noise. Hours later, we emerged after a powerful move of the Holy Spirit, with many people finding new life in Christ, many significant healings and much deliverance. In the evening, our brother reappeared from the district capital where he had spent the day. "What happened?" he asked. And we shared. He said, "In Santiago, some foreigners came. After they sent them to a house church, immigration arrived. They told them, 'If you continue to do what you are doing, we will expel you!' The meeting finished, and they returned to their hotel!"

"What about me?" I asked. "We were in downtown in a house church."

PASTOR HOSEA AND CLARI SENIOR PASTORS IN SANTIAGO, GUANTANAMO EASTERN DISTRICTS

He laughed and said, “That’s okay, you are safe, we don’t worry about you!”

CHAPTER 12

Dreams - Supernatural Encounters - Sikkim -Uganda - A Bag With Holes - Earthquake – Nepal -Myanmar -Nagpur, India

> Everything heaven contains has already been lavished upon us as a love gift from our wonderful heavenly Father, the Father of our Lord Jesus—all because He sees us in Christ. This is why we praise Him with all our hearts!
>
> —Colossians 3:1 ESV

I operate by faith speaking those things that are not as though they were and are. I use my imagination and see God do amazing things.

> If any man be in Christ, he is a new creation.
>
> —2 Corinthians 5:17 ESV

Dreams, visions, and supernatural revelation have been a focal point in my life. Because of dreams, so many things have happened. The dream of Bulgaria, and we visited Bulgaria, a simple, clear, directive dream, and we saw signs, wonders, and miracles. The vision Elisabeth received with a young woman calling her to the next room, saying, "Come over and help us," after, she received our prayer letter. Directional for her as she travelled for years with me and the teams and became my dear friend. Back in New Zealand, just after she passed, I attended the funeral celebration of her life. After I spoke, her family approached me to say, "You knew a grandmother and mother we never knew. Please, can we have a copy of what you said?" I missed her greatly, my loss and heaven's gain!

The dream of Morocco and Spain, and we travelled there, and God positioned us for His plan and purpose. With the dreams, He tested my obedience, leading, and guiding. Quite amazing that the only Roma churches open to women in the whole of Europe were in Bulgaria, the place of the dream. It opened up a tomorrow, a hope, and a future. The vision at Ashland that opened up the Himalayan region and touched thousands of lives. The Shenandoah dream, which opened up Wildwood, where we met Bruce, who opened up finance for the Himalayan journeys and opened up our amazing relationship with Nancy, the leader of a foundation that has assisted us for many years.

BRUCE

Wildwood played such a huge part as the dream unfolded. We ministered there during the week each year for years and returned many times to be part of Eight Days Ablaze. Our friendships with Bruce, Gwen and Dottie were so much part of my life. At Eight days Ablaze where we were part of the prophetic ministry team sitting at tables to prophesy over those who attended, often we prophesied late into the night and into the early hours of the morning. It was there we met Pastors from San Antonio Texas, as a result of which we visited San Antonio several times to see powerful moves of the Spirit. On one such visit we were involved on a Mother's Day with a women's meeting and there one woman was gloriously touched by the Lord. She had a heavenly experience and she as she lay on the floor with a leg raised in the air she was laughing and saying, "they are tickling me they are tickling me!" When she came back to us, she said, "there were tiny children, and they were dancing and playing all around me and climbing through my legs!" She was powerfully changed by the Holy Spirit and by this experience.

It was there at Wildwood we met China Bill who because he loved China spoke of it constantly as he had been there many times. He opened up an African church in New Jersey, and at a Teaneck ladies house meeting, heaven touched earth and several ladies had heavenly experiences bringing love and forgiveness into their lives.

Such powerful dreams, complicated or simple, opened doors, opened windows of opportunity. Positioned for God's plan, we listened to His voice as He unfolded His purpose and revealed the DNA within us. He showed us the way to open windows, unlock doors, and He poured out the supernatural.

- Dreams, visions, and revelation bring prophetic insight to birth the future. It shows this so clearly in the Bible.

> Faith inspired Joseph and opened his eyes to see into the future, for as he was dying he prophesied about the exodus of Israel out of Egypt, and gave instructions that his bones were to be taken from Egypt with them. Faith prompted the parents of Moses at his birth to hide him for three months, because they realised their child was exceptional and they refused to be afraid of the king's edict.
>
> —Hebrews 11:22–23 TPT

In another translation, it uses the words "prompted and actuated by faith." We are to be prompted and actuated by faith. Dreams do this in our lives. If you don't have dreams, ask the Lord to increase this dimension in your life, that's what I did (Genesis 50:24, 25; Exodus 13:19; Exodus 1:22; 2:2).

In a vision, He gave me a robe, a beautiful gown shimmering with glory. Jesus said, "It's yours, put it on." I did this, and it fitted like a glove, glorious shimmering glory, beautifully clothed in His righteousness, His glory. He was all glorious; the kings' daughters are all glorious within with inner beauty, shown as all glorious, nothing could stick to it or change it. It is a permanent-state glory, clothed in glory, walking in glory, releasing within us all forms of wisdom and practical understanding.

My prayer became, "Release within me, Lord, every form of wisdom and practical understanding. Unveil Your secret desires to me—the hidden mystery of Your long-range plan. Unveil Your secret desires to me, Your hidden long-range plan."

A BAG WITH HOLES? UGANDA.

UGANDA 2015-2017. The reason I have visited Africa, the reason we serve there, the reason I am alive, is for this purpose and this purpose alone: to learn how to love as Jesus loved. What a challenge Uganda has been! So different in every way from Asia.

Kevin asked, after the first trip, "How did it go?"

I declared in reply, "A bag with holes!"

"Sounds brutal!" said Kevin, but truly, that's how I saw it.

Margaret, our friend, a woman in her eighties, struggles to support Don's vision to take students from surrounding nations to impart missions' vision to reach the Islamic north and surrounding nations. When I first visited, I found an extensive property of eighteen acres but minimal productivity and ten nonpaying students! Hardly anything growing, no fences, just the brick dormitory building and the ablutions block in front of it, entirely unfinished. At a glance, easy to see this needed a team of men to start empowerment projects and finish rooms! The first place we've been where we could take a team of workers! Imagine a team of men who would finish the rooms, concrete the floors, finish the walls, and put windows in place with accommodation provided! I'm dreaming again! For a few hundred dollars, men would help finish students' rooms to achieve an increased student intake. Over five hundred students have graduated with Vision Bible School diplomas over the years. As we have finished several more rooms, student numbers have increased, with more courses introduced and property productivity. It's been an interesting experience with this bag of holes.

As a ministry, we have always sought to empower people, and with a quick glance, you could see the best way to empower this college. We started empowerment projects to assist and empower those there to become self-supporting. In a process of consultation with the Bible school team, we endeavored to assist achievement of what they desired. Because of this consultation, we bought several hundred seedling fruit trees, orange and mango. As is usual in Africa, the land leached of fertility through years of poor soil management. We began a rabbit project and were happy to put some netting as a low fence on a small piece of land. The following year, when I returned to continue the road forwards, we discussed with the team the possibilities of growing ginger, beans, maize, rabbits, and chickens. We planted more fruit trees as many had not survived the severe drought, which had rendered the ground like sand! In a visit to Kampala, we examined some rabbit farms and explored the possibility of raising rabbits and chickens. When I left that year, the team planted ginger and purchased several pairs of large pure-bred rabbits. They discarded the suggestion to raise chickens to ten weeks and sell as every day over ten weeks cost you money, in favor of another suggestion by a Ugandan to raise them to four months! Four months passed, and an e-mail arrived to say they abandoned the four-month chicken raising with no market, in favor of the two-month chickens and a favorable market! My original Holy Spirit suggestion now adopted. But the rabbits were doing really well, they had thirty large rabbits getting ready for the market with reproduction at an amazing rate! But they ran out of food for the rabbits and fed them the chicken food, and every rabbit rolled over, curled up, and died! They sold the chickens to the local market but needed to replace them with one day-old chicks. Because of travel time and cost to Kampala with accommodation, they bought the chicks locally! The chicks, diseased, failed to survive! The end of viable animal projects. Such a tragedy!

UGANDA COLLEGE

COLIN, MARGARET, DENISE AND VALERIE.

Pastor Lawrence, who lived with his family on the property filled with vision, expressed eagerness and willingness to empower the college. Happy, we sent him for several farming courses to enable the farming. Because of the desperate need for water, through generous giving and money raised through selling jewellery and bags, we raised sufficient money to drill a deep well. Students increased with progress imminent. In an assignment from the devil, a young man from a wealthy, prominent family visited the property to steal two oxen tethered at the well. Lawrence, sick in bed, woke to cries from his son, who spotted the thief. He ran to intercept the thief, but the mob heard the cries and rapidly arrived to beat the thief severely. Lawrence, with help from the neighbours, rescued him in a serious state, injured, and whilst they were seeking help, the mob returned to kill him! The police arrested Lawrence and his two neighbours for the murder and incarcerated them!

THE PRISON

The following year we visited Lawrence in prison, dressed in red, amongst others in yellow! Incarcerated for eight months with his two neighbours, they wore red as murderers! Our hearts broke, an innocent pastor imprisoned, wearing red, as did those there for rape and murder! We had to get him out! He stated, "I stay here unless they release the three of us."

Eventually, after we paid a large sum of money to release the men, the officials dropped the court case, but now Lawrence can never return to the property because that prominent family who seek revenge seek to kill him and his entire family!

For years, I had known about Uganda. Friends, Don and Margaret had planted the work in Soroti. Don appeared at church one day with grand plans for a series of buildings on this property. At the time I thought, "Wow, where is the money going to come from for such a gigantic project?"

Several years passed, and I said to him one day, "Do you think we should work together?"

He quickly replied, "Oh no! You work in Asia and I in Africa."

A man's man! The thought of working with a woman likely too much, though we were friends. But I suggested it. Over twenty years later, after he died, I had the three dreams, and I remembered we had spoken about this. After he died, I spoke with Margaret, and she said, "I don't know what to do about Uganda. I need answers!"

Dreams are very significant. God often speaks in dreams. We need to listen to our dreams, listen for the voice of God.

Three years after he died, God spoke!

I woke with the same dream, three times the same night! When you have the same dream over and over, God is speaking. Trying to reach me! The dream—plain, direct, and to the point—clearly a God-given dream!

In the dream, Margaret and I in Soroti, Uganda, in the Vision Bible College classroom!

Several weeks after the dream, from another nation, I contacted Margaret. Excited, she plied me with questions: "When did you have the dream? What night did you have it? How long ago?" After my reply, she said, "That very night everyone connected with the college fasted and prayed."

I explained to Margaret, "I am not the answer to the problems in Uganda, but it seems God is stirring me to go!"

The principal of the college later told me, "That night God spoke to me and told me everything changed!" In God's plan, I have been several times to Uganda to empower the college and the work there.

After many trips to Soroti and more work being done, we built a metal chain link concrete post fence with a gate around half of the property with a room for a gatekeeper. The college employed a watchman with dogs to protect the property. Fertilizer purchased, restored much of the land to a fertile state, a banana plantation established alongside the fruit trees, we put solar on the pump and built a big tank stand. Shortly after I visited, thieves stole the solar during a storm! Some time after another visit, I became very disheartened to discover that under cover of another storm, robbers came, cut the fence, and stole many posts! The live tree fence around the property continues to grow despite repeated efforts by neighbours to destroy it. The dogs poisoned by unknown people but likely those on the fence line!

The latest report says they're growing lots of oranges, bananas, and mangoes and feeding the students with four tons of cassava harvested and maize and crops grown on the property. The student intake has increased to forty, with students now paying fees. Though much work still needs done, the bag of holes is a bag of holes no longer, despite the many difficulties. Jesus always wins. Nothing is impossible to Him, only to people. He asked us to go beyond the possibility, the realm of the possible to the impossible, and what an impossible situation, yet God! Despite the many issues and problems, progress continues with great endurance and perseverance.

On one visit, "Come! Let's get out," the senior leader said. We followed his words and example. We visited the village with him and the leaders from the college. It took an hour to go by car. Rural Uganda, dry, a disastrous drought, the ground like sand because the rains had not appeared. Famine everywhere! We filed after him into a building where 180 secondary-level students were sitting an exam. He interrupted the exam, and they invited me to speak.

"I am from New Zealand. I am here in God's plan. This is a special day, an exam day determining your future. How many of you pray?" I said.

Every teenager raised their hand. This was a Christian school.

"How many of you read the Bible?"

All raised their hands.

"How many of you go to church?"

Again, all hands raised.

The last questions came. "How many of you have given your lives to Jesus Christ? How many of you have asked Jesus to be your Lord and Savior? How many of you have been born again?"

No hands raised! What a joy, what a privilege to lead every student to newfound faith in Jesus Christ! Rejoicing, the group climbed back into the waiting car.

FIRST SCHOOL

CHILDREN GIVING THEIR LIVES TO JESUS

"How did you make it so easy?" The bishop asked.

"It's only people who have made it hard," I replied.

Twenty minutes later, we stopped at another school, this time one thousand pupils of every level. After talking with the principal, he called the students! The entire group gathered; some in the tropical sun, others sheltered under the gigantic trees. Unforgettable. After, they sang to us with great gusto! Again, I asked the questions!

"How many of you pray?"

Everyone smiled in response, hands waving.

"How many of you read the Bible?"

Again, all responded.

"How many of have given your lives to Jesus Christ and have been born again?"

We prayed for the entire group. Another Christian school, every student knew about Jesus, prayed, read the Bible, and went to church. They had religion but no relationship with the Lord Jesus Christ. A special day, everyone born again!

BISHOP EBIASALI WITH BEATRICE

We flew into Kalay, Myanmar, to see rice fields filled with mud, water lying everywhere, fallen trees, and huge boulders. The land entirely destroyed. In July-August 2015, the cyclone Komen destroyed Chin State. The rains compounded upon ongoing flooding and contributed to the worst flooding in the country in a century. About 1.7 million people were forced to evacuate as flood waters inundated houses to their rooftops. About 510,000 houses in the country were damaged or destroyed, and many residents lost their source of income as 667,221 acres (270,000 hectare) of crop fields were damaged. The floods killed 132 people (Wikipedia, https://en.wikipedia.org/wiki/Cyclone_Komen).

ONLY THE PRAYER HOUSE ON THIS RICE FIELD WAS SAVED

Thousands homeless! Destitute! Something had to be done. We are His hands and feet to bring His presence and glory. Fancy meetings don't cut it, we must love and care. After we prayed and asked donors to help over US$10,000 came in, and we bought aid. Samuel prayed for wisdom for how to help. Alone, I travelled to assist him, and together with Moses, we travelled to Kalay on the border. Worried, he did not want to eat or drink because of contamination. People lived everywhere in blue tarpaulin tents, homes destroyed, food scarce! Roads destroyed. Some men trekked three days into Hakka, the capital, carrying bags of rice. Terrible destruction to roads and bridges, they travelled through mountains of mud and gravel. The road so bad we flew to return from Kalay to Mandalay!

We travelled to a village high in the hills towards the India border, destruction everywhere. The Lord warned this village to prepare for a disaster. They fled to higher ground, away from the river. Within seconds of their departure, the river rose and destroyed the entire area. Mobile phones are amazing; they caught on video their homes, the bridge, everything taken by the river!

We arrived at the site. Had we been a minute later, the well would have been drilled beside the toilets! There is little knowledge in these regions regarding faecal and ground contamination for fresh water. God's timing is always perfect.

THE WELL ABOUT TO BE DRILLED

Tarpaulins, food, and building materials so necessary, but most of all, Jesus's love as we are His hands and feet! All the people lived in desperate conditions, some with nothing! Just a tarpaulin to sleep under. They all gathered, and after a brief greeting, we explained what it means to follow Jesus. Hundreds of them gave their lives to Jesus that day. Pleasure came to so many who had nothing. I took a bag of several hundred wrist bracelets verses. They lined up eagerly, anxious to receive them.

The pastor shared a natural dam in the hills broke and totally destroyed a village. The people woke at 2:00 a.m. with a tremendous noise. They could not find the cause! At 3:00 a.m., they heard it again.

They were all outside their houses, puzzled, looking. They searched everywhere but could not find the cause! At 5:00 a.m., again, they searched for the noise! One hundred acres of mountain, the dam, and mud descended on them. They were all saved as they were wide awake and climbed in the trees. Even people of eighty years were in the trees. Samuel laughed and laughed as he told me a lady over eighty must've been desperate because she scrambled way up in the tree, escaping the onslaught of the water, the mud, and the slime.

Samuel, Moses, and I visited areas where the people were without food and could not eat the mouldy rice sent by the government. Other places had little food to feed thousands of people. Blue tarpaulins lined the roads as newly-homeless people sought shelter and fields once productive with rice, now filled with mud, huge logs, rubble, and gigantic broken trees. They showed us how mud filled their homes up to ten feet deep! Enormous logs washed down stream-destroyed bridges. Families sought help in the monasteries on higher ground as homes became uninhabitable.

THIS IS ALL SHE HAD...

DISASTER AID. FCM RAISED 10,000 USD TO HELP.

A RICE FIELD DESTROYED

Sick, I flew back from Myanmar! Sick in Bangkok. Cholera, severe diarrhea, my mouth coated white, infected with thrush, on much medication. After collapsing in the bathroom, I lay on the floor at the back of the plane all the way from Bangkok to Japan. Samuel later apologised, "I shouldn't have taken you there!"

I replied, "Rubbish, we needed to do it!"

After my return to the USA, whilst staying with our friends in Tamaqua, Pennsylvania, I collapsed with malaria! Bad things happen to God's people, but none of us will die until the day God decides!

> Your faith and love rise within you as you access all the treasures of your inheritance stored up in the heavenly realm. For the revelation of the true gospel is as real today as the day you first heard of our glorious hope, now that you have believed in the truth of the gospel.
>
> —Colossians 1:5 TPT

That year he pursued me, this leader of a Myanmar movement. "Please come for our annual conference?" he persisted.

"Where is the conference?" I asked.

"Chin State," he said, "two days' travel by road."

Dreadful roads, mud, rough gravel, hills, two days in a van, not an easy prospect.

"No way!" I said. "Too difficult for this woman! I pass on that one."

But he continued to pursue me by e-mail and the Internet. But when the story changed, I considered the matter and agreed. The conference in Yangon was doable as I would be close in Bangkok. To be available for this exceptional conference, I would join him in February in Yangon the day before it started.

As I arrived late at night, the intrepid leader, who met me and booked me in at the hotel, said, "Sleep well, we're leaving in the morning for Chin State!"

Shocked, I replied, "I thought we were in Yangon!"

"Oh no!" he replied. "No, always in Chin State!"

After I rose early, I phoned Toi San Aw (Samuel), my spiritual son who I had watched grow to maturity.

"Hi," I said. "How are you?"

He replied, "So when does it start?"

I said, "It's not here, it's in Chin State Thantlang, thirty miles from the capital Hakka!"

There was a shocked reply. "You can't go there! The road is frightful, too bad! Mud, gravel, tough! You are a foreigner! You can't go there!"

"I have to!" I said. "We leave in an hour!"

"I'll pray for you!" Samuel sighed and said.

An hour later, we left for two days' travel in a van, eating, sleeping, only stopping for the bathroom and food! Roads like I had never seen before, rougher than rough, eating dust if the windows opened. Sitting, sleeping, listening to music, waiting for the journey's end! Thinking, wow, we have to return this way. A journey of endurance. A brief stop at Hakka to visit people in United Nations tents made homeless after the cyclone destroyed their homes. Along the road in the distance was a hunter with a cat slung round his neck! "A small tiger," they said.

ROADS TO CHIN STATE

We stopped on a steep incline in a small town far from anywhere. "Here we are," they said.

We all piled out. With foreboding, I looked up.

"It's up there," he said, pointing upwards. "We are staying up there!"

I looked up three floors at the steep stairs! With dismay, I said, "I can't go there."

"That's where we're staying," he said.

Up the stairs, I climbed with knees that did not want to climb stairs! At the top, we washed with a bucket, boiled the water, used a large flask in this cooler climate.

This was a Pentecostal church without pentecost. Truly a divine appointment orchestrated by God. Five thousand people from across the nation danced and worshipped, hungry for the word of God. What an opportunity to serve, to minister His love and presence. The Lord touched hundreds, and the Holy Spirit filled them at the altar call after I preached.

After a wonderful morning, we shared lunch in a downstairs room eating things like heart, intestine, dog, and worse but some normal foods! Our leader, the bishop, said, "This afternoon there is a healing meeting at 1:00 p.m. We can't be there. We have told the people to come for prayer. It's upstairs. You can do it."

On enquiry as to "why me?" the reply was "So many people have been healed at my church in Yangon when you prayed."

"Okay!" Surprised, I obediently said, "But I need music, a microphone, and an interpreter."

"No problem," he said.

At 1:00 p.m., with a pastor interpreter, I climbed the steep stairs to the church above. Open-mouthed, amazed. My eyes widened as I saw the crowds. They packed the huge church full of people, hundreds. No room for anyone else. We struggled to get through the crowd to reach the front. Climbing up to the pulpit, we looked for the microphone! No microphone! No music! No atmosphere, only God! But at least there was an interpreter.

We braced ourselves, smiled at each other, and began shouting. About fifteen minutes into our delivery, a senior pastor came by, took pity on us, and provided a microphone, which the translator used. After delivery of the message, I gazed at the people. How could I pray for them all? Too many people! I looked out at all those people and said, "If you're sick, got pain, whatever the problem, touch your body and receive by faith. We are a people of faith. It's not about how you feel or what you see. Receive by faith."

They touched their bodies, and we prayed. "The name of Jesus, the blood of Jesus, receive your healing by faith. He heals you now. Thank Him for your healing. Receive by faith. It doesn't depend on what you feel. Receive by faith. Raise your hands if Jesus has healed you," I requested. I looked out at the people, and they raised all their hands.

"Please go to the meeting," I said. "It has started now." The worship resounded from the meeting at the tent below.

No one moved. They all sat there and waited. The translator and I gazed at them in dismay. Well, I guess now we must pray; we concluded.

We invited them to come for prayer, and they mobbed us! Sitting on a small stool, people came from all directions, and we touched and prayed for all, many at the same time. It was endless, so many hundreds of people all wanting prayer.

A crippled man carried his crutches and left them on the platform. A man approached, tears streaming down his water-logged cheeks as he spoke for the first time in three years because of a previous stroke. So many miracles. It was utterly wonderful.

A child, unable to speak for three years, spoke. Truly, this place was God's appointment, God's plan, God's purpose unlocked.

A man, who married an ex-worker, suffered with kidney failure. His wife wanted them to go to Thailand for a transplant. They travelled very far for prayer, convinced he would be healed. Prayed for in the meeting, he later shared when he visited late that night for prayer, he felt better, stronger, and could now eat normally. We prayed and blessed this precious couple.

Late that night others came. A pastor, unable to escape the meeting, came for prayer; his arm had a problem, and after prayer, he was extremely excited to find his arm healed. God is wonderful. At midnight, after praying for many, we retired to bed. What a day. God delights to heal and deliver His beloved people.

> God will continually revitalize you, implanting within you the passion to do what pleases him.
> —Philippians 2:13 TPT

The following year, we returned to another Chin State area close to the India border, accompanied by my nephew Andrew and his daughter Gabriella. A smaller national conference, but again where we saw signs, wonders, and miracles. Late at night, after the close of the conference, they carried a crippled man lying on a pallet to where we slept for prayer. After prayer, he rose and walked!

We visited Myiktina after twenty hours by train (the worst in the world). It rocked and rolled all night. Later Samuel told me he thought it would come off the track as it was the first train since a terrible accident!

Such wonderful testimonies, the girl wept as she told us, "God told me He loved me. Jesus told me He loved me, Jesus gave me a large circular golden cup. After that, I saw the last supper cup of communion, and Jesus gave it to me and said, share it with others. Jesus said, 'I love you so much.'"

A lady who told us, "I was running and running until I arrived in a very dry place, and all the ground was crisp, meaning the people's hearts were dry and crisp and fragile, needing the good news, needing encouragement and prayer. God told me to preach the gospel and encourage them and pray. My spirit went up to heaven, and I was participating in praise and worship and dancing, then I was praising and joyful. I was dancing, saying, 'Hallelujah! Hallelujah!'"

An older lady who came in weighed down and sad, left rejoicing. She said, "I felt the love of God deeply, more than I have ever felt it. More than I ever had before, I understood God's love was more than a husband and a wife. Nothing can stop it. I never understood this before. It was a revelation to me. When I was praying, I was just praying what I need, but today I understood this, and when I did, I felt so happy and so sorry. I had a revelation of God's love."

The Nepal economy, terrible since the earthquake devastated the nation. People queued for hours to get kerosene for cooking and cars line the streets waiting for gasoline! A magnitude 7.8 earthquake struck Nepal on 25 April 2015, toppling multistoreyed buildings in Kathmandu, the capital, and creating landslides and avalanches in the Himalaya mountains. Nearly nine thousand people died, and over twenty-two thosuand suffered injuries. [Apr 3, 2018 2015 Nepal earthquake: Facts, FAQs, and how to help | World ... www.worldvision.org > disaster-relief-news-stories] The amazing thing about the earthquake is that it happened at midday on a Saturday. Churches meet from 10:00 a.m. to midday, Saturday. No people in churches died that day, as churches all finished at 11:55 a.m., and every person had left the buildings when the disaster happened! What a miracle! Our God is the God of the miracles. His timing is excellent.

In 2016, Nagpur called. Why did it call? After several years of pain in my knees, one knee in particular, I visited a specialist on arrival back in New Zealand. He greeted me to ask how I felt, and I said, "Fine!"

I gave him the X-rays, we discussed the problem, and he announced, "Your knee is finished!"

I said, "Well, what can I do about it?"

And he said, "You need to see me at outpatients."

I asked, "When?"

"Two or three months," he said.

"That's no good! I came to see you to speed the process. Surely that helps?" I asked.

"Not at all," he said. "I'll book you at outpatients!"

I researched surgery around the world. With my busy life, I had a plan, a DNA. I could not stop for all that time! There remained much work yet to do.

I called orthopedic outpatients and spoke with the charge nurse. "What are the criteria for having surgery speedily? How can I get a speedy appointment?"

She replied, "It's a two- to three-month waiting list, except if you meet the criteria."

"What is the criteria?" I asked.

She replied, "A, B, C and D!"

I asked again, "What does it take to get A or B or C or D?"

She replied, "Oh, nobody ever gets an A and B. Everybody always gets C and D."

Stunned, I said, "What do you mean, nobody ever gets an A and a B? How long will I wait for the surgery?"

"Oh, perhaps two years!" she said.

"Oh! I can't wait that long!" I said. "I'll go to India!"

An alarmed silence greeted me, and she said, "Don't do that! What happens if you have complications?"

I replied, "Don't worry, the moment I have complications, I'll be on your doorstep to see you!"

She laughed and said, "I'll see you in outpatients!"

The conversation ended. I researched Asia, decided on India, and as I had a current visa, with Ros as a companion, we travelled to India!

After a week of holiday and strengthening exercises, swimming in the south of Thailand, we flew to Nagpur. Surprised to find no one there to meet us, some helpful onlookers phoned the hospital to ask who would come to collect us! Shortly after the call, someone arrived, and they transported us to the hospital with apologies. This an important religious holiday. Most English-speaking staff were on leave! We cleaned the room on arrival, and the staff, embarrassed, asked the maids using our materials to finish the task! And this the third world! Grubby!

Two weeks and I sealed the deal! There in the orthopaedic hospital in Nagpur, I had both knees replaced on the same day, not one, but two. After investigations for the first knee and surgery scheduled, I asked the surgical team, "Please, can you check the other knee?"

When they did, they said, "The knee is finished, but it will last another couple of years, so if it's not a big problem, you can wait another couple of years."

I thought about this, and in that moment, I decided! After all, now in Nagpur, I paid the money for one, I had enough for two! I travelled, I had a companion, we were there. Why only do one leg? Why not have both fixed? Why not finish the thing and live a normal life?

An incredible talking point attracting much attention as the computer sat on the bedside table showing pictures of the nations on my screen saver. Visitors and patients alike paused at my door and gazed into the room. They asked constantly, "Where is that?"

At the first interview, I sent the doctor away. His English inadequate for the required health check. I told him if they did not do better, I would leave! After several apologies later from senior staff members everything became okay.

NAGPUR HOSPITAL

Limited English created some issues, and a wonderful younger doctor often retreated to my room to escape the busy life. He shared that when I rang the bell, the nurses in their station below froze and ran to get him for help to understand what I wanted! What a joy to share with him the way to new life in Jesus and show him tremendous videos of supernatural experiences and miracles. With a beautiful soft spirit, he later told me he was hungry to hear of miracles, signs, and wonders. On my return to New Zealand, we sent him a Bible to assist his search for a deeper spiritual relationship with God. Of another faith, he trusted Allah and had a tender heart very open to the touch of God. We held precious times with other staff members, and when we came to leave, the maids wept and to our shock, tried to kiss our feet.

I asked the surgeon, "Could I have both knees done?"

He said, "This is the largest orthopaedic surgery in your body, greater than any other replacement! We don't do them both at once on the same day, usually a week or weeks apart. But if your health is okay, we could make an exception."

I phoned Kevin in New Zealand and said, "I'm having both knees done!"

They did extra investigations, put the surgery back another day, and on Sunday, 30 March, I had total replacement of both knees, with two weeks in hospital for follow-up care and physiotherapy! Amazing really when I recall that I travelled by faith to Nagpur in Central India, knowing very little about the hospital or about the situation, never dreaming I would have both knees done and under local epidural! They didn't do general anaesthetics there! Had I known in advance, it would have affected my decision. But they put me to sleep with a sedative. When I woke halfway through, I said, "It's a little sore!" Immediately asleep again! I never dreamt I became only the eighth foreigner that year to have surgery!

Infection control paramount in this grubby place, yet clean by other hospital standards. Every day the nurse entered my room swinging the bottle of Dettol. We laughed as every day, from head to toe, they washed me in Dettol antiseptic.

The organisation, through which we had arranged the surgery, phoned our room each morning to ask what we wanted to eat! Difficult, as neither of us enjoyed Indian food! Sometimes twice a day, we agonised over what to eat!

A visitor in a neighbouring room advised us of hotels and places they could purchase food, and after that, we did better. She spoke English well as a university lecturer and took us round the city to see the sights! Ros didn't believe in microwaves, but that changed as every day we heated the food in the microwave!

Mobilised on day 1, walking stairs on day 4, I dispensed with the walker and discharged on day 14 to fly to Bangkok for two days, then home to New Zealand! I travelled to Nagpur for more than the surgery, an amazing time of bringing God's presence into this hospital through the many divine appointments there.

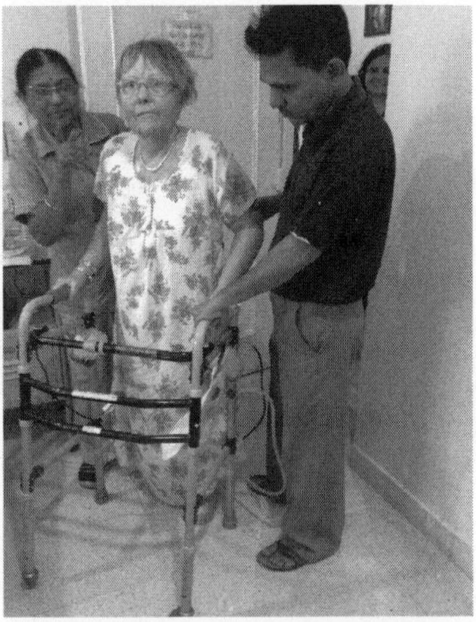

DENISE AFTER SURGERY

OUT TO DINNER WITH ROS AND THE LADY WHO HELPED US

I climbed one hundred stairs each day and walked the floors in Bangkok, where we stayed two days to take a break from travel. Positioned for His purpose and plan, we met the Pakistanis! God opened a window with these people illegal in Thailand, believers, loving Jesus, needing love and help. They had fled after suffering persecution in their homeland. A season later developed where we ministered and visited them in their homes.

Four days after arrival in New Zealand, I discovered a lump at the top of my leg, and off we travelled to emergency. Obviously, a clot! After a blood test, the staff said, "It's a clot!" and asked me to give myself an injection of an anticoagulant Heparin and said, "We will manage this in the morning! It's 10:00 p.m., and the radiologist has gone home."

I asked, "What will happen if I have a problem in the night?"

They replied, "Oh, no problem, just get the ambulance!"

I said, "What if the ambulance doesn't come?"

They replied, "It will come!"

And I said, "Why is that?"

They said, "Because you'll be breathless!"

We returned home and prayed. The next morning at ten o'clock, we returned to the hospital for management of the clot. When they examined my leg, the clot, which they had measured four inches by three and half inches, could not be found! After much ado, they said, "We made a mistake, you're fine, go home!"

Later that week, I visited my family doctor, a believer, who said to me, "You had a clot in your leg! Your blood work shows it!"

I said, "Yes!"

He said, "It's four by three and a half inches!"

And I said, "Yes!"

He replied, "You had a miracle—you had a clot and then no clot!"

Our God is the God of miracles. Nothing is impossible with him. He healed my leg because he knew my lifestyle would've changed, that everything would've become impossible in the DNA, in the vision that He had given me! What a marvelous Father we have, God who delights to do miracles.

I took a month off to recover, walked two miles and climbed one hundred steps every day. We travelled to Rarotonga in the Cook Islands to take a break before we returned to serious ministry. There, in Rarotonga, in the business class lounge, we met Martin and Wendy, our ex-pastors from the early days of ministry! He said, "I tell your story everywhere I go!"

I asked, "What story is that?"

He said, "You came to my office one day and said God has given me an international miracle ministry with signs, wonders, and miracles! As senior pastor, I had the power to release you or shut you down! In that minute, God spoke and told me, 'That's My plan.'"

It's so important to hear God's voice. Listening involves action. We can listen, we can even hear, but if we do nothing about it, what is the point?

Someone I knew called me the iron woman, and when I arrived in Myanmar in August that year, Samuel said, "I thought you would not come. It would be too much this year!"

And I said, "Nothing is impossible with God!"

CHAPTER 13

The Latter Years - The Himalayas - Heavenly Stuff - Myanmar 2019 - Jase's Visit - The Heavenly Compound - Vanishing Ink - The Wedding

We were shocked when he showed us his arms and back with many chop marks, huge scars from attacks with axes and knives. A humble man who had suffered much, Pastor Adam came from an extremely persecuted area. He shared stories of suffering when the radicals from another faith had terrorised his village and other areas. Children fled to the jungles. Families were separated. Parents were murdered, chopped, and burnt to death. He had suffered much; lost his church, his home, all his belongings destroyed by the radicals who devastated entire Christian areas throughout the region. A tremendous musician, we enjoyed his fellowship, and the people loved his music and ministry. He shared tragic stories of Christian children dying after being offered sweets laced with poison.

PASTOR ADAM WITH MARIAN AND PASTOR DAN

Without faith in Jesus, women in the Himalayan region were and are nothing more than chattels. Once they marry, the society regards them as used goods. Religion and the church say the woman should serve her husband, the church, and her family. Years ago, and occasionally today, though against the law, when the husband died, they burnt the wife to death on the funeral pyre alongside the husband's body. The society says she has little identity of her own. She only realises her identity through her husband! Single women believers may not have careers as they are told by the church they must marry, have children, serve their husbands, families, and the church. How sad we were to discover this in the discussion groups of the teachings. A single lady cried as she shared her painful reality imposed by the church. When we taught on Jesus brings freedom to women, relationships, and intimacy, it appalled me to discover a total devaluing of women. Though the women carry the baby through the pregnancy, the belief amongst women over thirty is they impart nothing to their baby whilst in the uterus. The common belief is the husband imparted the sperm and the seed. The woman is only the surrogate or host for the pregnancy. In the eighteenth century, scientists discovered the woman carried the seed and the man the sperm. But isn't it amazing that God spoke of this in Genesis 3:15. Most Bible translations refer to the seed of the woman and the seed of the man. This recognises that the women carried the seed. The world devalued women in all of society and still does in many parts of the world today.

We read,

> Then God said, Let us make man in our image, after our likeness. And let them have dominion over the fish of the sea and over the birds of the heavens and over the livestock and over all the earth and over every creeping thing that creeps on the earth. So God created man in his own image, in the image of God he created him; male and female, he created them. And God blessed them. And God said to them, Be fruitful and multiply and fill the earth and

> subdue it, and have dominion over the fish of the sea and over the birds of the heavens and over every living thing that moves on the earth.
>
> —Genesis 1:26–28 ESV

This passage shows us the man and woman were there together in the garden. God gave them the mandate to rule and reign together, together carriers of the glory to have dominion, not over each other, no one subservient, to fill the earth, to multiply. God blessed them. They were made in His image, image-makers, to live like Him in relationship with each other and Him. We are empowering women and men, not to compete but to walk together in love and unity, releasing each other to be God's image-makers.

In this past twenty years, I have done over 120 conferences in the region and seen women empowered, supernatural events, and God's glory manifest. In Darjeeling, angels visited when Paul, our son, walked the path from the pastor's house, and gold dust fell on the worshippers' heads in the meetings.

At the hotel in Agra, near the Taj, we asked the manager where we should hang our washing as after all the travel, we needed clean clothes. In a cooler downstairs room, it was a problem to get washing dry. He looked up at the roof and said, "It's not good up there because the monkeys come. They will steal your washing and throw it around."

During the night, the monkeys came. They threw everything around just as he said. That's everything: plants, chairs, tables, a colossal mess Those monkeys caused a lot of damage to the restaurant furniture, everywhere including all furniture near the foyer, and they threw our washing round the yard. The first worker to arrive used long sticks to chase the monkeys away. They loped straight back up over the walls, the balconies, and the roof. We learnt don't leave washing outside at night.

At the church in Agra, we experienced the easiest miracle, I think, I have ever seen. After the preaching and ministry, I approached an older man sitting on a form waiting for prayer. Knowing nothing, I prayed in the name of Jesus and told him to get up and walk! Unable to walk for six months after high fevers, he did just that. He walked!

AGRA

THE CRIPPLED MAN WALKED AGRA

In January 2017, at a church just an hour from Siliguri, we travelled as usual in the jeep. Another outstanding day in an exceptionally-restrained religious atmosphere! But we change atmosphere! The Bible school students came for prayer at the end. Someone had visited and prophesied and prayed for them previously! Since that visit, demons oppressed all the students, but when we prayed, all were set free. A girl, set free from drugs, healed from sexual abuse and sexual sin, gave her life to Jesus after many words of knowledge regarding situations in her life.

Three young men spoke of demonic oppression. We had words of knowledge about surfing the Internet and pornography with their mobile phones. One man shared when he spoke in his heavenly language, he flew around the room! He did not have a heavenly language but a demonic tongue! After prayer and deliverance, the levitation finished! All were set free. Deliverance is hard work. Jesus brought deliverance when He brought the kingdom of heaven to earth. Everywhere He travelled, demons manifested. One of the greatest features of His ministry was the deliverance. Pioneers know the power of the blood to bring deliverance from demons!

I took teams every year to bless and minister in the nation high in the Himalayas. We have seen much deliverance, with tremendous moves of freedom in the Holy Spirit. Eventually, we stayed three days, which allowed for two full days of teaching and ministry. To be anonymous each year until recently, we stayed at different hotels in the city. Because another group entered and immigration authorities visited, shut the meeting, and challenged their tourist visas, our tour guide changed our visa to health and fitness to technically allow for our activities.

In the Sunday service, I noticed a man shaking and trembling as I walked around the church. Others around him thought it the touch of God, but it was demons! With a word of knowledge, we prayed and commanded pornography and fornication to leave! After repentance, he testified to immediate freedom! I challenged the congregation, "How many of you are watching pornography on your phones, watching on the Internet, watching sex scenes in videos and movies?"

It shocked the pastor when at least half his congregation responded to repent and be free. How shocked we were that there in the back blocks of North India and the Himalayas far from life in the fast lane was pornography and people surfing the net, watching inappropriate materials on TV and their phones!

Over the years, we have seen an enormous change in the spirit and life of this restricted church. For more than fifteen years, we visited the house church and saw great moves of the Holy Spirit as we taught on the kingdom of power, that we are children of the King, supernatural, here to do the works that Jesus did. We brought the presence of God to a church ever only exposed to conservatism and saw them released.

After a prophetic word over a young man in the worship team, the following year, after the Holy Spirit blasted him, he testified to God touching and changing his life and the word being fulfilled.

Each year we travelled until COVID-19! Only one year did we miss because of national elections. With a restriction on numbers gathering, they forbade public meetings.

A feature of recent ministry there, is children ministering to one another.

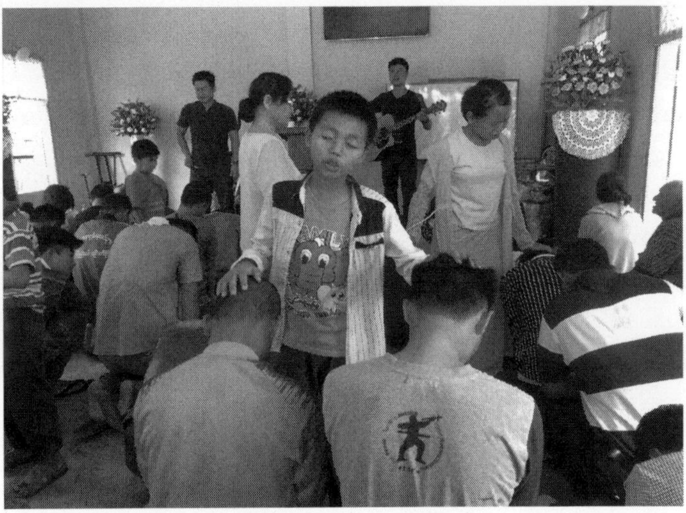

A CHILD MINISTERING

Sikkim 2019, Wednesday

We left majestic mountainous Gangtok at 8:30 a.m. for the seminar. The mountains were very clear, and we had magnificent views of Kanchenjunga. We experienced great worship on our wonderful last day.

Maurice and I prophesied over a man. His journey would involve bumps in the road, speed humps. He should slow down carefully before proceeding and take great care. He testified that as a driver of a truck, he cancelled his work to attend the seminar. God touched him mightily as the word changed his life, and he received an abundance of work. A lady testified she saw Jesus, encountered heaven, and received armfuls of flowers, beautiful orange and yellow poppies, red tulips, brilliant roses, purple velvet pansies, and an abundance of purple flowers of all kinds. We left at 3:30 p.m. for the journey back to Siliguri. Despite warm clothes, this became a rather cool journey, as a convoy of army trucks made the journey painstakingly arduous. Instead of the usual three hours, it took four to five hours.

The nation of Nepal in 2019 passed a non-conversion law, where anyone converting or being baptised goes to prison. Draconian punishments are now law, but in the 1990s, believers suffered seven-year sentences!

I asked our friend Gopalje, a senior pastor in Kathmandu, "What will you do?"

He replied, "The government has the problem! It's not a problem to us!"

His pastor Prem Pradhan spent years in prison for his faith for leading people to Jesus. Prem Pradhan, led to Christ by members of Bakht Singh's people in a city near Nepal, became Nepal's first modern convert and later Nepal's first apostle. By the end of his life, Prem had spent half of his Christian life in prisons. His crime? Preaching Christ and baptising others (Amazon).

We built a relationship with the Rathnababu family in the south, and after several years, in our desire to see transformation, we started sewing and children's computer initiatives in the church. Thousands of fisherfolk live in this slum area. They are low caste and despised with little possibility or hope. Slum children receive ghetto-type schooling. They have few possibilities. Children by age twelve work in the gravel pits, girls are trafficked or work in slave labor and servitude, boys work on the boats! They rarely have opportunity or access to computers. There are more than one hundred widows in the church. Empowered through this initiative, they live without shame. When a woman is widowed, she suffers abuse, ridicule, and shame from the local community.

EMPOWERING THE WIDOWS

In 2019, an older woman (the pastor's mother) in white twirled, jumped, clapped, and shouted with her eyes tightly shut and her sari draped round her head. I along with Marian thought the entire group who jumped, shouted clapped and danced and twirled had gone crazy! We had to retreat from praying for them it was so dangerous! She shared that she experienced heaven magnificently and saw Jesus. He gave her a gold ornate embossed bowl filled with exquisite diamonds and multicoloured precious gems. He told her the church would never lack again!

In the remote mountains of Central India, a remarkable outpouring of the Holy Spirit touched a community and revealed the reality of Jesus and His kingdom. Fifty people were caught up into heaven and experienced wondrous visions like the apostle Paul.

> And I know that this man . . . was caught up in an ecstatic experience and brought into paradise, where he overheard many wondrous and inexpressible secrets . . .
>
> —2 Corinthians 12:3–4 ESV

Jesus commissioned the release of these encounters to reveal His mission to reunite heaven with the earth (Talk to me in Paradise).

For many years, I waited to visit this remote region, this heavenly compound. Repeatedly, I wrote to our friends but always impossible to do so until the right time and place. God's timing is always perfect. When we steward God's glory, He has perfect timings and places to orchestrate His plan in fulfilment of His purpose. God wants to unlock and fulfil the planned revelation of the DNA within us, naturally and supernaturally. For as it is in the natural so it is in the spiritual.

When I knew where we would travel, I contacted our friend Jase, who lives near "as the crow flies" to where we were going to minister and suggested he might like to join us for a few days as Paul who he knows would travel with me. He replied he could spare a couple of days to come to the resort area. On arrival on his bike, he looked up at the sign in the big tent. "Look!" he said. "Look at all your names! Thank God my name is not there!"

I said, "We've told them again and again never to put our names on the posters! In fact, never to have posters! But they take no notice!"

"It has to come down!" he said.

Immediately, we removed it. He said that some friends of his had been expelled just six months previously from this place for preaching and we were holding a conference!

JASE ARRIVING

To Myanmar we went this time to Taungyi, a military city in Shan state with a cooler climate as it is at a higher altitude. What a blessing that visit was, with Pam a friend from Seymour Indiana. At the smaller conference there, we heard so many testimonies from previous visits to the area. Many women testified to healings previously on other visits to the city.

"My name is Daw Baby La I" am Kachin my Kachin name is Emerald Nu.

I live in Taungyi and go to the Kachin Baptist church.

In 2005 I met with Denise Reid at the Conference in the Anglican Church and now again at this 2 day conference. On the first day they taught about the Holy Spirit

The main Scripture was Acts 1:8. After lunch there was the foot washing, at that time many people came -people had their feet washed. I looked at the dirty water in the bowl! In my mind I did not want to participate. I felt disgust! But I decided to do it. I dedicated myself and came to the front for prayer.

As I washed three peoples the Lord touched me and I was crying.

One of the ladies gave me a word from Eph 6: 15 my feet shod with the Gospel of peace —that my life was to be as evangelical socks. I did not really understand this. I confessed and declared it. I cried and after that Denise called for the baptism in the Holy Spirit — 2 groups were separated one group already baptised and another group to be baptised in the Holy Spirit

At that time, I was already baptized at 18 years old.

But I needed more and decided to go to the group not baptized.

Then I was filled with the Holy Spirit -my hands felt like electric shock and it came through my whole body.

The force was so strong I could not stand.

After praying I felt the electric shock still in my body.

At that time in front of me was a girl who needed deliverance

God spoke to me to lay my hand on the girl.

But I am not a minister, so I was scared to do that. My hand automatically did it — it was God. The girl was delivered.

After this I felt electric forces for ten or fifteen days. My life was changed. I had a greater passion for the Gospel. Later God gave me a gift to speak and preach the Gospel

As a result of understanding Acts 1:8, I began to move in power deliverance and healing as in Acts 1:8"

I am Kachin Baptist my name is Taung Bu I live in Taunggyi, Shan State. In 2003, 2004, 2005, Denise and the team came to Taunggyi. I came to the Conference, and she hugged me at the gate. I felt loved warmly. At that time my life was fear, and worry, bitterness, shame and hopelessness. They taught on the Holy Spirit and when they taught on deliverance, she told us to cough. I coughed continually and I was free from all those things. I shouted loudly for a long time and all that was oppressing me left and I was free. My family and my life were hopeless, and one lady prayed for me and gave me a prophetic word that God called me to do ministry. That word gave me comfort and hope. She called Dr Johnny to interpret, and Denise drew the picture of the cycle that I was the author of the hopelessness, and someone saw a clay pot and that pot was smashed and became a gold pot. Those were the prophetic words that changed my life. Wonderfully I felt free, and they kept coming. Every year I went to the meetings. From that time, I participated in the prayer ministry. Because the Lord sent this ministry I received the touch from God, The Baptism in the Holy Spirit and now when I came to this conference I wanted to testify of the greatness of God.

A woman who was deaf in one ear and had pain and discharge from the ear all her life was totally healed when Pam prayed. Here is her testimony. "My name is Daw NANG Dawng I am Kachin Baptist I was the first believer in my family I had ear problems from birth with pain, loss of hearing and infection. My parents consulted many doctors with very little effect. There was little help, with much pain and pus. I had lots of headaches and shoulder pain all my life. There was constant pus until now at 65 years. I have suffered all this time and could not hear! God told me to go in front for prayer and by the grace of God when I came to the front, I was touched by the Lord. I cannot speak in English, I went to the front, took the lady's hand and put it on my ear. She prayed for me, and I was healed Praise the Lord. When the break came, I tested my ear, it was very clear I could hear! I tested it again with my mobile phone. I had never used my mobile phone with that ear, now I could. I could hear! I heard and was so happy, for the first time in my whole life I could hear— today is so special to me. I put my finger in my ear and there for the first time it was dry with no pus."

My husband said if I had been born one hundred years earlier, I would have been a suffragette. I admired the courage of the women in movies, who chained themselves to lampposts, went to prison, did hunger strikes, some even died for the cause. I watched a movie about the suffragettes, and one woman threw herself in front of a horse racing at Ascot, England. Bold, brave women who did not count the cost but sacrificed all. They suffered for the cause of women to get the vote. Recently, we discovered in our family history that my grandmother and other lady family members with the DNA from their bold brave ancestors were suffragettes when the women received the vote in New Zealand, the first nation to give women the vote. On 19 September 1893, the governor, Lord Glasgow, signed a new electoral act into law. Because of this landmark legislation, New Zealand became the first self-governing country in the world in which women had the right to vote in parliamentary elections (nzhistory.govt.nz > politics > women's-suffrage).

Sacrifice was a way of life for them. They sacrificed all for the vote.

What will we sacrifice for Jesus? Many believers I am in relationship with have suffered.

Pastor Laja in Kachin State Myanmar went to prison for twenty-four hours because his children's home burnt down with no loss of life, only the building destroyed. He spent the complete twenty-four hours evangelising until the moment of his release. When released, the officials said, "Come back anytime we need you here!"

Marilyn, Linda and I went at the pastor's request to a Christian refugee camp on the edge of a war zone. We took food for the 125 people who fled the war zone. When the army came to their village, they burnt their crops, destroyed their houses, poisoned the wells, and the families fled. Living in a valley, the opposing armies fired across their houses, and during the day, they hid in the dugout areas as their houses were full of bullet holes! Though they lost everything, they escaped with their lives! The church in this area built a camp for them. They had no food. They prayed for three days, but no one could help. They prayed, and we arrived with food. Unaware of their situation, the day of travel, we discussed we could not go there with nothing. A small church in New Zealand with many members on welfare gave money to Linda to help a needy situation, which provided the much-needed money to buy the food! When we walked around their tiny camp, our hearts broke as they had nothing, and the well dug since their arrival was beside the toilets! Our supernatural Father provided a miracle of provision. The government do not permit foreigners to visit in (black) war zones. Immigration authorities, after finding us there, checked our passports whilst we prayed! Sadly, we could only pray about the water contamination!

Reader, can't you tell I love Myanmar? Our entire family has been there. It's such a great place to go, the people are so special and the accommodation A1 okay.

From day 1 in 1990, I just wanted to live in Asia. Suddenly realising why I never felt I fitted in New Zealand, I was the right size, people were my size, I felt I fitted there! I love Asia. I felt this was my destiny, my home, and finally, I had found it. If it had not been for Kevin and our family, I would have gone, lived there forever!

Rahab Ministries was always a focal point of a visit to Bangkok. It was on one such visit with Patricia translating, I prophesied over a young woman, telling her she would become a leader of the ministry! Two years ago, this young woman reminded me of this. Now that woman is a leader of Rahab. I had completely forgotten the incident, but she will never forget as it changed her life forever! Prophetic words do that.

RAHAB MINISTRY

In Myanmar, 2019, the team of six returned to Mandalay.

After God touched her, this keyboard player lay on the sanctuary floor. Now eighteen years old, I had watched her grow from a small child. Her dancing, at only four and five years, delighted the worshippers. As she danced with the worshippers at the church front, she brought us into His glorious presence where heaven touched earth. She had many encounters with the Lord, experiences with heaven, seeing Jesus. But now, deep inside, mindful of how unusual she had become to those around her, she craved to be like her unbelieving friends. When His love changes us, can we ever be the same as those who don't know His love? That day she changed. God answered a mother's cry! We are different when Jesus changes our hearts. We bring that change wherever we are. He transforms us to be transformers amongst those around us.

Her mother stood beside her, crying. "Praise God. Thank You, God," she announced. "I asked for an answer as she had lost her way. I prayed for God to change her." Excited at the timing, she had her answer from God. That day my young friend returned to a biblical perspective with new joy and freedom.

THE YOUNG WOMAN

Forgiven healed and delivered. "I wanted nothing! I only wanted to sleep!" said the demonised girl.

The three-day seminar for forty-five students was finishing. Committed to a psychiatric institution after she drank a witchcraft concoction given to her by the boyfriend, authorities institutionalized her for three years! Discharged on medication, abandoned by family and friends, she lived on the streets until the church rescued her! Every day we prayed for her as she lay on the floor in a drugged stupor! She testified at the training closure that she didn't want Jesus. "I was sleeping on the floor, and Jesus, glowing bright in white clothes, stood beside me. He took me across a bridge and through an enormous pearl gate. Two huge angels accompanied me. Everything was so beautiful, gold, pearls, diamonds, everything shining," she said. "Jesus stood in front of me, and He drew a large coffee-coloured heart and said, 'Your heart is in my hands!'"

SET FREE [SHE IS AT THE END OF THE FRONT ROW RIGHT]

A bomb exploded at a Yoma Bank branch in Lashio, a nearly lawless city in the northern part of Myanmar's Shan State, on Wednesday. No one claimed responsibility, but the frontier region is plagued by ethnic violence. Twenty-two persons were injured the week we were to travel there! (Credit... en.wikipedia.org › wiki › 2018_Lashio_bombing) We cancelled Lashio's conference because of the bombings and the bridge destruction.

In Pyin Oo Lwin, we gathered for a wonderful conference, where the military base was bombed just the week before our visit.

A rebel group attacked a military academy near Mandalay, Myanmar's second largest city, the military said Thursday. The Defence Services Technology Academy (DSTA), located in Pyin Oo Lwin, a scenic hill town in Mandalay Region, was hit by five heavy artillery or motor shells early this morning, said spokesman Brigadier General Zaw Min Tun. "It killed a civilian and wounded a soldier in the academy compound," he told Anadolu Agency by phone. He added that a military checkpoint in Pyin Oo Lwin and a military base in Naung Cho in Shan State were also attacked by a group of unidentified armed rebels Thursday morning. He said the attacks were likely in response to a recent military raid on drug factories in Shan State. Some local media reports said the attacks were carried out by the Ta'ang National Liberation Army (TNLA), a member of the Northern Alliance military coalition composed of ethnic insurgent groups which still engages in armed conflicts with the military in border areas. [Anadolu Agency 15.08.2019 Kyaw Ye Lynn]

"No problem," said Samuel. "We will be at the other end of the city!" A hundred and fifty persons attended, mainly young men, many of whom ex-drug addicts.

"Jesus! Jesus, I saw him!" he exclaimed. "It happened, it happened," he cried. "I so wanted to see Jesus, and it happened!"

"I want to see Jesus!" the pastor in Pyin Oo Lwin said.

"I can't give you Jesus," I replied. "You need to ask Him. Often we have not because we ask not!"

He sat with us at lunch after the morning session. We talked more. He returned for breakfast, asking more questions, hungry to know what God was doing. The following day at the testimony time, he shared with the group of 160 people what had happened for him. They laughed when he said, "I didn't want to come! A woman was preaching! God woke me in the night and spoke, told me to come. I'm so glad I came. I am healed! Sickness filled my body! And most wonderful of all, I saw Jesus."

THE PASTOR

"God, I want to experience you," he said. He expected an answer. "Let me see the heavens," he said.

We received and released by faith from heaven the power of the Holy Spirit to this ex-drug addict. He received a heavenly language when the Holy Spirit baptised him in fire. He laughed, waved his hands, and smiled as he shared, "I climbed a ladder. From the top, I noticed a beautiful rainbow waterfall. There was a house, made of pieces of jade with precious stones all over it. I reached the door. As I turned the large gold handle, I heard a voice, 'Come in.' On entry, I saw Jesus sitting at the table. Jesus requested me to come and sit there with Him. He said, 'My son, don't worry anymore, I want to give you one present. Here is the Bible. If you stay and build your life upon this book, you will never slip.'"

THE YOUNG MAN

Praise God for the many divine appointments on this trip to Myanmar.

Several ladies testified, one to fire all over her body after prayer, another went evangelising about a month before where there was much demonic activity. In the weeks that followed, she suffered a persistent cough, which she could not get rid of, but when she coughed during the deliverance prayer, she was free with no more cough.

An ancient man was thanking God that we came. He had been praying as most of the churches needed the gifting and power of the Holy Spirit. He saw the face of Jesus, and it filled his heart with great joy. Every morning, at two to three o'clock, God used to wake him up and have a conversation with him. He said, "I want to thank you all for bringing God's revival to our church and to our community!"

A grandfather brought his many grandchildren and shared, "It blessed me to see the children praying for the people. Never has that happened."

I woke to see my sister Lyndsey wiping away tears. I asked, "are you Ok?" She replied, "I said to the Lord, Denise speaks of the heavenly experiences and so many are having them, Lord I want to see you and go to heaven. I walked through a door and there I was at the beautiful river of Revelation with trees and fruit on either side. And there was Jesus standing beside me. He looked up at the tree and said as he picked a vibrant green leaf, Take this and eat it, it's for your healing and the healing of the nations!"

ONE OF THE CHILDREN PRAYING

Yangon was exceptional. After a night on the bus and a wonderful day of sightseeing, we visited special friends. Brother Ronnie, the leader of the huge Brethren network of churches in his late eighties, prayed for each team member as we knelt before him. A giant of faith and vision, he imparted to each of us as he laid hands on us. For the first time in my journey of knowing him for thirty years, they invited us to lunch with him. So memorable for this giant of faith to spend time with us.

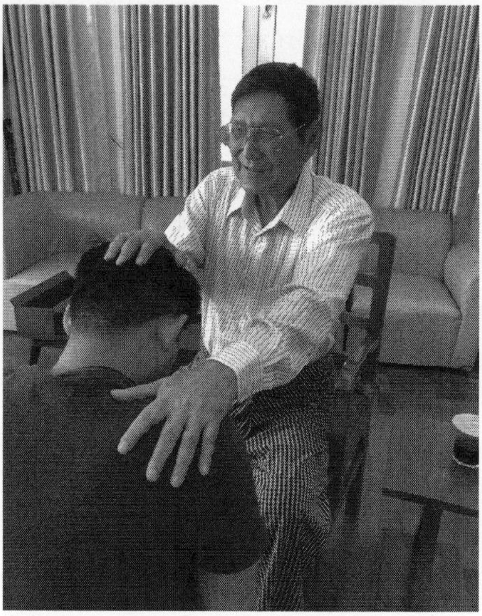

BROTHER RONNIE

We journeyed on to see the Zin Hla's in the satellite city. They had been waiting all morning for our arrival with many workers there to greet us. Our special friend, husband, and father Pastor U Zin Hla passed on to heaven some weeks previously, which saddened us, but to see his son arise to take over the ministry delighted us. This special man who after periods of severe illness, suffers no more. Sadly missed in Myanmar for his unique, powerful deliverance and prophetic intercessory mantle, he left a great legacy with his son and workers, now empowered to do what he did. How special when the new leader his eldest son testified to having fasted and prayed for a week before asking Brother Ronnie to pray and anoint him for the ministry. I have watched this young man grow to adulthood and seen him rise to statehood in Christ, now the leader of a major Myanmar ministry and only in his early twenties!

Divine appointments are part of my life.

Every day, when staying with our family in New Zealand, I walk on the beach. Just five minutes from where they live is a beautiful long beach where in the summer, I swim to exercise and enjoy. On one beautiful summer day, I was halfway along this beach when I noticed a man and woman standing looking at the ocean. I paused to greet them. They greeted me, and I walked on. On my return, after walking to the end of the beach, they were still standing in the same spot!

I stopped to talk, and they asked, "Do you know what that is out there?" They pointed to an obscure pole out in the ocean.

"No," I said. "I don't live here, I'm visiting! I am a missionary and just visit here!"

"We are pastors," they said.

We talked some more, and I said, "I am an Assemblies of God pastor and missionary travelling the world."

They said, "We are New Life pastors from the south of the city."

Hearing this, I asked them, "Do you know a friend of mine? He is a New Life pastor and works in a remote area in India. His name is Jase . . ."

They said they did, and we were all excited. As a result of this conversation, we checked out when they had a vacancy for us to visit the church and when we had a free Sunday. Amazingly, both dates matched, and on 14 April that year, we visited their church to minister.

After two amazing services, when the Holy Spirit moved powerfully with the presence of the Lord, filling the place and a time of tremendous ministry, we sat together, sharing in the foyer, eating a belated lunch.

"Well, were you surprised at what you got?" I asked.

"Not at all," they replied. They went on to share, "We never go to that beach as it's very far from where we live, an hour and half away, but that morning the Lord impressed on us that we must go there as He had something, someone for us to meet. When we met you, we knew that God had a plan! We knew God wanted to do something new!"

God is amazing listen to Him. Do what He shows you to do even if it's only an impression or a feeling. Divine appointments open up new doors, new possibilities, forge the way ahead, Kevin parked the SUV outside the house in Iowa after the long journey from Indiana. Downstairs was a table covered in fabric and patterns for sewing! I asked Dorothy, "what are you making?" her reply surprised me, "bags for girls!... To help young women with their monthly cycles." After all my years in the nations I had never realized the desperate need ladies and girls had for these!

BAGS FOR GIRLS IN UGANDA

Kevin tried to start the car as we needed to go for our appointment to see Pastor Dave, but.... The Ford would not start.. totally dead... no life at all! Stranded in Iowa, they loaned us their van to return to Indiana for a meeting. After our return we discovered the Ford had died. The car was abandoned after it accrued an account of over 700 dollars and no solution found. Ed gave us his well-used Toyota van and paid the garage account! After this divine appointment we began to take bags to assist the young women in the nations... I was shocked and stunned that in thirty years of ministry in the nations I had never realized this most urgent need for the assistance and empowerment of the young women. What a change that visit brought!

A visit to Kakinada for a pastors' leaders conference to minister and dedicate the new church with a team of six from the USA and NZ, I paused, hugged, and prayed for a tall man. Later he testified, "I suffered pain in my entire body for months, and from the moment I was hugged and prayed for, the pain left. I'm healed."

THE TEAM ARRIVAL IN VISHAKAPATNUM

THE MAN HEALED AFTER A HUG!

SEWING INITIATIVE

I wrote to Jase in the heavenly compound and asked if we could visit. He replied, "We have two groups coming at that time!" After persistence, he said, "Okay, how many?"

He knew I would bring people with me because we empower the nationals. It's no good just going and doing amazing conferences, amazing stuff, without empowering the nationals to travel with us so they catch what we carry. I told him six persons, then maybe eight, and the day before, we told him eleven persons. Each time I knew he would groan! I offered to stay at a local hotel, but no, they would accommodate us at the heavenly compound! After the service, and lunch we travelled along the coast, and finally, to the train. With no time to stop for dinner, we travelled all night, shaking and rattling through the countryside, to wake at 3:00 a.m., worried we might miss the stop after the hill! But which hill? And in the dark. The train stopped for two minutes at this station, and we had eleven people plus twenty enormous bags! We waited for an entire hour, actually from 2:00 a.m., standing in the cold with the door open, watching for the lights of the station. Jase had warned me if we missed the station, we would be an hour down the track before we even realised. But we didn't miss the station, we made sure of that! Organised, men and bags were at one door, ladies and others at the first door! As we scrambled off, the guys threw the bags! All achieved successfully in two minutes with Jase there in the dark to meet us for four days at the wonderful heavenly compound.

At 5:00 a.m., in the dark, the children greeted and sang for us! What a highlight of our trip to travel to where children visit heaven every day and have done so for over ten years! CCTV in the buildings for child protection, with one hundred children including the fourteen babies. In this compound, they seek to bring heaven to earth with the flowers, gardens, animals, birds, fish, tortoises, an emu, dogs, pond, and surroundings. There is never a cross word, children don't fight or squabble, babies don't cry, all is peace and harmony.

Each day, when Kizz finished her work, she joined us upstairs in the chapel, whilst Jase shared the stories of their journey, the stories of heaven. She would enter to fall on the floor and visit heaven. She rose on her knees and moved round the room with her eyes shut, sharing and releasing to the team what Jesus showed her in heaven. On one occasion, the incredible fragrance of roses permeated and filled the entire room. I have smelled nothing quite like it! So fragrant, so beautiful, the fragrance of heaven.

In the evenings, the entire group gathered. We worshipped and prayed, and the children danced with untiring vigor, often having heavenly encounters. On one such evening, Jase called to my attention a young woman Sukanti, and in Jase's words from *Heavenly Kaleidoscope* foreword, "Recently, during a worship service on our campus in rural India, I observed Denise minister to a young woman who, minutes earlier, was brought to us for care and protection by the local police. This woman's eighteen-month-old daughter had just been kidnapped. As the worship music played, I observed Denise embrace this distraught woman in her arms and hold her for a prolonged period. I saw Sukanti relax, soften, break, weep, and then eventually smile. I remember thinking, That's God's love manifesting right there! Denise was clearly partnering with the Holy Spirit that day to channel God's love and healing into her broken soul. Sukanti is a transformed woman now because of Denise's love; a mother's hug, a grandmother's embrace, the arms of Christ. They were one and the same; so simple, but so powerful."

Several months later, in a communication with Jase, in excitement, we discovered a tremendous answer to our prayers for this girl and her small child. The police contacted the compound to tell the family the child had been located three hundred kilometres away, and they needed Sukanti to travel with them to uplift the child in a sting operation! What a miracle when they uplifted the little girl and restored her to her mother nine months after her abduction.

Another night, after a presentation by the team of a jungle doctor animal drama, Jase received a phone call! He called us. Quickly, he said, "The police have called. They are at the gate. They won't come in until we tie up the dogs as they fear the dogs. Go to the bedroom and lock the door. The entire compound must be silent! They must not know you are here!"

SUKANTI

Fourteen police stations in the district have decided this compound is the place to take abused women. They did not desire to become a women's refuge, but God decided! Quickly, everything shut down, with us in the bedroom quietly praying, the children silent! They unlocked the gates, tied up the dogs, and the police entered. Imagine almost one hundred children silent! The police entered the downstairs area with a young woman and looked around, again and again. They commented, "What amazing music and singing, so beautiful!"

There was no music or singing! Just the sounds of heaven! They heard the heavenly music and the angels singing.

Another evening at the end of the service, Jase said, "Let's go outside."

With a small group of children, we gathered in the dark in front of the building. The children dropped on the grass in a heavenly experience as Jase prayed. Quickly, they rose and took off running, with eyes shut, in the dark, across the grass, through the gate, down the long path, almost to the property wall where they spun. Of course, we ran after them. Imagine, in the dark, we all ran, following this group of children! Now beside the pond, we ran in the dark, laughing as we thought about snakes! After all, this was Rural India! In pitch-black, up and down, eager to keep up and not miss anything, we stumbled over the ditches alongside the pond. We followed the children with their eyes closed until we reached the memorial plaque placed beside the pond, after heaven touched earth.

The entire group stopped here. Whilst the children talked and prayed, we prayed. Then round the pond, past the tall eucalyptus trees, through the fence, back to the front of the house where they danced and played, before coming back to us, and all with their eyes shut tight! So many miracles have happened at the pond! Heaven has touched earth so often there.

MEMORIAL PLAQUE

Have you ever patted an emu? Walked with an emu? Had an emu put his beak on your cheek? The morning of our departure, I desired to pray at the pond. As I left the building and passed through the gate, the emu joined me to walk, not just with me but touching me, his beak on my face, his body right against me! Startling and unusual, but not so if these are heavenly animals! This emu, with his beak on my cheek, walked alongside me all the way down the path. I could pat his feathers, alongside the pond, round the pond. He stopped when I prayed at the pond and walked with me all the way back to the building where I started! The guys watching in amazement jumped off the concrete veranda and lined up to walk with the emu. It could only be supernatural, this emu walking with us! A team member sadly said later, "I feared the emu and shooed it away!"

I just want to return! Wouldn't you?

Ten hours in and ten hours out on rugged roads to Southern Chin State, a colder place in Chin Hills, for a transformational conference. Myanmar's heat did not penetrate in the Chin Hills.

Vanishing ink, I met a lady in the hotel at Kanpetlet who said she was writing a book about the women in the area, how the ink was vanishing.

Everywhere we looked in this big conference of over four hundred people, women appeared to have blue faces. What was it? We gazed closely, and to our horror, we discovered it was tattoos! Tattoos all over their faces, the eyelids, their lips, their nose and cheeks, the entire face tattooed! I could not imagine or comprehend the suffering! Imagine the pain! We visited a village, and there was a lady with her family; her face tattooed! We stopped to talk to her and wept when we heard her story. Four family members held her down at fifteen years of age and forcibly tattooed her face. There was no choice; if she ever wished to marry, she had to undergo the tattoo. They tattooed her eyelids, her cheeks, her lips, her complete face! She said it was terrible, the pain and suffering during and after. Some children died, she told us as tears welled in her eyes! They were only eight years of age when they did this to them; the trauma and shock was too great! It started after the king visited 100-150 years earlier. He had seen all the beautiful women and took some as concubines. The families decided they didn't want to lose their beautiful girls to the king, so they tattooed their faces so that the king would no longer be interested. When the missionaries came to the area in the 1980s-1990s, they stopped the tattooing as they recognised that this inhumane practise was obsolete, not acceptable, and caused great suffering and even death to the women and children. I wept as she shared her story as she wiped tears from her eyes.

THE LADY WHO SHARED HER STORY

Excited and amazed, the people told us that with other conferences, all the conservatives who attended always left after the first morning, but this time they stayed 'til the end. It was God. When we learn to steward the glory, we do things God's way. The Lord had shown me to build a biblical perspective of the supernatural from Genesis through to Revelation and share relevant stories. A platform was successfully built and evident. The team ministered to hundreds of people day and night.

Nelson, my friend from Allentown, groaned as he said, "My stomach hurts I have cried, shouted, and hugged when I prayed for so many people." Hundreds of people prayed for, hundreds healed, delivered and ministered too.

NELSON AND A BELIEVER

She lay on the floor in the family house on a blanket with a flat pillow. We were visiting in the village; we visited the woman with the tattooed face and looked at photos of the area, and the guys were using bows and arrows in this little tourist area. As I moved towards the car, a young woman took my arm and pulled me into her house. Inside in the dim light, I saw the little girl about six years of age lying on the floor! Totally normal before a severe fever two years before, but after the fever entirely disabled. The mother had attended some meetings with her family. I fetched Samuel to enable communication. Like me, he wanted to do something to help. We looked around the small house and found some pillows to sit her up and talked to her. It was clear she could hear us, I moved her arms and legs, and we could see she began to respond. We prayed for her, and Samuel got out his mobile phone and showed her things. Her eyes flickered in interested response, and she watched everything on the phone! How we wished we could have left some toys, books, music, anything to enable these parents in this isolated area with poor medical facilities to aid this small child's recovery. We felt so helpless! We prayed, saw the response, advised the parents and had to leave her in the hands of the Lord! I wanted to see her get up like so many others have, but we left her there and prayed. The amazing thing with miracles I've found is that in the days that follow, often on the third day, the miracle begins, and by three months, the healing is complete. COVID-19 arrived, so we have never heard how she is.

THE CHILD

THE TEAM

We travelled back from Chin State to the wedding of Moses and Hau Sac (Jasmine, we now call her). Such a precious time, to be there for the wedding was my delight. Grace loved and raised her from four years, a true orphan. I have watched her grow up to be a fine young woman who now speaks English fluently after a stint where she ran away and lived in Singapore for a couple of years. She returned to the family at a critical time for Moses. That very year was one of family disaster when a month after our visit, disaster struck his family. His drug addict brother murdered his sister and her small daughter! Moses was suffering terribly from the pain of losing three family members when Jasmine returned. How happy we were to see this blossoming relationship. They recently had their first most beautiful baby girl, Christabel.

MOSES AND JASMINES' WEDDING

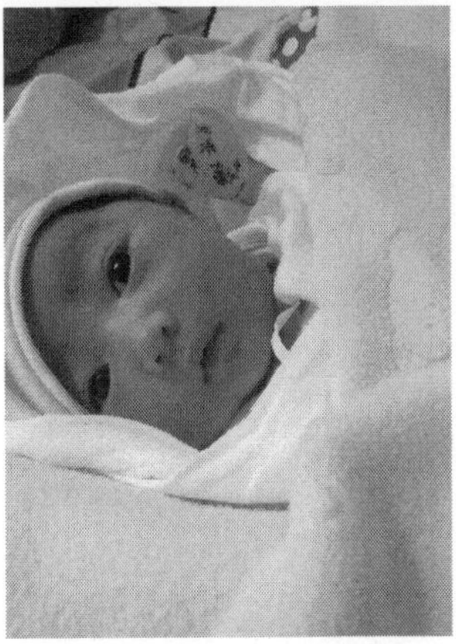

BABY CHRISTABEL ONE DAY OLD

CONCLUSION

> The entire universe is standing on tiptoe, [yearning to see the unveiling of God's *glorious*] sons and daughters!
> —Romans 8:19 TPT

The world is waiting for the sons and daughters of the living God to rise to take their place to demonstrate his presence: to unveil their true identity, that when we were born again, we became a totally new creation. The old life is finished and gone, we are seated with Christ in heavenly places and rule from there to bring heaven to earth, by our faith, prayer, and praises (2 Corinthians 5:17; Ephesians 2:6).

This special book has been a long time coming. I hope it has blessed and encouraged you as you have read the stories of my life and journey to steward the glory, with my hand in the hand of Jesus. With just do it, do the crazy thing, the signature of my life, I became a crazy woman doing whatever I felt to do in obedience to the voice of God. I have an amazing husband who released me to do just that, and in fact, he encouraged me in situations where I would have given up. *Unlocked* draws attention to the supernatural, the unthinkable, the impossible set aside for you, not for your glory, but for His.

I have introduced you to the supernatural as a lifestyle and want to encourage you to move into the purpose for which you were given life.

Jesus came to bring heaven to earth and walks in the world as He unlocks heaven to earth through you and me. He walked amongst us to bring hope and a future, with freedom from sin and degradation, freedom from the boundaries of religion, the law and unbelief. Jesus demonstrated what the Son of God could do on earth and you and I are in that same position today. As children of the Living God, we bring the love and life of God into every situation. We change the atmosphere.

Rise up and understand your real position to be an image-maker carrying His glory, not ordinary, not a worm, but as a son and daughter of the Living God, extraordinary. He in you and you in Him

(1 John 4:17). As He is, so are we in the world, not as He was when He lived amongst us but as He is now in you and me.

There are thousands waiting to be unlocked, on the other side of your obedience for you to touch, speak, and pray because His presence flows through you. Give away what you've got, you are the hands and feet of Jesus to bring His transforming love into every situation.

As I look back over my life, I see keys discovered, revealed, unveiled and unlocked as I moved forward with lady bird steps of faith. The day came with the realisation that as I took giant steps, my faith became active and greater than I ever could have imagined asked or thought. Though I confessed to having little faith and an inability to believe, as I declared and decreed the word of God over my life, my faith grew. Once miracles signs and wonders arrived, my faith became unstoppable. The declaration and proclamation of the word empowered and released me, then it empowered and released the teams who travelled, and it empowered and released thousands to whom we ministered in the conferences across the Himalayas, Asia, and throughout the world. When you recognise the power, there is in faith declarations of the blood of Jesus, the name of Jesus, and the power released with these declarations, life changes. As by faith we proclaimed, "Jesus is here. He's touching you now. Jesus is kissing you, and He is hugging you . . . He's healing your body!" Jesus did it in the meetings.

So what can you the reader learn from all this? Shall I list all the things? But that would be too boring. To unlock miracles signs and wonders, the supernatural, my relationship with the Lord was the key. From the beginning, when God first spoke with the call to Myanmar and later the four corners of the earth, I studied the word of God, I spoke the good verses over my life, I prayed those verses over my life. I rose early in the morning and lay on the floor, crying out to God to change my heart, that I might be like Him. As I listened to His voice as He spoke to me in my spirit, through the word, through e-mails, people, dreams, visions, prophetic words, I recognised it's not enough to hear the word of God, I needed to do what it said. So many people listen and hear but never obey. Obedience is the key. I urge you to learn a new walk of obedience and love, love that flows out from your intimacy with Him.

Just do it, the cry of my life, is an abiding principle to unlock His purpose and plan. After a law-abiding life, as a perpetual tourist, much of what I did was illegal. I operated on a green light, to keep going and doing, recognising that until a red light came, I would continue to do what I would do, regardless of the consequences. For you, as the reader, recognise that you have a green light, a light that says GO! Stop delaying, stop making excuses, start acting, and move into what God has for you. There is so much more for you.

Fasting and prayer unlocked a huge key for breakthrough. I suggested to everyone seeking to come on the teams that they fast for a minimum of three days prior to travel. Many fasted for twenty-one, twenty-eight, and forty days. For the first ten years of ministry, I led a fasted life, only eating about twice a week. If you want breakthrough in your life, fast and pray.

> In obedience and recognition of God's purpose and plan in the biblical mandate as revealed in Genesis 1:26-28, then God said, "Let us make man in our image, after our likeness. And let them have dominion over the fish of the sea and over the birds of the heavens and over the livestock and over all the earth and over every creeping thing that creeps on the earth." So, God created man in his own image, in the image of God he created him; male and female, he created them. And God blessed them. And God said to them, "Be fruitful and multiply and fill the earth and subdue it and have dominion over the fish of the sea and over the birds of the heavens and over every living thing that moves on the earth."

Together, God commanded the man and woman to be fruitful, to multiply, to have dominion, to rule and reign, to carry the glory, to fill the earth with people like themselves made in His image. Special notice is taken when mention is made for the very first time in the Bible. God's intent in His first mandate, His first great commission was that man and woman, His image-makers, were to fill the earth with people like themselves. So when Jesus announced the great commission in Matthew 28:18-20, it was not new, not optional, but a command reflected throughout the whole Old Testament. In obedience to the Lord, I recognised the open door in the nations, and I needed to continue going until that door shut!

> And Jesus came and said to them, "All authority in heaven and on earth has been given to me. Go therefore and make disciples of all nations, baptizing them in the name of the Father and of the Son and of the Holy Spirit, teaching them to observe all that I have commanded you. And behold, I am with you always, to the end of the age.
>
> —Matthew 28:18–20

To multiply what we carried, we encouraged nationals to travel with us in the teams to catch what we carried and recognised if this did not happen, our time was wasted. When leaders from Asia wrote, wanting us to visit them, I remained focused on the call to the Himalayan region and suggested they join us to build relationship to see what we did in order to empower them to do it. Operating out of relationship was the key. After we built relationship, I visited them. Everywhere we travel across the region, we take a team of nationals, sometimes ten to twelve leaders who do the ministry, dramas, and teach prepared materials. To assist and empower, we meet their costs. After we purchased bags of drama materials for each team in every nation visited, we saw them transform their gospel presentations and crusades. As we encouraged oppressed women to rise to their true identity, we saw boldness and additional levels of team outreaches.

It's not enough to teach. The national brothers and sisters are excellent teachers of the word. They need the ministry and power of the Holy Spirit. At every stage, we have sought to bring the empowerment of the Holy Spirit, often sacrificing the teaching to allow extra time for ministry and prayer. In the conferences, we seek to build an atmosphere where heaven touches earth and those attending learn how to bring heaven to earth in their daily lives and churches.

Recognition of my identity in Christ was a freeing, liberating, transforming experience, which unfolded and unlocked as we saw God's glory poured out. I want to challenge you, do you know who you are in Christ? Does heaven touch earth in your life?

Recently Rachel said to me we have paid a high price for the ministry, and as I replied I discussed with her the price. For us as a family all the cancers when the devil tried to kill us and stop God's purpose. The allergies and health issues family members have suffered, the head injuries to both Kevin and Rachel around the same ages, the sicknesses on the field due to the conditions in which we work. The attack against both girls our grandchildren to bring death situations, crippling them. The loss of family relationships as we have been gone for so many years. The hardships, the pain and difficulties suffered with surgery and recovery even when things did not go well, not giving up and abandoning the journey. Yes, there has been a price for the anointing and power of God. Indeed the Scriptures show us in:

> Rev 3:18 I counsel you to buy from me gold refined by fire, so that you may be rich, and white garments so that you may clothe yourself and the shame of your nakedness may not be seen, and salve to anoint your eyes, so that you may see.

There is a cost a price for what we do.

I see evidence in the Scriptures for the price to move in power and glory. All the apostles and those who worked with them paid the ultimate price. Was it worth it? You may ask and I could only reply, "yes a thousand times yes." How blessed I have been to see the Lord do so many wonderful miracles, signs and wonders. How blessed I have been to love Jesus and be His hands and feet. To bring love and care in nations where believers suffer for Him. How blessed and priviledged I have been to do what I have done: and meet, serve and work alongside the precious brothers and sisters in the fields. So many who I have loved have fallen and no longer walk in His ways, and even died, yet we carry on persevering, as God never said it would be easy.

He just asked me to love and serve, to pour out for Him: and that I will continue to do, as in Jesus there is no retirement, no laying down the task. How blessed I have been with all the amazing people who have travelled on teams, and those who have supported and sowed seed into what we do. We could not have done it without them all.

He promises that those who wait on the Lord will renew their strength they will run and not be weary they will walk and not faint they will rise up with wings as of eagles Isaiah 40:31 ESV

You may ask 'Would I do it again?' My reply would be again and again absolutely without any hesitation.

For more than thirty years, I have listened and obeyed the voice of God. Reader, you need to listen to the voice of God and do what He says. I have sought to do this and to follow the leading of Holy Spirit. In this time, there have been the highs and lows in relationships and events.

So many sad things which broke my heart, happened amongst leaders with whom we served, because of demonic activity, self-will, and disease. You see, doing what we do, we love the people, it's not about missions as many people do that. This is a love relationship where we love the people and love those with whom we serve.

A pioneer breaks ground, is single minded purpose driven, focused, unstoppable. Nothing stops a pioneer. I would say that this would be true of my life. Facing formidable odds, odds that would have stopped so many, I have not allowed them to stop me. Focused on the task, with my eyes fixed on Jesus I have pursued with passion the vision born of God. He promised he would never leave me nor forsake me. Believing this, by faith I have moved in with purpose to the task regardless of pain or suffering or issues with my body as it is not in my strength but His on whom I depend. He promised to enable and pour His love through me: that if I loved Him and did what he said, He would empower me. I can say with confidence Jesus has done just that and will do that for any who will sell out their lives to Him. I put my hand in His and never looked back! Will you do that today as you read these words?

One thing has been loud and clear in my journey: I will not die until the day God decides. He has much work yet for us to do. In these days of great fear and foreboding, we do not fear as Jesus is with us. He brings his hope and love into every situation. None of what we did was about staying safe as that is not a key factor when we love God. God's value is not safety, and that has been a challenging factor for me this past year. He promises to help and watch over us. As you have read, war and bombs did not stop me, cancer did not stop me, rebellions, disasters, sickness did not stop me, so I continue to ask myself, why did COVID-19 stop me?

The world quakes, shakes, and looks for vaccines, looks for answers, isolates, but we, as a people, are victorious, no matter what the circumstances. We walk by faith, not fear, we walk in victory. We do not bow to fear, intimidation and control. As a people of hope who bring light and hope into darkened situations we change the atmosphere. This is a new day, and we have never walked this way before. Nations have closed, and until they open again, we cannot go: but we can keep in contact, encourage, send devotionals, see them on zoom and messenger, and send messages! We can make sure they are aware that they are not abandoned, not forgotten. For many nations, there currently appears to be a red light but we are ever watchful for a change waiting again for what God will do.

Unlocked shows you God can take anyone, no matter how tough their life background has been, and make them His servants of power and fire to change nations and people's destinies. Reader, in my story, I have shown you how I took steps to unlock and embrace God's plan for my life. How to become part of God's incredible army of saints unlocking and manifesting the power of God across the earth. You too can embrace His plan to become part of His army moving in supernatural power and authority to bring change and transformation.

Unlocked brings to you a glimpse of the wonder, the magnificence, the glory, the power and the immenseness of our Father, the Lord of Lords the King of Kings: our Father God and His Son Jesus Christ our Saviour, who paid the ultimate price on the cross to take our sin and make us a total new creation. A new creation supernatural with no previous history, no longer sinners but saints.

Let me remind you of the power of God's word, the power of our words for life or death. We are atmosphere changers because we bring God's light in to every situation.

Job 22:28 You will decide [declare, decree, proclaim] on a matter, and it will be established for you, and light will shine on your ways.

Jesus Christ Himself gave us our true identity as sons and daughters, born again by the Spirit of the living God, seated in heavenly places with Him, bringing heaven to earth by the power of the precious Holy Spirit. Unlocked opens a door to the friendship and release of the power of the Holy Spirit our friend and guide. Unlocked releases our identity as supernatural people to bring heaven to earth through our lives in a lost world.

A special daughter in Christ wrote to me, 'Supernatural woman,' she said. That's what we are to be, Supernatural! Supernatural men and women changing the world, transforming atmospheres to bring His glory into every situation and place.

Let me encourage you. If you do not have a faith in Jesus after reading my story, I would challenge you to ask Jesus, the Son of God, to reveal Himself to you. Ask Jesus to come into your life, to take away your sin and be your Savior and Lord. Unlock His purpose and plan for your life as I have done with mine.

You can contact me on deniseereid@gmail.com or our website: http//fourcornersministries.com.

There are three other books stories from my life and those who have journeyed with me. You can access them through our website and through http//DeniseReidbooks.com

Denise has three other books recently published and available.

HEAVENLY KALEIDOSCOPE

Arm yourself with inspiration and revelation regarding the supernatural power of God. Be empowered to a new level of living as you read heavenly stories of nations and personal supernatural experiences Denise Reid has had in her walk discovering God's purpose and plan in her life. Be inspired as you taste and see, as you catch a glimpse of those, she has taken on teams to empower nations.

You will be captured and encouraged by the experiences of the many, who have received frequently changing visions and experiences to whom Denise and teams have ministered.

You will be challenged to rise to your identity as a powerful believer, as a ministry gift to the body of Christ releasing God's kingdom on earth.

Available on www.xlibris.com You can contact Denise Reid at denise@ fourcornersministries.com or deniseereid@gmail.com.

ENDLESS SAFARI

A safari is an animal adventure, into the unknown, to see and experience things you never have. Exploring new places, doing different things, experiencing constant change. An adventure into the unknown, always following a guide. You think you know what is to happen but all the time it changes. You have the ticket, you've paid the money, you've received the plan. Embark with Denise on this endless journey into the unknown, encounter with her glorious experiences, and gain the trophies of supernatural encounters in new relationships in exotic places. Be empowered to embark with a green light to move on in your own endless safari. Awaken your heart to the challenges facing you as you follow the guide.

Reader, are you a dreamer? When we dream, impossibilities become possibilities. When the old is revisited and the prize achieved, relationships deepen and trust in the guide becomes paramount.

Available on www.xlibris.com You can contact Denise Reid at denise@fourcornersministries.com or deniseereid@gmail.com.

CHANGING GEARS

If you test a new car, you have to get in it to drive it. If you try a new dress, you get in it to try it. We are often inspired by words like heavenly experiences, encounters with the glory. This is the how-to, how to get in it, to experience it. The thrill of encountering the supernatural. How far, how fast, how wonderful, and where do I fit? When you read about cars, bikes, rifles, you always talk about the size, the make, the gears, the distance, the speed, and the velocity, but for ladies, the colour and the greatness of the purchase. These are Denise's experiences of changing gears of how to move into your true identity, how to see the heavenly, how to encounter the glory.

Available on www.xlibris.com.
You can contact Denise Reid at denise@fourcornersministries.com or deniseereid@gmail.com.

PGIL2021USA